David Patrick is Post-Doctoral Researcher at the International Studies Group, University of the Free State, South Africa. He completed his PhD in History at Sheffield University.

'This empirically rich and conceptually sophisticated study is essential reading for anyone interested in media responses to genocide and mass violence'.

Professor Adrian Bingham, University of Sheffield

'David Patrick has written a path-breaking account of how genocidal mass violence was publicised and framed by Western media. Focusing on the Holocaust, Bosnia (1992–5), and Rwanda (1994), he examines the ways in which the Anglo-American press reported on three different instances of genocide, and what this tells us about Western attitudes to mass violence. Prominent among the findings of this erudite and measured study is how coverage of the Bosnian and Rwandan genocides was skewed towards the former. Acknowledging Derrida, Patrick too concludes that the dead are counted differently "from one corner of the globe to the other". Crucially, *Reporting Genocide* identifies a process of desensitisation towards human suffering. Reports and images that shocked the world in 1945 had 50 years later become merely one item among many in the Western news media'.

Ian Phiminster, Senior Research Professor,
University of the Free State

'This is an urgent and provocative intervention into discussions of how genocide is reported. In concentrating on events in Bosnia and Rwanda, Patrick identifies strands of continuity within media representations across historical eras. The rigour of the book's textual explorations shakes us out of complacent views of Anglo-American newspapers as benignly liberal, demanding that our news media engage more systematically beyond their all-too-narrow presuppositions and frames of reference if they are to provide truly authoritative context in our troubled times'.

Professor Martin Conboy, University of Sheffield

Reporting Genocide

Media, Mass Violence and
Human Rights

DAVID PATRICK

BLOOMSBURY ACADEMIC
LONDON • NEW YORK • OXFORD • NEW DELHI • SYDNEY

BLOOMSBURY ACADEMIC
Bloomsbury Publishing Plc
50 Bedford Square, London, WC1B 3DP, UK
1385 Broadway, New York, NY 10018, USA
29 Earlsfort Terrace, Dublin 2, Ireland

BLOOMSBURY, BLOOMSBURY ACADEMIC and the Diana logo
are trademarks of Bloomsbury Publishing Plc

First published in Great Britain 2018 by I. B. Tauris
This paperback edition published in 2021

ISBN: HB: 978-1-7845-3722-7
PB: 978-1-3502-4815-1
ePDF: 978-1-7867-3293-4
eBook: 978-1-7867-2293-5

Typeset by Newgen Knowledge Works Pvt Ltd
Printed and bound in Great Britain

To find out more about our authors and books visit
www.bloomsbury.com and sign up for our newsletters.

Contents

Contents

Acknowledgments

There are a number of people who have influenced the various versions of this book, and I extend my genuine thanks to each and every one of them for their respective inputs and suggestions. I am grateful to my former supervisor, Juergen Zimmerer, for first taking on the responsibilities of my PhD proposal. His early guidance, regarding choice of sources and overall structure, greatly influenced this project. There are several other people from my time at the University of Sheffield whom I would like thank for their help in the production of this research. Beky Hasnip and James Pearson were a source of technical support whenever I needed them, and this was a huge help on countless occasions. To Matt Carnell and Mark Seddon, I extend my appreciation for their comments on very early aspects of this work, and for their numerous suggestions regarding relevant literature. I would also like to thank Henning Pieper and Jennifer Pahmeyer, both of whom were invaluable in providing me with a source of discussion and specialist critique of my early research. To Alex White, I extend my sincere gratitude for his help in informing the legal aspects of the original thesis. A special debt of gratitude is reserved for Umit Ungor and Gerold Krozewski, whose support, encouragement and suggestions are most genuinely appreciated. Their respective expertise helped to underpin many of the key concepts which initially informed this study, and were thus highly influential in what this book eventually became. I am also sincerely grateful to Adrian Gallagher, for his guidance and suggestions at every stage of this project. To Paul Behrens, I extend my genuine thanks for his help with early drafts of the chapter on Rwanda, and for his subsequent advice on the larger themes of this work. I would also like to thank Linda Melvern, who provided a series of excellent suggestions regarding Rwanda in the early stages of this research. Special thanks go to Sir Martin Gilbert, who discussed this work with me when it was in its infancy, and who was most welcoming when I travelled to London. To Tim Cole, Hannah Holtschneider

Acknowledgments

and Jolyon Mitchell, I am grateful for their input and advice – particularly on the more theoretical aspects of the project – in the early days of my PhD. I am also very grateful to Ben Shepherd, for his advice on sections relating to the German military, and to Chris Nottingham, whose encouragement and support was enormously appreciated when I first began to consider the main ideas of this project. To James Smith, I am most thankful for him allowing me to frequently discuss various ideas, and for sharing his advice on a number of occasions. I extend a most sincere thanks to Martin Conboy and Mark Levene, who were integral in the completion of this initial research. Their suggestions and support during the final days of my PhD were invaluable, and the production of this book would have been impossible without their respective inputs. I owe a particular debt of gratitude to Adrian Bingham, who helped immeasurably in this overall project. His suggestions in terms of both sources and methodology were invaluable, as was his general guidance throughout my PhD. To Ian Phimister, I extend my most sincere and genuine gratitude, for his endless support across the duration of this project. In the production of both this book and the thesis upon which it is based, his encouragement, advice, patience, expertise and support have been enormously appreciated; and without his influence this book would not have been possible. To my colleagues at the International Studies Group, I extend my gratitude for providing me with various forums to discuss and present my work. Suggestions regarding literature and theoretical standpoints have been most welcome, as has the provision of a department which it is a pleasure to be a part of. Special thanks go to Kate Law, Andy Cohen and Helen Garnett; all of whom have assisted the production of this research, in some manner or another. I am also indebted to Jack Hogan, whose assistance with the final stages of this book was vital. His help with proofing, structure and expression are all hugely appreciated. To the staff at the (former) Colindale archives, I extend my gratitude for making the frequent trips there both productive and enjoyable. Similarly, I thank the specialist staff of the Mitchell Library (Glasgow), for all their help and assistance at various times during this project. I extend special thanks to Tomasz Hoskins, Arub Ahmed and all their colleagues at I.B.Tauris. The process of producing this book has been made much more manageable by their professionalism, patience and general assistance. To the anonymous

Acknowledgments

reviewer of the original manuscript, I am indebted to the various suggestions regarding content and structure; many of which have contributed to a much more focused monograph. To Mark Cameron, Alex Blair, Alex McMurdo, John Millar, Paul Black, Stuart MacMillan, Scott Muldoon, Stuart Latimer, Allan Muirhead, Adam Copeland and Derek Law, I am grateful for their patience in letting me discuss this work at various times, and for providing the social distraction which such research necessitates. To Tamsin de la Harpe, I extend my appreciation for her support and understanding throughout the creation of this monograph. I am greatly thankful to my grandmother, Janet Tully, for her endless support and encouragement throughout the years. To my father, Steven Patrick, I extend my sincere gratitude for all his help and assistance over the course of this research. Finally, I extend a most special note of appreciation to my mother, Margaret Patrick, whose unwavering support, assistance and encouragement has been a constant source of strength; throughout the duration of this project, and beyond.

1

The Crime of Crimes?

Do people really care about genocide? On the surface, the answer seems an obvious 'yes'. Official acknowledgement of historical instances, such as Germany's recent decision to properly recognise the Armenian genocide, continues to grow year on year. Memorialisation of certain events – particularly the Holocaust – gains ever-wider prominence, with celebrities and various public figures eager to be seen commemorating these dark pages in human history. And in the realm of popular media, the likes of *Schindler's List* and *Hotel Rwanda* achieve both box-office success and near-universal critical acclaim. Evidently then, one might assume, crimes of this nature are an affront to the purported liberal values upon which postwar Western civilisation has been built. But as the following study seeks to demonstrate, this may be little more than a self-delusion on grand scale, with the Anglo–American response to genocide being as susceptible to media-framing and the limitations of realpolitik as virtually any other contemporary issue.

Encompassing the darkest aspects of human nature, history is littered with brutal examples of genocide, and it is a darkness which continues to manifest itself in different forms to this very day. But although mass murder may be 'as old as the human race,' it is only in recent decades that interest in such crimes has led to a separate school of study.[1] Before this academic development, however, genocide had grown to be considered by many as a crime which surpassed all others, a process which had its genesis in the importance placed upon the notion of 'human rights' in the aftermath of World War II. To quote Berel Lang:

> On any ranking of atrocities, it would be difficult to name an act or event regarded as more heinous; genocide arguably appears now as the most serious offence in humanity's lengthy – and, we recognise, still growing – list of moral or legal violations.[2]

While there are a number of different ways in which genocide can be defined, this study will use Frank Chalk's interpretation of genocide as being 'a form of one-sided mass killing in which a state or other authority intends to destroy a group, as that group and membership are defined by the perpetrator.'[3] Though terms like 'ethnic cleansing' and 'mass violence' will also be utilised throughout, this work is essentially focusing on violence which takes place within a more general process of repression and persecution, which is aimed at a predominantly civilian population.

Yet acts of genocide themselves are not the main focus of this study, with documentation and analysis of genocidal mass violence already an established field. Much less developed is research into how such atrocities are publicised and framed by the media when they occur. Though descriptions and coverage of global atrocities have a long history, it is only in the last 70 years – and even more so with the advent of international communications technology in recent decades – that such events have been reported on virtually as they were taking place. In turn, ordinary people in the West are now *accustomed* to seeing such things in the media. Certainly, as Zelizer notes, 'Nearly every time we pick up a newspaper, turn on the television, or listen to the radio, we learn of another instance that has been added to the repertoire of horrific acts.'[4] As will be explored in the pages to follow, however, there is little by way of correlation between greater *knowledge* of such crimes and an increased *response* to those same atrocities.

By focusing on the Holocaust, Bosnia (1992–5) and Rwanda (1994) – three historical occurrences which are generally accepted as examples of 'genocide' – this research is able to refine its analysis and, in doing so, provide more specific conclusions regarding media framing of genocide than would be the case if the scope of this study had been expanded to focus on violence and suffering more generally. Taking these three examples of genocide as its key case studies, this research engages with two primary questions:

(1) How has the Anglo–American press reported on different instances of genocidal violence in the twentieth century?
(2) What do the findings of this research reveal about Western attitudes to mass violence?

Structure and Approach

For the purposes of this study, and to provide chronological consistency within the book, Chapter 2 focuses on the Holocaust and its subsequent place in Anglo–American culture. The first half of this chapter engages primarily with the Anglo–American response to the liberation of the Nazi concentration camps in April and May 1945 – a crucially important landmark in terms of Western exposure to genocide. Though the Holocaust was not the first genocide of the twentieth century – the cases of the Herero (1904–8) and the Armenian (1915) genocides being two notable prior examples – it was the first instance in which its revelation provoked an enormous surge of press interest and, as a result, it was seen to have a much wider popular impact than previous examples of this crime. Utilising newspaper reports from the time, supplemented by a range of other primary sources, the main purpose of this section is to highlight the societal impact which accompanied the horrific revelations following the Allied advance into Nazi Germany.

With this first section engaging with the idea that the liberation of the camps in the spring of 1945 proved to be something of an 'introduction' to genocidal crimes for many in the Anglo–American world, the second section of Chapter 2 details how the Holocaust – as a distinct entity – came to become increasingly central to Western consciousness in the decades which followed the end of World War II. Indeed, it should be remembered that the Holocaust (as it is now understood) did not become widely recognised, or appreciated, automatically with the discovery of the camps. Instead, a series of popular representations in the years which followed – a process which arguably reached its zenith in the early 1990s – had a critical influence on how the crimes of the Nazis were to ultimately achieve a level of recognition unlike most other historical events of the twentieth century. Chapter 2, therefore, first engages with the general response to the liberation of Germany's concentration camps, before detailing how the Holocaust came to be increasingly well-recognised over the course of the twentieth century – arguing that this latter process ultimately had an impact on the Western conceptualisation of genocide itself.

Chapters 3 and 4 provide the analytical core of this study, and engage primarily with the Anglo–American press response to the crisis in the Balkans (1992–5) and the Rwandan genocide (1994). Detailing the manner in which eight specific newspapers reported on these two instances of mass violence, these chapters seek to highlight trends which emerged in the reporting of two of the most infamous cases of genocide in the late twentieth century. Using both quantitative and qualitative analysis, both case-studies utilise a 114-day sample, ensuring that any notable comparisons can be used as evidence in supporting the conclusions within the study as a whole. Though there are several recent studies which have focused on the Western response to these two events, few have looked at them in relation to a wider notion of the apparent importance (or lack of) placed on this crime within the Western world.

The decision to use only British and American newspaper titles was taken primarily on the basis of ease of access, but also because the United Kingdom and the United States – both permanent members of the UN Security Council – are seen to be (at least rhetorical) supporters of human rights. Further, the press in both of these countries exist within a free-market system. Having few constraints on what they can put into print, any trends or patterns which emerge from this research can therefore be attributed to the decisions of the press themselves, rather than as a result, for example, of direct government manipulation. As something of a disclaimer though, it should be noted that these same titles – whilst indeed being generally free of state influence and the like – do exist within this free-market system as economic enterprises, and so are expected to take into consideration the economic viability of covering a given news item. This is of particular relevance in relation to the reporting of foreign news events – such as the violence which took place in the Balkans or in Rwanda – and therefore must always be regarded as an important factor when discussing the response of the Anglo–American press to events which take place overseas. This consideration, in itself though, is favourable to the overall analysis in Chapters 3 and 4, since the decision to cover the expense of sending journalists to one region (e.g., Sarajevo) whilst not expending similar resources to report on a comparable situation in a different region (e.g., Kigali) can be cited as evidence of a variation in the manner in which the two occurrences were constructed as being somehow different in terms of their importance to the Anglo–American news agenda.

A total of eight newspapers were selected for analysis within this research, four from the US and four from Britain. The American titles chosen were the *New York Times*, the *Los Angeles Times*, the *Washington Post* and the *Chicago Tribune*; whilst *The Times*, the *Guardian*, the *Daily Telegraph* and the *Independent* were selected from the British press. With reference to the British titles, it should be noted that – for the purposes of seven-day coverage – a Sunday equivalent was chosen for each, these being: the *Sunday Times*, the *Observer*, the *Sunday Telegraph* and the *Independent on Sunday*. Each of the titles selected are regarded as occupying the quality end of the newspaper market, and as such are expected to be a reliable source of news – particularly that which deals with international matters.[5] A number of these newspapers command sufficient respect that they can be legitimately regarded as being *agenda setters*, in that their editorial decisions and coverage on a range of matters, both foreign and domestic, will generally influence what stories and issues other branches of news media give priority to. This phenomenon is especially pronounced in the United States, where the *New York Times* (and to a lesser extent, the *Washington Post*) can be viewed as being both a key source for policy makers *and* an informal determinant of policy itself.[6] Tabloid newspapers – despite their comparatively large circulations – were rejected as sources as they tend to focus predominantly on domestic matters, and so a lack of coverage of the likes of Bosnia or Rwanda in publications such as the *Sun* would not be particularly revealing to the focus of this study.[7]

For each of the two case studies selected, a sample size of 114 days was chosen. This number was arrived at by the fact that the Rwandan example was selected first, and stems from the 100-day duration of the genocide plus a further two weeks added in order to include the refugee crisis which followed the violence. Taking as its starting point the day immediately following the assassination of President Juvenal Habyarimana, the period of analysis for Chapter 4 therefore is 7 April – 29 July 1994. Given that the sample size for the Rwandan case was 114 days, it was decided that for purposes of direct comparison the sample size for Bosnia would be the same. This presented some difficulties, however, as the crisis in the Balkans lasted more than three years and a random sample of 114 days would not be suitably representative of how the press covered major developments in Bosnia and the surrounding region. To counter this, four specific events were chosen around which in-depth analysis could be conducted – with each specific period being either 28 or 29 days in length. Following a review of secondary literature concerning Bosnia, the four events selected were ultimately chosen because they involved a notable instance of mass atrocity. The first period selected is from 1–28 August 1992, which details the discovery of functioning concentration camps in eastern Bosnia. The second period (29 January – 26 February 1994) takes the Markale market bombing as its focal point, whilst the third period (7 July – 3 August 1995) highlights press reaction to the fall of the Srebrenica safe haven. The final section of this analysis, which combines with the previous three to form the basis of the third chapter, is concerned with the 28 August 1995 shelling of Sarajevo which led to NATO retaliation, and engages with the period 21 August – 18 September 1995.

By researching the various ways in which genocide has been responded to and publicised by the press at different junctures in the twentieth century, this research seeks to expand on a field of study which has developed over recent decades, aiming to provide fresh perspectives on how the Anglo–American world confronts what is regarded as the crime of crimes. On a more functional, empirical level, this research seeks to make a major contribution in terms of analysing the press response to both Bosnia and Rwanda, detailing the overall trends and themes which appeared in the case studies chosen. At the same time, it also aims to highlight how the accumulation of Holocaust awareness in the Anglo–American world was seen to influence the manner in which these 1990s atrocities – and genocide as a concept itself – were framed by the British and American press. Whilst such analysis has been attempted by others, this research seeks to expand on these existing works by embarking upon a wider exploration (both in terms of sample size and number of newspapers selected) than anything previously undertaken.[8]

Ultimately though, this study begins from one simple premise: that the overall response to genocide in the late twentieth century was not consistent with the by-then established Western commitment to the protection of human rights. Whilst the claims of some academics that Rwanda and Bosnia were ignored by the Anglo–American world are an exaggeration, it remains the case that both these horrific events were often of little interest to Western media. At other times they were misunderstood, de-contextualised and misrepresented by a number of respected British and American newspapers. Indeed, to borrow a quote from Samantha Power, 'We have all been bystanders to genocide: The crucial question is why.'[9]

2

Bringing Darkness to Light

Anglo–American Awareness of the Holocaust,
1945–95

This chapter engages with the evolving place of the Holocaust in mid- to late twentieth-century Anglo–American popular culture, in an attempt to highlight how this particular event – through mass-media representations, memorialisation and other depictions – came to occupy a unique place within Western society. Not only widely recognised within both Britain and America, the Holocaust – as a particular *example* of the crime of genocide – has also become intrinsically linked to the popular understanding of what 'genocide' entails. The first half of this chapter is concerned with the reaction, both in the press and in wider Anglo–American society, to the discovery of concentration camps in Germany and other parts of Europe in April and May 1945. This period is discussed primarily because it presents a series of notable observations in relation to the overall media response to the liberation of the camps – particularly the fact that journalists seemed genuinely shocked by what was discovered, in a manner unlike the vast majority of 1990s reporting of similar crimes. Further, this section aims to highlight the fact that – through newspapers, radio and cinema – this period can be interpreted as the first instance of genocide to be presented to the Anglo–American public in such a concentrated manner. The second half of this chapter then highlights the various ways in which, through media depictions of related concepts, the Holocaust, as a distinct event, came to be increasingly well recognised over the course of the later twentieth century. It will be shown that Holocaust awareness reached something of a cultural peak in the early 1990s; almost at the exact same time as the media were reacting with general indifference to mass violence in Bosnia and Rwanda. This chapter, therefore, seeks to highlight the degree of shock and disbelief witnessed in 1945, whilst also detailing how the Holocaust came to be both increasingly recognised as a distinct event *and* intrinsically linked to the concept of genocide itself.

The Liberation of the Camps: 1945

A resulting cultural dynamic of the progression into the communication age, in the sense that a multitude of peoples can now bear collective witness to major events through various forms of media, has been that a small number of these occurrences have left such an imprint on the wider public consciousness that they have come to be something of a collective reference point for different generations. These media events often take the form of national celebrations – such as a royal wedding or the memorialisation of a war's end – but can also be related to contemporary political or social developments.[1] In the post-Cold War era, one could make the argument that the 9/11 attacks would fit this criteria, with earlier examples being the Kennedy assassination, the moon landings, or even 'popular' events such as *Live Aid*. These, and many others, are examples of such media events – which, despite only actually happening directly in front of a small number of people, were covered extensively by the media and as such left an indelible impression on society at large. One such occurrence – arguably one of the most shocking and deeply felt – came in the spring of 1945, when the invasion of Germany revealed to the world the horror of the liberated Nazi concentration camps. The revelations of what had occurred inside the likes of Belsen and Buchenwald generated a media frenzy and, though the word itself had not yet come into common use, *genocide* was presented to the world in a manner which was infinitely more concentrated and vivid than anything which had preceded it. The atrocity stories which poured out of Germany were soon being widely discussed throughout the

Anglo–American world, and a watershed moment in media exposure to such atrocities had been reached.[2]

What was Uncovered

Considering the magnitude of the carnage which greeted the advancing Allied forces, it comes as little shock that the majority of witnesses during this period – both first-hand and through the media – were completely unprepared for what was uncovered as the camps were liberated. In September 1942, responding to reports describing the fate of Jewish populations in occupied Europe, an unconvinced *Catholic Herald* stated that 'for the exact truth we must wait till the war is over.'[3] With *Fortress Europa* crumbling, the spring of 1945 saw Allied soldiers uncover this truth amidst the remnants of a camp system within which 'death had become as common as breath.'[4] Although the revelations within each camp varied, there were a number of commonalities between the discoveries at each site, and a plethora of evidence of Nazi crimes was presented throughout the collapsing Nazi empire. In addition to the overcrowded barracks that had housed prisoners from all corners of the formerly-occupied territories, entire warehouses full of their former possessions were also uncovered, often containing the likes of hair and teeth alongside the expected jewelry and hard currency.[5] More immediate, and disconcerting, to a number of combat-hardened veterans were the innumerable bodies which were strewn about the grounds of these locales. In varying degrees of decomposition, bodies in their hundreds and thousands were generally the first welcome that many Allied troops received, with Roger Dixey, present at the liberation of Belsen, later recounting that, 'It was on such a huge scale it was rather like trying to count the stars.'[6] An illustration for the scale of this comes in the estimation that of the 715,000 camp inmates at the beginning of 1945, around 238,000 had perished by spring of that same year.[7] Some attempts had been made to contain this through cremation and mass burial, but the majority had been dumped in open pits or simply left where they had fallen.

Those prisoners who were fortunate enough to have survived their incarceration, both long-term 'political' prisoners and those recently marched westwards from the extermination camps in Poland, presented their liberators with a clear indication of what the Nazis had intended for the 'unwanted' peoples of Europe. The physical condition of most prisoners was near-starvation, with emaciation to the extent that differences between men and women were often difficult to distinguish. Almost every piece of correspondence from this period references the sickly-thin appearance of the camp survivors, with a contemporary stating that the likes of Buchenwald represented 'the lowest point of degradation to which humanity has yet descended.'[8] Though conditions were horrific in most instances, some camps quickly earned a particularly infamous reputation for brutality and horror. In Dachau, for example, almost half of all recorded deaths in the camp's entire history occurred in the first four months of 1945, even though the camp had been operational since 1933. During this time, the number of deaths in the camp ranged from 2,625 to 3,977 per month and, to add to the instant infamy of Dachau, 50 locked railway cars packed with 2,000 recently deceased prisoners were found upon its liberation in late April.[9] In Buchenwald, 21,000 male prisoners, of various nationalities, were discovered and many were suffering from the effects of the infectious diseases which had blighted the camp. Barracks which were designed to hold 300 people were found to be imprisoning more than 1,000, a situation that led to an acceleration of the worsening of conditions.[10]

One aspect of the liberation process which added to the overwhelming sense of shock which accompanied each new discovery was the rapidity with which each subsequent camp was liberated. Of the 22 principal camps – separate from the six extermination camps in the east – most were uncovered within the same three-week period.[11] Following the liberation of Buchenwald on 11 April, the likes of Ebensee, Thekla and Ravensbruck (where 23,000 women had been liberated) had all been revealed to the world by the first week of May 1945.[12] Because of its reputation as being the first 'major' camp to be liberated, Buchenwald quickly became the epicentre of the vast media operation which developed to publicise the atrocities. Journalists, at the encouragement of General Eisenhower, congregated at the site, each attempting to get the most news-worthy 'scoop' for their own outlet. One, unintended, impact of this was that it ensured an even swifter response to the discovery of perhaps the most infamous concentration camp of them all: Bergen-Belsen.

Providing, in the words of Reilly, 'the most visual images to encapsulate Nazi barbarity,' Belsen tested the coping abilities of virtually all who encountered it.[13] Belsen was unusual in that it had been officially surrendered to the British as part of an agreement with local Nazi authorities. This was done predominantly for health reasons, as the camp had become overwhelmed by both typhus and tuberculosis.[14] Conditions within Belsen were thus worse than anything which had previously been discovered, with Camp One of the establishment soon being referred to as the 'Horror Camp.'[15] Upon liberation, some 10,000 corpses were strewn around the grounds, in addition to an estimated 60,000 survivors. Many of those who had managed to stay alive long enough to witness their hour of liberation were beyond medical treatment, and death continued to be an ever-present in the camp. The daily average of those dying remained at several hundred per day in the immediate post-liberation days, and it was not until 11 May that the death rate fell below 100.[16] Estimates vary, but such were the conditions in the camp that around 14,000 inmates died *after* liberation. Indeed, it is little wonder that Robert Abzug would later remark that 'Bergen-Belsen was in a class by itself.'[17]

That such 'scientific Satanism', in the words of one contemporary, should have presented itself to the liberating armies resulted, in part, from the primary function of the camps.[18] In contrast to the extermination camps in Poland, the camp system in Germany had not been designed, initially, to kill multitudes of people. Unlike Auschwitz or Treblinka, they therefore lacked the capacity, in terms of burial or cremation, to properly dispose of corpses in such numbers. Losing a war on two fronts, the German High Command also diverted resources and manpower away from the camp system during this period, meaning that supplies of food, building materials and the like began to seriously dwindle towards the final weeks of the war in Europe.[19] Conditions in Belsen, in particular, deteriorated rapidly during this time, with the availability of food and even water being disrupted by both supply problems and due to aerial bombing within the local area. Amidst such conditions, some 35,000 Belsen inmates died in the four-and-a-half months prior to liberation, with more than half of these deaths coming in March 1945 alone.[20]

Certainly, it has been argued that the deterioration and death which surrounded the world of the concentration camps by the end of the war was also an almost inevitable result of Nazi ideology. With the war lost, many ardent Nazis regarded the elimination of the Jews as one aim which was still achievable. Military shortcomings may have not, as Breitman argues, actually *stimulated* the murderous role of the camps, but it *is* likely that the genocidal programme of the previous four years had made such an end to the war more plausible.[21] Perhaps the most illustrative quote for this phenomenon comes from Josef Goebbels, who declared in 1945: 'If we have to leave, we'll close the door behind us with a slam that all the world will hear.'[22] As the borders of the Reich shrank ever-inwards then, several camps therefore became little more than holding-pens for thousands of unwanted people, and it was these 'unplanned remnants' which presented themselves to the world in the spring of 1945.[23]

Faced with such monumental horror, it was quickly decided by the Allied High Command that the extent of Nazi brutality should be relayed to the world. Primarily at the insistence of Eisenhower – who said of the press, 'Your responsibilities, I believe, extend into a great field, and inform-ing the people at home of things like these atrocities is one of them' – an unprecedented media operation gathered momentum with the explicit intent of informing the Anglo–American world of the nature of the discov-eries.[24] With few exceptions, not since *Kristallnacht* in November 1938 had the press given such concentrated attention to Nazi war crimes.[25] Certainly, the (short-lived) flood of information which soon flowed out of Germany was such that it ensured that 'Belsen' and 'Buchenwald' quickly acquired common usage within Britain and America to refer to subsequent humani-tarian disasters. Indeed, it could be argued that, by the early summer of 1945, a new threshold for human suffering had been reached.[26]

Media Responses to Liberation

When the Anglo–American media acknowledged that the revelations within the camps were unlike anything previously discovered on the Western Front, a determined campaign began publicising the camp atroc-ities. Whilst it has been noted retrospectively that some outlets did not give the story the blanket coverage it warranted (the New York Times, for example, devoted only two front page stories to the liberation period), it remains evident that from mid-April to early June 1945 the concentration camps were a major story, covered by a variety of sources.[27] Though 'national preference' was given to those camps which had been liberated by one's own troops – for example, Buchenwald and Mathhausen commanded greater coverage in the United States than was the case for Belsen, which was discovered by the British – focus was given to most atrocity stories that emerged during this time, on both sides of the Atlantic. By late April a range of journalists had travelled to Germany to witness the devastation for themselves, and 'Horror stories that made the stories of Edgar Allan Poe read like fairy tales' were soon being transmitted to the public at home.[28] Even though it is true that some outlets did not provide front page coverage to the atrocities, many compensated for this by devoting full inside-pages to the story. Indeed, many would produce two- and three-page spreads on occasion – an indication of the importance given to these discoveries during a time in which column inches, due to wartime restraints, were at a premium. Both newspapers and magazines showed significant interest in the camps, and all during a period in which a series of other important events were taking place – not least the deaths of Roosevelt and Hitler, and the end of the war in Europe itself.[29]

To supplement the journalistic presence, it was also decided that official delegations from the British and American governments should be in attendance. On the personal invitation of Eisenhower, eight US Congressmen and 18 American newspaper and magazine editors were summoned to Buchenwald. From Britain, a total of eight M.P.s and two peers, selected from dozens of parliamentary volunteers, also attended this endeavour.[30] Although primarily a fact-finding mission, it was also believed that the presence of such well-respected individuals would help to combat the rumours of faked atrocities and staged photos which had already began circulating in Britain and America. These trips were given special prominence in the Western press, and the responses of the various representatives were publicised in several outlets. The fact that Mrs Mavis Tate, the only woman in the British delegation, had been in tears during the entire visit was highlighted as an indication of the horror witnessed by those on the scene, and an American representative, Gordon Canfield, was quoted as saying that the camps were 'barbarism at its worst.'[31] There is even evidence that some members of these groups shared a kind of dark fascination with the camps, with Senator (and later Vice-President) Alben Barkley stating that it would be desirable to see more camps in order to 'get the best possible picture.'[32]

Although journalists tried to convey the horror that they were bearing witness to, several had difficulties in finding the right words. Many were battle-hardened reporters who had spent months covering the Allied advance, and this prior experience was often used as a disclaimer regarding the conditions in the camps. This is seen, for example, in the following extract – which is typical of journalistic attempts at the time to contrast this catastrophe with some acceptable reference point: 'I have visited many battlefields in this war, and Belsen is an immeasurably more terrible sight.'[33] The harrowing conditions within the camps led many correspondents to cease even *trying* to properly articulate the scenes. Many would only give a brief overview of the situation being presented to them, before stating that the full truth of the environment was simply too awful to print.[34] Such journalistic shortcomings are arguably unheard of in today's world, for the idea of something being too horrible to print is now a thing of the past. The prevalence of such statements within reporting from 1945, however, demonstrate that it was a genuine response to a level of horror which was beyond anything which had preceded it. The statement from a contemporary editor that 'language breaks down' in the face of such atrocity does seem to be accurate for this period, in contrast to the mass violence of the 1990s, by which time such linguistic challenges had apparently been all but eradicated.[35]

With such difficulties in finding adequate expression with which to describe the likes of Belsen, it was inevitable that photographs would be used in an attempt to compensate for the shortcomings of the written word. Indeed, a number of these photos have since become instantly recognisable and immediately connected to the Holocaust. To contemporary readers, however, several of these pictures would have been far more graphic than anything they had previously seen. Several showed bodies stacked together, in varying degrees of decomposition, whilst others portrayed a lone survivor – emaciated and wide-eyed – staring into the camera. These were of course not the first pictures of atrocity and death to be circulated in the Anglo–American world (photographs of dead bodies had been appearing in print since the American Civil War era), but their clarity and volume were something new. Even so, many of these photographs came with the same disclaimer as that expressed in written testimony (that they could not do justice to the *reality* of the camps), but were used nonetheless, often to corroborate the truth of the more shocking stories.[36]

One 'function' of such photographs was to prove that the influential people discussed in the previous section were indeed present, *and* as further proof that the claims were neither fabricated nor exaggerated. In an interesting development within print journalism, this period proved to be one of the first times in which pictures were constructed as being more important, on occasion, than their accompanying words.[37] The importance of these pictures was further evidenced by the decision of the *Daily Express* to hold an exhibition in London, which showed a selection of the most gruesome images. Free to attend, the exhibit opened on 24 April and was open to the public from 10 a.m. till 7 p.m. daily, and a smaller version went on to tour other venues.[38] Described at the time as 'a terrible and convincing exposure of German brutality,' such an exhibit was somewhat exceptional and illustrates the new mode of understanding which had been provoked by the discovery of the camps.[39]

Broadcast radio was another medium through which such discoveries would be publicised. Though many of the details being transmitted were not new to those who had access to a daily newspaper, the testimony of radio veterans like Richard Dimbleby, or his American counterpart, Ed Murrow, carried significantly more weight than the plethora of essentially unknown journalists who were filing similar stories. The familiar voices of these men had been entering ordinary people's homes for years and so any expression of revulsion on their part magnified the impact of their broadcast. In addition to this, the medium of radio was highly effective as it, inevitably, carried more emotion than simple text. In many radio dispatches from the camps, the challenge to the reporter in keeping their composure is obvious, meaning that even simple statements – most famously Dimbleby's assertion that his Belsen experience had been the 'most horrible of [his] life' – had the potential to impact on audiences at home.[40] Similarly, Ed Murrow's 'quiet, graphic, unemotional recital' was said have caused such revulsion in listeners that many felt physically sick.[41]

Perhaps the most dynamic and affecting method of publicising the camps came through an even more novel outlet for contemporary consumers – cinematic representation. Even though print media had already described the conditions in the camps in detail, often accompanying the stories with graphic pictures, the newsreels which began showing in late April proved to be more traumatic for the Anglo–American public than anything that had come before. The first ever British newsreel had appeared in the summer of 1910, and by the mid-1940s patrons were accustomed to being informed of news developments during regular visits to the cinema.[42] Little could have prepared this same cinema-going public for what was to be revealed in the spring of 1945, however. The newsreels, such as 'Horror in Our Time,' showed a variety of traumatic images, including unedited scenes of decomposing bodies.[43] Interviews with ordinary soldiers were also recorded – partly to prove that the images were not faked – in addition to footage of the perpetrators themselves being rounded up and paraded.[44] Undoubtedly the most widely remembered sequence, though, and one which has become a virtual cliché in subsequent documentaries, was that of a British soldier using a bulldozer to push bodies into a mass grave. Images such as these stuck long in the memory, and none more so than those captured at Belsen, which was filmed more extensively than any other camp.[45]

Whilst the material being produced for the newsreels was clearly harrowing, it was also the case that the producers were determined to document these scenes in a manner which would do the camps a degree of justice, even if capturing the full horror on celluloid was an impossible task. To aid this, government regulations regarding filming were also further relaxed in order to provide maximum publicity to the camp horrors. In addition, extra allowances of film stock were provided to camera crews in order to show 'full scenes of conditions in concentration camps in Germany.'[46] During this period, noted filmmaker Alfred Hitchcock was drafted in to help this process, though the footage he collected was largely suppressed until its release in early 2015.[47] Further to this, a determined advertising campaign was launched to publicise the showing of the news-reels. Even before the various films had been edited and distributed to cin-emas around the country (in the case of Britain), newspaper readers were already being informed of the aforementioned concessions being made in order to properly document the atrocities on film.[48] With a belief that moving images would have greater impact than the entire body of printed exposure, dates and times for cinematic presentations were advertised widely by early May, and readers were strongly encouraged to brave seeing them. Even amidst complaints from several that the scenes had been so awful that they had been forced to leave the cinema, editorials and other prominent sections of the press continued to push for maximum attend-ance – with one such article in *The Times* stating that the distribution of the evidence was 'fulfilling a public duty'.[49]

The liberation of the camps was covered extensively through mid-April and into early may, and the British and American press had gone to great lengths to encourage people to view the emerging footage of the atrocities, but difficulties remained in distributing such material as widely as would have been hoped. Primarily, a number of cinema owners simply refused to show the films. Usually, this was because they were worried that doing so would affect overall profits, with one such proprietor stating that he was running an entertainment business and not a 'chamber of horrors'.[50] In addition to this, several cinemas also stopped showing the film in response to mass walkouts, with an establishment in Manchester justifying the ter-mination of any further screenings on the grounds that more than 100 peo-ple had left during the first showing. With similar occurrences across the country, it was even reported that soldiers had been posted to some thea-tres to force patrons to go back in and finish watching till the end.[51] These setbacks did not prove to be insurmountable though, and over the weeks following the screening of these newsreels many cinemas were consistently reporting near-capacity audiences. Indeed, by 1 May, 'all box office records had been broken in the London news theatres'.[52]

The manner in which the liberation of the camps was publicised and reported on by the media at this time is particularly important in relation to an overall appreciation of how the Holocaust became such an estab-lished cultural reference point in the Anglo–American world. Through transmitting a series of shocking revelations to the public at home, this period represents the first time in which crimes of this nature (and certainly scale) were presented in such vivid and accessible terms to a mass audience through the media. Further to this, the imagery which was captured during this time has in subsequent years become, in itself, iconic through its use in documentaries and the like, and has thus helped to solidify an idea of what features constitute genocide – namely, camps and tens of thousands of victims.

The immediate impact of these same horrific discoveries was noticeably different from that which would accompany later revelations of genocidal mass violence, as will be detailed in the subsequent chapters concerning reporting of 1990s genocide. The remainder of this section is devoted to charting notable trends in the coverage from the time of the liberation period, partially to highlight a discourse which was different from that which surrounded the later reporting of Bosnia and Rwanda. Perhaps most significantly, in reports from 1945 there is a clear sense of disbelief and genuine shock at the revelations of these crimes, whereas in 1990s media-reporting of genocidal conflicts the violence itself was rarely the focus of the story for any length of time.

Stylistic Themes in Reporting

With the benefit of hindsight, a number of trends present themselves when this body of publicity – predominantly the print media from the time – is closely analysed. One of the most immediate is the number of reports which, consciously or not, utilise language which dehumanises the victims themselves. For one, suddenly presented with the sight of sometimes thousands of dying prisoners, journalists often lapsed into applying animalistic labels to the people they were reporting on. Inmates were referred to as locusts, apes and dying rabbits, though this 'veritable thesaurus of diminished humanity' did not end with allusions to the animal-like traits of the prisoners.[53] Even representatives from the more respectable outlets resorted to using such language, with one *Washington Post* observer referring to 'the shambles of humanity who were the prisoners,' whilst another from the same publication noted that there was 'no self-respect among these people – driven in a few months backward a million years toward primordial scum.'[54] Though it should be remembered that, in contrast to journalists who would cover atrocities later in the twentieth century, there was little precedent (in terms of an established Western historical memory, at least) for suffering on such an immense scale. Western awareness of such atrocities prior to this was generally limited, and so this linguistic regression into degrading analogies cannot be entirely condemned. As Leff notes, physical revulsion and emotional traumatisation were almost inevitable responses to witnessing the remnants of the concentration camp universe.[55] Falling 'outside the realm of expression,' these barbaric crimes were beyond comprehension for many and, being unprecedented in nature, there was little in the prior history of reporting which could be utilised in order to adequately convey the scenes of atrocity.[56]

Another common thread within the press coverage of the time was the use of what would now be described as sensationalist framing. Essentially, the already-awful scenes were further exaggerated and embellished by unconfirmed reports, rumour and hyperbole. For example, it was soon claimed that the conditions discovered in April and May 1945 were representative of the suffering and death inflicted upon masses of innocent people ever since the very beginning of the Nazi regime in 1933. One report even went as far as to claim that American prisoners-of-war had been subjected to equally brutal treatment throughout their own internment in Europe, though it would later be established that POW camps, for Western Allied soldiers at least, were in no way comparable to the conditions endured by concentration camp inmates.[57] In addition to this, perpetrators themselves were often depicted in an almost cartoonish fashion. Being particularly prevalent in, though not exclusive to, the popular press, there were myriad examples of the use of terms such as 'The Beast of Belsen' or the 'Mad Doctor of Belsen' by the end of April/May 1945.[58] Such exaggeration and sensationalism may have simply been the result of journalists wishing to embellish their story and thus sell more newspapers, though it is likely that such journalistic practice was also, in part, a means of painting the Nazis as utterly barbaric.

This is a key consideration within the overall scope of this research – that the events of spring 1945 proved to be a watershed in Anglo–American exposure to genocide. In stark contrast to the press response to mass violence in the 1990s, by which time the preceding half-century had seen journalism establish a lexicon of atrocity, the disclosure of the Nazi crimes was so intensely shocking that even veteran journalists struggled to properly express what they bore witness to. By the time that Bosnia and Rwanda were erupting into genocidal bloodshed – though dehumanising language continued to be used to describe the victims – this no longer seemed to be a factor, with the violence itself usually framed as being of only secondary importance.

General Responses to Press Disclosures

With this wave of dramatic and intense publicity coming into the public domain in a relatively short space of time, it was perhaps inevitable that the discoveries from within the crumbling Reich would become a topic of discussion throughout the English-speaking world. In both Britain and the US, the camps were soon being discussed on high streets, in bars, in offices, on public transport and even in schools.[59] Such was the impact of these revelations, particularly following the release of newsreel footage, that it became virtually impossible to find someone who was not aware of the horror being uncovered in Germany. Whether as a result of some 'foul fascination' with the atrocities – as one Mass Observation diarist noted – or simply because the government and press were publicising the discoveries in an unprecedented manner, it is clear that the concentration camps grabbed the collective conscience of the British and American people in a way that few events prior to, or indeed since, were able.[60]

That the revelations from the likes of Buchenwald were being widely discussed almost immediately is evidenced by the vast number of letters which were submitted, in both nations, by ordinary people who wished to voice their opinion on the discoveries in Germany. Though obviously not having experienced the camps first-hand, a number of citizens felt compelled to share their feelings on the subject, and newspapers were inundated with an overwhelming amount of correspondence. Even weeks after the original disclosures, newspaper editors highlighted the fact that they were still receiving hundreds of letters addressing the discovery of the camps, further evidence of just how discussion-worthy this information was for many people. In reading both letters and other contemporary sources, the level of feeling generated by the publicity of the camps soon becomes apparent. Germany's regression from 'civilised man to barbarism' triggered a public outpouring of shock, disbelief and anger which has rarely, if ever, been replicated.[61] Also, in a concentrated manner which has seldom been repeated in response to subsequent atrocities, ordinary individuals felt compelled to convey their own deep personal horror in learning of the concentration camps. One of the more poetic letters, from a Mrs Spencer, asked, 'How can I put into words the fury and anguish and pain that is in my heart today?' – a sentiment which was repeated elsewhere in other correspondence.[62] A lead article in *The Times* stated that the pictures of the camps had sickened all who saw them, whilst Ronald Tritton, who was Director of Public Relations at the War Office and thus no stranger to reports of carnage, recorded in his diary that he had been 'almost physically sickened' by the revelations, adding that he 'felt shaky and very upset.'[63]

A general sadness, that such things could even take place in the modern world, was also a common response. Even after several years of war, people were both upset and disgusted that human beings could commit crimes which could surpass in cruelty and barbarity what had already been the most destructive conflict in history. To this end, Robert Burns' lament that 'Man's inhumanity to man makes countless thousands mourn' has seldom been more appropriate.[64] In the modern Western world, with a consistent stream of atrocity and destruction being presented daily through a variety of media sources, it is easy to underestimate the emotional impact which Belsen and others had on the collective conscience of the Anglo–American world at the time of their disclosure. The very fact that 'Belsen remains a byword for human evil and depravity, a benchmark in the moral history of the world' is primarily because these crimes were genuinely shocking to virtually all who confronted them at the time.[65] Again, this is in stark contrast to the general reaction to the later carnage in Bosnia and Rwanda, where the violence was instead generally met with, at best, indifference.

The sadness and shock generated by the camp revelations, however, soon turned to fury. The anger which followed the initial outpouring of sympathy and disgust was first and foremost directed at the German nation, and its perceived descent into barbarism. This perhaps resulted from the fact that Germany, once home to some of Europe's finest universities, had previously been seen as one of the most 'supremely cultured' nations in the world.[66] That such a nation had descended to the point of attempting to eradicate entire peoples, simply on the basis of their racial origins, was seen as a failure of progress itself.[67] The prior 'cultural standing' of Germany thus further compounded the impact of the crimes for which they were shown to be guilty. Whilst the destruction and chaos presented within the concentration camps was shocking in itself, the fact that they had been perpetrated by a once-great nation lent further significance to the revelations of 1945.

Within days of the first reports of the liberation of various camps, a substantial number of ordinary people in the Anglo–American world, echoing the convictions of several prominent journalists, started to insist that this was a crime for which *all* German people (and not simply the actual, physical perpetrators) were responsible. Though such an extreme view could arguably be put down to the intense emotional reaction which erupted in April 1945, it persisted throughout that following summer and no doubt influenced general feelings towards the Germans for a great many years afterwards. Even those not in uniform were characterised as being guilty, and the assertion that 'It is surely obvious that no discrimination is possible between the German military, intellectual, or Nazi mentality' was not the belief of a lone extremist.[68] As will be explored in greater detail in the chapters to follow, characterisation of the German nation in this manner contrasted with the later stereotyping of participants in the mass violence of Bosnia and Rwanda. In the 1990s, the people of these respective regions were portrayed as being savage and inherently violent; with the extension of this argument being that the carnage there was simply the latest example of a trend that went back centuries. With Germany, however, the fault seemed to lie in the fact that it had once been held up as a great nation, and had failed to live up to this mantle. German atrocities, whilst being seen as evil and barbaric, were thus interpreted as being a temporary abomination from a cultured, Western nation; whilst later instances in Bosnia and Rwanda were (mistakenly) explained as being entirely in keeping with the violent histories of those regions.

Nonetheless, the hatred directed towards Germany in this period remained both immediate and strongly worded. Even members of government, in addition to newspaper editors and prominent opinion-makers, were quick to voice such negative opinions about the country and its people.[69] Whilst there are several examples of this conviction being expressed, perhaps the most illustrative is from the following letter to *The Scotsman*, published on 26 April 1945:

> Unfortunately, it is impossible to regard these two groups as completely separate and unrelated divisions of the human race. The awkward fact remains that the Nazis are the brothers, husbands, sons, fathers, cousins – yes, and even (sad to relate) the sisters of the 'good' German people. This rather complicates matters, as it is difficult to determine where the 'noble' German ends and the ignoble Nazi begins [...] I think it might be accepted as an axiom that the individual members of the British race would much rather die (or, at least, allow themselves to be clubbed into insensibility) than commit those fearful cruelties on helpless people [...] With the evidence before us, I should like to ask Mr Cuthbertson what proportion of the German people, he thinks, would adopt the same steadfast and humane attitude. Precious few, I should think, if any.[70]

Such was the shock and disbelief that these crimes could exist in the contemporary world that the emotive reaction they triggered led many observers to argue that the entire German nation were to blame for the excesses of a few.[71] Again; though it would be later intimated that the inhabitants of, for example, Rwanda and Bosnia had a historical proclivity for violence, this was generally explained within a framework whereby the perpetrators were *savage* or *mindless*; whereas the German nation, in part due to its previous cultural standing, was caricatured as being inherently wicked.

Following closely from the general belief that all of Germany was responsible for the very *existence* of such vile establishments, it was quickly debated whether there was in fact something inherently cruel within the German psyche. Though it has been accepted in the decades following the Holocaust that one does not have to be psychologically abnormal in order to become a *genocidaire*, this was not the general belief during the spring and summer of 1945.[72] It was widely debated in a number of outlets as to whether a social or cultural propensity for evil was somehow innate within the mind of every German, with one *Daily Mirror* article arguing that 'A race which can produce so much foulness must itself be foul.'[73] A similar opinion was voiced by Representative Clare Luce, who openly questioned whether there could be 'any good in any German' – though it should be remembered that this polemic outburst was made only a short time after she had witnessed the horrors of Buchenwald first-hand.[74] Even professional psychologists and analysts weighed in with like-minded views, with one letter citing Jacques Riviere's opinion that 'while the German may, with one side of his mind, know an act or principle to be evil, he too often, on the other side of his mind, does not feel it to be wrong.'[75]

The flood of publicity documenting the atrocious discoveries in places like Nordhausen and Buchenwald thus generated a great deal of general contempt for Germany, and once the *guilt* of the entire German nation had been established – at least in the opinion of a sickened Anglo–American public – a concentrated outpouring of hatred and disgust was expressed in increasingly extreme tones. Michael Burleigh neatly sums up this phenomenon by arguing that, 'past sentimentality towards the German race and nation was superseded by utter contempt for a people which had failed the test of greatness.'[76] More often than not, this contempt was articulated in the form of calls for what should become of Germany following the war's end – some of which seem, to the contemporary reader, both violent and excessive.

It has been argued that, in the present day, photos and reports of atrocity no longer provoke the same emotional response as they perhaps once did – in effect meaning that they struggle to make a dramatic impression on public sentiments – but this was certainly not the case in Britain and America in 1945.[77] A deep anger swept both nations and soon a variety of proposals were being suggested with the aim of punishing or rehabilitating the German foe. Provoking a debate that would continue long after the war's end, a policy of re-education of the German people was one such measure which was often expressed. In an attempt to eradicate what was viewed as 'the evil in the souls' of German citizens, it was strongly encouraged that details of the camps should become required reading throughout postwar Germany.[78]

Others questioned this, however, citing Germany's past standing as a centre of educational excellence as proof that such measures would not have the desired effect.[79] A similar, and more immediate, measure that *was* enacted was the decision to force as many Germans as possible to see the camps for themselves. With a view to also silencing those Germans who continued to dispute the authenticity of the Allied claims, it was suggested in a variety of quarters that ordinary Germans should be exposed to the atrocities first-hand. Indeed, on several occasions this policy was actually practiced, with Allied troops forcing German locals to tour the scenes of devastation – even going as far as forcing men and women, many of whom were on the verge of collapsing, to desist in covering their eyes.[80]

It could be argued that those members of the German population who saw the most immediate deterioration in their condition, as a direct result of the concentration camp revelations, were the prisoners-of-war being held in Britain and America. In what had previously been a rather comfortable existence, several of these prisoners saw their situation change dramatically in the wake of the stories emanating from their homeland. Hundreds of thousands of these detainees were forced to watch news footage of the camps and this, in turn, generally led to a souring of once-amicable relationships with their respective camp guards.[81] Also, largely in response to the scenes of starvation from the camps, a torrent of correspondence challenged whether it was justified that German prisoners still enjoyed greater food privileges than many civilians were benefitting from.[82] It was even discussed in some quarters whether violent retaliatory action should be taken against these prisoners, though it was quickly insisted upon that the Allies would abide by the Geneva Convention. This is not to say, however, that German inmates did not feel the brunt of Allied disgust at what was uncovered in their fatherland.[83]

By far the most extreme suggestion in response to the discovery of the camps, however, was that which advocated extermination of at least some sections of German society. On both sides of the Atlantic, calls for this most violent of reprisals were heard nationwide, with some being more vindictive than others. Amidst calls from frontline servicemen and others that all German males should be killed, opinions were also publicly voiced which called for the complete extermination of the German people.

As Reilly has pointed out, the irony of punishing mass extermination with *further* organised violence was, however, clearly lost on a number of these individuals.[84] Proponents of complete extermination were in the minority though, with a more widely held view being that Nazi leaders and cohorts should be sentenced to death. One vocal advocate of this was Joseph Pulitzer, a descendent of the man who founded the journalism prize which shares his name. As editor and publisher of the *St. Louis Post-Dispatch*, he argued that the 'entire German General Staff, German industrialists and financiers, and almost all, if not all, the members of the *Gestapo* and the S.S. should be put to death as war criminals,' and was seemingly undeterred by the fact that this may have amounted to some 1.5 million individuals being executed.[85] Perhaps more indicative of this ill feeling towards those perceived as the architects of the concentration camp system was the fact that a poll taken in late April 1945 indicated that 19 per cent of respondents agreed with killing *all* those individuals implicated in the extermination process.[86] Such vengeful views towards the German people, illustrated in these calls for violent retribution, indicate the intense feeling which was generated by the disclosure of the camps. As will be highlighted in later chapters of this work, such an emotional and vocal reaction was not replicated in response to the genocidal turmoil that would be presented to the world in the 1990s.[87]

Another response which was commonly voiced in the spring of 1945, and one which could be argued as being the only one with any form of redemptive quality to it, was the belief that the discovery of the camps had provided a concrete justification for fighting the war in the first place. The camps were soon presented as a warning of the dangers of totalitarian regimes, and so began a crystallisation of the assertion that the war had indeed been an almost mythic battle of *good vs evil*. Described at the time as 'the lowest point to which humanity has yet descended' and 'a fearful reminder of what the disease of sin in its ultimate form [...] can bring men to do,' the carnage uncovered by the Allied forces was soon cited as evidence that the struggle and sacrifice of the preceding years had indeed been worthwhile.[88] Certainly, the fact that the Holocaust has been described in the intervening years as perhaps *the* defining moral event of the twentieth century has its origin in this early belief in the moral legitimacy of the

Allied action.[89] Arguably those most directly affected by this phenomenon – in essence a sudden belief in the righteousness of the war itself – were the frontline soldiers. As was mentioned earlier, the military high command ordered all soldiers within the vicinity of the various camps who were not committed to immediate engagements to visit the sites of atrocity for themselves, and many would later recall that the experience gave them a concrete reason for fighting the war. A British soldier who was present at Bergen-Belsen remarked that 'When you actually see them for yourselves, you know what you are fighting for,' a sentiment which was often repeated in the contemporary correspondence from the front.[90] Perhaps the most illustrative remark however came from General Eisenhower who, in a now oft-quoted statement, observed: 'We are told that the American soldier does not know what he is fighting for. Now, at least, he will know what he is fighting against.'[91]

A Unique Response: Disbelief

A further notable trend which was revealed through this research was the consistent, and deliberate, attempt to emphasise that the reports emanating from the camps were genuine. From the first accounts which were transmitted to various news outlets, there are a number of articles which are clearly at pains to stress that the reports were completely genuine. Certainly, there were reasons why the Anglo–American public may have been sceptical of these early revelations (to be discussed later), and it seems apparent that the contemporary press in turn went to great lengths to publicise the veracity of their reports. Often in bold headlines, terms such as 'PROOF' and 'IRREFUTABLE EVIDENCE' were commonplace on both sides of the Atlantic, with others printing graphic pictures alongside captions such as: 'Evidence That Cannot be Refuted.'[92] Arguably the most illustrative example of this phenomenon was the title of the *Daily Express'* aforementioned photographic exhibition. Set up in Trafalgar Square to encourage maximum attendance, the selection of 22 photographs documenting camp conditions was advertised under the evocative title 'SEEING IS BELIEVING.'[93] Again, this trend contrasts with the reporting of genocide in the 1990s, by which time the reporting of atrocities on this scale rarely, if ever, came with a disclaimer asserting their credibility. Thought of in a different sense; what had to be constantly reiterated in 1945 (due to its horrific nature) was, by the 1990s, no longer beyond the comprehension of Western audiences.

Aside from the use of such terms in headlines, correspondents themselves were also keen to stress that their claims were authentic. Perhaps realising that the stories being produced were beyond what many could reasonably accept (even after several years of war), many of the early reports consistently asserted the authenticity of what was being described. In addition to citing the testimony of individuals who would be respected and trusted, most notably senior politicians and press-editors, a common method of emphasising the veracity of such accounts came in the form of reiterating that these horrific things had been witnessed, *first-hand*, by the author.[94] A number of these articles utilise the 'I saw' style of reporting; consciously and deliberately indicating that these depictions of brutality were indeed from personal experience, as opposed to simply repeating the unverified claims of another individual. A most explicit example of this trend was produced by William Frye who, in a front page article, used the expression 'I saw' more than a dozen times – evidently in order to underpin the truth behind his descriptions of conditions in Belsen.[95]

Disbelief at what had suddenly and viciously presented itself to the various liberators during the fall of Nazi Germany is a theme which runs through several reports from the time. Even to those who had already experienced the trials of war, the sheer horror of what was discovered in Belsen and the like was beyond the comprehension of many.[96] Letters home often emphasised this, with their authors stressing that the terrible conditions being described were indeed an accurate account. One such letter came from George Walker, a British soldier present during the liberation of Belsen, who, obviously realising that his account would prove difficult for many to accept, accompanied his correspondence with the following disclaimer: 'This letter will read like fiction, but I swear that as sure as there is a God in heaven what I have told you is the Gospel truth.' The realisation that the reality of what had been discovered would be hard for many to grasp was echoed by a nurse, who was also serving at Belsen, Kathleen

Elvidge, who stated in a letter home that what she had witnessed had been so horrific that those at home 'probably would never believe them.'[97]

The impact of the discovery of the concentration camps also had an effect on the members of the press who were present in the days and weeks following liberation. Despite the obvious potential for a career-enhancing story, a number of hardened journalists would later state the difficulties they had in coming to terms with and accurately disclosing what they were bearing witness to. Many simply could not tolerate such anguish and asked to be re-assigned, whilst others admitted to weeping or vomiting uncontrollably.[98] In relation to the notion of disbelief, the recollections of Richard Dimbleby are particularly illuminating. Though his 12-minute report detailing the conditions within Belsen has now become one of the iconic broadcasts of the twentieth century, he initially had difficulty in convincing his superiors at the BBC that his depiction of the camps was indeed completely accurate. He recalled insisting that he must 'tell the exact truth, every detail of it, even if people don't believe me' but found that his employers had a great number of reservations concerning the accuracy of his report. Indeed, it was only upon telephoning the BBC, with the threat that he would never again produce another broadcast unless the report was aired in full, that they relented and produced an un-edited version.[99] Given Dimbleby's impeccable reputation at the time, that his employer would question the veracity of his broadcast provides clear evidence in highlighting the difficulty in *processing* the full extent of the Nazi crimes in the immediate wake of their disclosure.

Whilst it could be argued that the regular insistence on the authenticity of such reports was partly in response to those sceptics who continued to argue that it was mere propaganda, it is perhaps more likely that these linguistic methods were used because members of the press realised that their readership would struggle to accept that these crimes were even possible. Again, contrasting this with predominant forms of press representation in the 1990s, whilst later horrors would continue to be described and photographed in detail, their authenticity was seldom, if ever, called into question. Expressed another way, emphasis on the accuracy of such reports was redundant by the time of the Rwandan genocide, as horrors of virtually any magnitude had by then become an accepted aspect of the political landscape as depicted in the media. As will be discussed more fully in the chapters relating to the coverage of Bosnia and Rwanda, such crimes had ceased to be truly shocking by the early 1990s, and even those journalists who *were* affected by what they bore witness to in these instances never intimated that they found this level of violence to be beyond belief. Indeed, it appears that what had been shocking in 1945 had since become business-as-usual less than half a century later.

It might seem strange to the current generation, long-since exposed to a multitude of atrocities through the media, that disbelief was a common and persistent response, but it must be remembered that there were a number of contemporary factors which contributed to this. One of the most pertinent reasons is that the liberation of the camps was the first time in which genocide had been presented to the Anglo–American world in such a concentrated manner. Though there had been instances of genocidal mass violence in the early part of the twentieth century, with the 1915 massacres of Armenians being a notable example which has in more recent decades been imbibed with a particular infamy, these were not assimilated by the Western public in any way which could be compared to the discoveries in April and May 1945.[100] Certainly, even the Armenian genocide, which provoked 145 stories in the *New York Times* in 1915, struggled to retain any meaningful position in the wider public consciousness. Hitler's 1939 rhetorical remark of 'Who today, after all, speaks of the annihilation of the Armenians?' was indeed accurate, with later descriptions of this event describing the fate of the Armenians as 'the hidden holocaust.'[101] Part of the reason why these particular genocidal events did not establish themselves in Anglo–American memory was because British and American citizens, in the form of soldiers and journalists, were not as intimately involved in their discovery. With the exception of the likes of Henry Morgenthau and his dispatches on Armenia, few first-hand accounts were produced by Anglo–American sources and so, perhaps understandably when one considers the advances in communications technology achieved by 1945, these particular stories were quickly forgotten.[102] Of course, genocide had taken place at numerous junctures in history before this time, but never in a period where the media could highlight it with such immediacy or vivid accompanying imagery.

Another related aspect also helps to explain why the camp discoveries provoked such disbelief – the fact that the horror which presented itself was far beyond what many ordinary people considered the
Nazis to be capable of. Though few at the time would regard the Nazi
regime as being tolerant or progressive, many would conceive Nazi
actions during the 1930s – such as the well-documented *Kristallnacht*
– as being the peak of their civilian atrocities. Indeed, in the words
of Richard Breitman, 'Few could believe that Nazi inhumanity would
or could get worse.'[103] Of course, the very existence of concentration
camps within the Nazi system was hardly a secret, and Western outlets
had documented them since the opening of Dachau in 1933. Indeed,
many did not see them as being particularly note-worthy, with 'Oh,
the English invented them in South Africa with the Boers' being a
common response to such revelations.[104] The 'function' of the camps
during the 1930s also helped to allow many lay observers avoid giving
them serious thought, as it was commonly assumed that the majority
of the inmates were political opponents and those suspected of being
a genuine threat to the Nazi regime. Essentially, because the evolving
function of the concentration camps system was largely hidden from
the Western world – a factor which will be discussed shortly – many
continued to accept this characterisation until the invasion of Germany
itself. When one considers the unprecedented nature of Nazi brutality,
this reason – illustrated in the following passage from Laurel Leff – can
perhaps be better understood:

> The notion that the camps held political and military prisoners
> and slave labourers had an appeal apart from the availability of
> the sources offering it. It introduced a modicum of rationality
> into scenes so ghastly that they defied reason.[105]

A related element which helps explain the difficulty that many had in com-
prehending the scale and barbarism of the Nazi camps was the *unprecedented* nature of the violence itself. Donald L. Niewyk once remarked
that 'nothing short of clairvoyance' could have mentally prepared the
Jews for what was to befall them, and this statement is equally true for
the Anglo–American audiences that were suddenly presented with such

brutal facts at the conclusion of the war in Europe.[106] Predictably then, terms like 'unparalleled' and 'unprecedented' were, and continue to be, common in myriad written responses to the Holocaust, with one contemporary editorial illustrating this phenomenon well:

> There have, however, always been some for who the honour of human nature have withheld complete belief from the reports, finding it easier to suppose that suffering has caused hallucination in the victims than to imagine a degradation of the soul that could descend so far below the animal level of cruelty.[107]

To those generations born *after* the Holocaust, the difficulty in perceiving evil on such a scale may not be particularly challenging – certainly, as Samantha Power notes, 'The Holocaust is too present in Western schoolbooks and culture today for genocide to be "unimaginable."'[108] However, such barbarity was largely incomprehensible before 1945, with the notion of the extermination of an entire people being beyond the darkest expectations of most Western citizens. Although genocide had occurred throughout history, it had never before dominated the media spotlight as it would in April and May 1945, and many struggled to incorporate this new reality into existing perceptions of the world at the time. The deliberate and organised annihilation of hundreds of thousands of civilians, as an end in itself, went 'well beyond previous experience,' and so there was little, if any, reason for the Anglo–American public to foresee the level of violence which would engulf Nazi-controlled Europe. Indeed, Himmler himself remarked in 1940 that the 'physical extermination of a people' was both 'un-German and impossible' – further illustrating the fact that the horrific revelations following liberation did not fit any existing Western schema.[109]

Finally, another crucial factor – what one might term the 'shadow of propaganda' – also drove this tendency towards disbelief. Atrocity propaganda had been a virtual constant in Western conflict for almost a century, rearing its head in both the American Civil War and the Boer War, but it was the experience of World War I which provoked a widespread public skepticism of such reports when they emerged in the early 1940s.[110] For one, the infamous 'violated nuns and babies' which had been described in British propaganda during the 1914–18 conflict ultimately proved to be largely fabricated, and this led to a number of contemporaries to dismiss similar accusations when they surfaced during World War II.[111] In a number of instances, fake atrocity stories were perceived to be simply an expected part of modern warfare, but not something which one was to accept unconditionally. Particularly among those who were old enough to remember World War I, there was a distrust regarding reports of organised mass murder within the areas of German control and influence – and this was undoubtedly a major factor in explaining why the *extent* of the Nazi terror was not appreciated before the discovery of the camps by Allied soldiers.

As Laural Leff argues, the memory of fabricated atrocities during the Great War had left 'a broad legacy of suspicion about reports of enemy atrocities,' and this trend continued in some quarters even *after* the degradation of Belsen and Buchenwald had been recorded by a large section of the media.[112] Leslie Mitchell, the voice of *Movietone News*, later recalled members of the public outside an exhibition showing some of the photos collected from the camps displaying banners proclaiming: 'Don't be misled! These films are propaganda. They are fakes!'[113] Amidst the testimony of respected journalists and soldiers, countless photographs and numerous films, the ability to fully accept was being presented remained difficult for many, with one poll taken in May 1945 – some weeks after the first reports from the camps had emerged – stating that 85 per cent of the American public believed the evidence to be exaggerated.[114] Arguments like these, in turn, led to further emphasis on the veracity of these accounts, with a number of reports from the time explicitly stating that nothing in such correspondence was to be regarded as faked. An example of this can be seen in the following extract from *The Times*:

> Our own have suffered from an understandable squeamishness, but the eye is the king of the senses, and it is good that this nightmare of cruelty, this epic of brutality, should be on record to refute those who still talk glibly of atrocity 'stories.' The camera, it is true, can on occasions, lie and set photographs can be 'faked,' but the very size and scale of these German enormities carry their own guarantee of authenticity.[115]

Evidently, then, this notable trend towards disbelief in the wake of some of the more horrific atrocities existed, in part, because of an overall lack of appreciation about the nature of the Nazi camp system. In addition to this, it also resulted from a cultural mistrust of official atrocity propaganda, stemming from the experience from World War I. However, these factors accepted, it is nonetheless the case that a distinct tone of disbelief permeates a variety of responses from April and May 1945; something which, again, was rarely (if ever) seen within the media coverage of the examples to be discussed in later chapters. Essentially, by the time that genocidal violence in the 1990s was being reported on, disclaimers as to the veracity of reports and the scale of the carnage were all but redundant, as by then such atrocities had an established history of being depicted in the Western media.

A Landmark in Exposure to Genocide

The discoveries at the likes of Belsen and Buchenwald in the late spring of 1945, and their subsequent depiction in the Anglo–American media, were a critically important landmark in terms of mass exposure to crimes of a genocidal nature. Whilst not being by any means the first instance of genocide in history, it was the first incidence in which evidence of its occurrence was covered by such a wide array of media. Also of note is that, in contrast to media coverage of the mass violence in Bosnia and Rwanda, the liberation period was characterised by evident disbelief and shock from both journalists and their audiences. Further, the visual imagery from the time also helped to inform the subsequent iconography which has developed around the Holocaust (and, by extension, the wider concept of 'genocide') in the decades since.

As influential as it was, the response to the camp revelations is not, in itself, enough to explain the position of the Holocaust within contemporary British and American culture. This development was instead the cumulative result of decades of exposure to, and familiarisation with, the crimes of the Nazis through a variety of mass-culture settings; and it is to the most important examples of these that the analysis now turns.

Public Awareness of the Holocaust: 1945–95

By the early 1990s, the Holocaust had become an established phenomenon in Western culture, particularly in the United States. Regarded as both a hugely important event in twentieth-century history and as something from which it is believed important moral and ethical lessons can be drawn, the Holocaust is as an historical occurrence which is arguably unmatched in terms of cultural posterity. The position which the Holocaust now occupies was only carved out over several decades, however, with certain crucial events cementing its place within Anglo–American culture and popular memory. It is to these important developments, each of which were integral in presenting the Holocaust (and thus genocide in general) to an ever-wider audience, that the focus of this chapter will now turn.

Immediate Postwar Period

With the Allied victory in 1945, the Holocaust became history, increasingly distant, remote, forgotten; a chapter, reduced to a page, shortened to a paragraph, relegated to a footnote.[116]

So once wrote Martin Gilbert, and this is a fairly accurate description of the manner in which the response to the camp revelations was quickly superseded by other concerns. In itself, therefore, the intense publicity during the liberation period was insufficient to provoke a desire for a deeper understanding of the Holocaust in the Anglo–American world. Though it may seem strange that interest in the crimes of the Nazis faded so quickly after the concentrated and emotive coverage which had accompanied the liberation of the camps in the spring of 1945, it should be remembered that all parties involved were now emerging from a war that had been the most destructive in history. The Allies' victory had been a lengthy struggle, expending unprecedented amounts of blood and treasure, and thus few wished to dwell on the recent violent past.[117] Instead, a spirit of optimism dominated the Western world, determined to see the horrors of the Third Reich as belonging to a different era. In the United States, this took the form of the postwar boom, with strong economic growth and the expansion of suburbia. In Europe, where the ruined buildings were a constant visual reminder of what had gone before, most were simply interested in messages of 'rebirth, regeneration, and reconciliation.'[118] Further, despite the end of the war, and the defeat of the Axis Powers, new threats suddenly came to the fore. The two most important of these, which in many ways over the subsequent years reinforced each other, were the advent of the nuclear age and the re-emergence of Communism as a challenge to the West's self-perceived liberal democratic values.[119] In particular, the atomic destruction of Japan was seen as a potential warning of what future wars might entail – a thought that was, understandably, more disconcerting and thus important to most Westerners than the atrocities of the most recent conflict. Indeed, as Lawrence Baron notes:

> Following Allied victory, the destruction of European Jewry was widely subsumed under the generic category of war casualties and crimes. The mushroom clouds over Hiroshima and Nagasaki appeared to many as ominous as the smoke rising from the crematoria of Auschwitz.[120]

Added to these factors was the simple fact that few people wished to engage with the crimes of the Nazis in any concentrated manner, with many believing that returning to focus on the horrors which had emerged from the camps constituted a form of 'unhealthy voyeurism.'[121] Notably, this was a phenomenon which affected both those who had been exposed to such things through the media and, also, the actual survivors themselves. In the contemporary world, where Holocaust memoirs and personal documentaries are both numerous and accessible, this may come as something of a surprise. It should be remembered, however, that most of these same survivors – 100,000 of whom came to the United States following the war – simply did not wish, or feel able, to transmit their experiences to a wider audience. Even the young Israeli state wished to separate itself from the previous era of destruction, seeing the passive nature in which much of the Holocaust had been suffered by Jews as being at odds with the aims of the new Jewish homeland.[122] Ultimately, the immediate postwar period was one in which those who knew of the horrors wished to move past them, whilst the actual survivors of these crimes, with few outlets for expression, endured what has been termed 'a phase of intense private misery.'[123]

All of this is not to say, however, that the Holocaust – and the wider issue of human rights violations – failed to be given at least some consideration at various junctures. One of the most important of these came with the Nuremburg Trials, which opened proceedings on 18 October 1945. Of the original 24 accused, 18 would be found guilty of war crimes and/or crimes against humanity. Twelve of these individuals would also receive the death penalty, though Martin Bormann and Hermann Goering – through escape and suicide, respectively – would ultimately not see this sentence carried out. Though given coverage by the Anglo–American press, the proceedings had nothing close to the impact that the trial of Adolf Eichmann would later have, but they did allow the public to 'grasp the implications of [...] extreme anti-Semitic policies.'[124]

Another crucial development came in 1948, with the ratification of the Convention on the Prevention and Punishment of the Crime of Genocide. The result, in part, of the work of Rapahel Lemkin – who had first used the term 'genocide' in print in 1944 – the Convention was heralded as demonstrating a global commitment to a new value system.[125] Though hampered by problems of definition and terminology – a fact that underscored by the decision of the USSR, South Africa and Yugoslavia, amongst others, to refuse to become signatories – the Convention was passed on 9 December 1948. Brought into existence a single day before the Universal Declaration of Human Rights, it was 'the world's first [...] comprehensive and codified protection of human rights,' and as such was given prominent attention by several media outlets.[126] Inevitably, discussions of the new treaty often referenced the various atrocities committed under the Nazi regime and in doing so ensured that they were given at least some form of renewed publicity during this period.[127]

The emerging medium of television, still attempting to secure a wide public audience, also brought the suffering inflicted by the Nazi regime into the popular consciousness. Despite early restrictions regarding content, and a desire to show appropriate reverence to the subject, 'several dozen' productions that dealt with the destruction of the Jews in at least some capacity had been broadcast by the late 1950s. These included 'original dramas for prime time "playhouses", programs for ecumenical religion series, documentaries [...] and even several instalments of the popular entertainment series *This Is Your Life*,' and though most intentionally avoided the inclusion of horrific details and graphic images, they nonetheless helped to introduce the postwar generation to the crimes of the Nazis.[128]

Whilst not reaching anywhere near the levels which would be seen in more recent decades, the postwar period also saw the publication of several books that had a particular focus on the Nazi atrocities themselves. There was a steady progression of such works through the 1950s, with Willi Frischauer's *Himmler: The Evil Genius of the Third Reich* (1953), Edward Crankshaw's *Instrument of Tyranny* (1956) and Gerald Reitlinger's *The Final Solution* (1953) all paving the way for what would later become something of a cottage industry in publishing. In Britain, *The Scourge of the Swastika* (1954), by Lord Liverpool, was also well received, though the focus on the Holocaust was rather limited within this publication.[129] Perhaps the most notable example of this developing interest in the Nazi period came from William R. Shirer's 1959 publication *Rise and Fall of the Third Reich*. Despite being the thickest paperback ever produced at that point – with 1,250 pages – and costing more than a dollar, Shirer's book sold more than one million copies and vividly illustrated that there was a (re)emerging interest in the events which had occurred under Hitler's regime.[130] One book, however, would surpass all others in terms of its popular impact in introducing people to the Jewish tragedy; and it was not an academic account, but instead the diary of a young girl.

The Diary of Anne Frank

The importance of *The Diary of Anne Frank*, first published in Holland in 1947, in relation to raising Holocaust 'awareness' cannot be overstated. Recording the life of the young author between June 1942 and August 1944, the book has become something of a phenomenon. Perhaps most influentially, to this day it remains the first exposure of many young people to the plight of Jews trapped in Nazi-occupied Europe.[131] Though initially having difficulty in finding a publisher for the English translation, *Anne Frank:*

The Diary of a Young Girl (as it was titled when published in English) was a sensation when it was first released in 1952, selling out its initial run of 100,000 copies in the US.[132] Part of its attraction was that it was very much a product of its time. During the optimistic postwar period, the largely positive and universal tone of the book – which was partly a result of multiple editing decisions – was in many ways an appropriately accessible introduction to the suffering endured under the Nazis. Also important was the fact that *The Diary* put a face to the multitude of Nazi victims, and in doing so helped people to properly empathise with the protagonist in a way that was not possible with the nameless masses which would be encountered following the discovery of the camps. Certainly, John F. Kennedy intimated as much when he later stated that, 'Of the multitude throughout history who have spoken for human dignity of great suffering and loss, no voice is more compelling than that of Anne Frank.'[133]

That the diary became 'an important catalyst for the penetration of the Holocaust into the consciousness of many millions' was not solely down to the success of the book, however, but also as a result of later adaptations on stage and screen.[134] Developed for the stage by the husband-and-wife writing team of Albert and Frances Hackett, the theatrical adaptation opened in Broadway's *Cort* theatre in October 1955 and proved to be just as successful as the print version. Described by Peter Novick as a 'box office smash,' its first run in New York lasted for 717 performances, and in 1956 the play received critical recognition by winning the Pulitzer Prize, Critic's Circle Prize and the Antoinette Perry Award.[135] This success inevitably led to the play being performed in numerous cities in the United States and Europe, and versions of it continue to be produced up to the present day.

The box office takings of the play also prompted Twentieth Century Fox to secure the rights to a possible film adaptation, production of which began in March 1958. Directed by George Stevens, who as a Signal Corps officer had filmed the liberation of Dachau, the 1959 motion picture continued the success of the stage version. Starring (a clearly much older) Millie Perkins in the title role, the film went on to win three Academy Awards and was nominated in five other categories, including Best Director and Best Picture.[136] The movie was also an international success, and its impact later prompted Alvin H. Rosenfeld to proclaim that 'The "child's voice" that had been silenced in Bergen-Belsen had now become audible to large numbers of people around the world.'[137]

The mid-to-late 1950s may have witnessed the most intense period of publicity concerning Anne Frank and the telling of her story, but what is perhaps more revealing is the manner in which Anne Frank's legacy has endured and subsequently been adapted to a whole range of cultural forms. *The Diary* itself had sold in excess of twenty million copies by the early 1990s, and has been published in more than 40 countries, with the 'character' of Anne accounting for almost one-quarter of Holocaust films produced for children. The Amsterdam attic in which she hid for so many months was opened to the public in May 1960 and by 1990 was attracting more than 600,000 visitors annually.[138] Her name has been attached to 'a day, a week, a rose, a tulip, countless trees, a whole forest, streets, schools and youth centres, and a village', whilst her image has adorned 'public statues, stamps, and commemorative coins.'[139] Essentially, there are few mediums, particularly those aimed at young people, which have not invoked Anne Frank's memory. In many ways, hers is a palatable version of the Holocaust story, and one which has ensured that Anne Frank certainly stands, in the words of Alvin H. Rosenfeld, 'almost unrivalled [...] as a contemporary cultural icon.'[140]

Though Anne Frank's story would introduce millions to the daily plight of Jews hiding in Nazi-occupied Europe, it remained the case that *The Diary*, due to the location in which it was written, was largely bereft of details of the more murderous aspects of Nazi policy. Whilst both the stage and film versions would end with a depiction of Anne in Bergen-Belsen, the wider ideology of the Holocaust – as a deliberate attempt to exterminate an entire race using coordinated, industrialised means – was not apparent in the *Diary* or its various adaptations. These details would emerge, however, with what continues to be regarded as one of the most infamous legal trials in history – the trial of Adolf Eichmann.

The Trial of Adolf Eichmann

Captured by Israeli Secret Service personnel in Buenos Aires in early May 1960, Adolf Eichmann arrived in Israel on 22 May that same year. Whilst his interrogation began a week later the trial itself would not commence until 11 April 1961 – though this did not mean that his seizure was not discussed within sections of the media immediately after it came to light.[141] Eichmann may have been a suspected war criminal but the legal implications of his abduction nonetheless caused a great deal of controversy, with many commentators arguing that it violated international law. Newspaper editorials produced in the immediate aftermath of his capture were negative 'by a margin of 2-to-1,' with Eric Fromm describing it as 'an act of lawlessness of exactly the type of which the Nazis themselves [...] have been guilty.' If anything then, this early controversy ensured that the eventual trial would command extensive international attention.[142]

In many ways, and quite deliberately, the function of the trial was more than simply finding Eichmann guilty for his role in the Holocaust. Described by prosecutor Gideon Hausner as the Nazi regime's 'executive arm for the extermination of the Jewish people,' Eichmann was to become symbolic of all those who had been involved in this historic crime.[143] As the most senior Nazi captured since 1945, the defendant would be framed as representing not just himself, but the Third Reich – once described by Niall Ferguson as 'the most abominable regime ever to emerge from a modern democracy' – in its entirety. Indeed, David Ben-Gurion reiterated as much, saying of the proceedings: 'it is not an individual that is in the dock at this historical trial, and not the Nazi regime alone, but anti-Semitism throughout history.'[144] Building on this, the trial was thus used to provide a means of detailing the nature of the Nazi crimes which had taken place two decades prior. With the world's media in attendance, the Israeli state grasped the opportunity to reveal 'the full horrors of the Holocaust,' determined to highlight the scale and complexity of the extermination process.[145] Vital to this goal was the testimony of survivors – the majority of whom, it should be noted, had no personal experience with Eichmann himself – whose cumulative experiences would ultimately be used to present 'an epic retelling of the Holocaust narrative.'[146] In relation to the developing awareness of the Holocaust within Western culture, this aspect was crucial. Specific details of the atrocities which had taken place within the Nazi empire had been under-developed in most popular mediums to this point, and so the full extent of what had occurred during the Holocaust was not readily apparent to many until *after* the revelations of the Eichmann trial.

Speaking before the trial, Ben-Gurion asserted that 'We want the nations of the world to know', and, given the intense media coverage of the proceedings, this aim was to some extent achieved.[147]

Given the intention of the prosecution to not simply secure a guilty verdict but to also publicise the details of the Holocaust to a global audience, it was essential that there be a sizable media presence in attendance. Reporters from 50 countries filled the courthouse in the opening days, with 450 out of 750 available seats being awarded to journalists. To aid the immediate dissemination of the proceedings, simultaneous translation was also provided, ensuring that the grim details emerging from the trial could be reported on and circulated in the shortest possible time.[148] Integral to reaching a large audience however was the role of television, a medium which was present in over 90 per cent of US homes by 1960. Arguing that 'where there is no publicity there is no justice', the judges at the trial had encouraged the proceedings to be televised from the beginning and, given the time difference between Israel and the United States, citizens of the latter had 'the privilege of watching the trial almost live.'[149] The use of television maximised the number of people who would could follow the proceedings – particularly in Britain, where the press were sometimes accused of not devoting sufficient attention to the trial – with a Gallup poll taken four months before the final verdict citing that 87 per cent of the American public were familiar with the event.[150] Though media interest in the trial decreased as the trial wore on as a perhaps inevitable result of its lengthy duration, the press returned in great numbers for the verdict – in which the defendant was found guilty and sentenced to death. Eichmann's execution, however, divided opinion 'on a global level', though this in turn further ensured that the trial remained in the public spotlight long after the sentence had been carried out.[151]

A further aspect of the trial's influence was that the details of the proceedings helped to redefine the public image of those who had been *responsible* for the Holocaust. Eichmann's ordinary appearance and insistence that he had simply been following orders introduced the idea of the 'desk killer', which was far removed from the generalised notion of the Nazi killing machine as being made up of sociopaths and those predisposed to violence.[152] The seminal academic work relating to this was Hannah Arendt's *Eichmann in*

Jerusalem, published in 1963. Although an account of the trial itself, Arendt's thesis on the 'banality of evil' – a phrase which continues to resonate to this day – was hugely significant in altering the perception of Nazism and organised mass violence in general. Over 200 books and articles were written in response to this important work, and it was highly influential in initiating 'the growing tidal wave of works on the Holocaust and other genocides.'[153] Not only was there a notable increase in scholarly contributions to the subject of Jewish suffering but, perhaps more importantly, the trial itself and Arendt's subsequent analysis also encouraged a rise in the number of survivors who were willing to share their own experiences with those outside their immediate circle. Certainly, as Cole notes, 'what had been silenced and suppressed gushed out and became common knowledge.'[154]

Perhaps the most important change that resulted from the concentrated focus on the trial was the birth of *The Holocaust* as a distinct event in its own right. As Kushner has noted, 'before the 1960s at the earliest the Holocaust as a self-enclosed entity had not yet entered into the general consciousness or memory of the Western world,' and so the proceedings against Eichmann were surely highly influential in changing this.[155] The destruction of the Jews had until this point been largely subsumed within the larger narrative of World War II, being seen by many as one crime among the multitude of atrocities committed by the Nazis. Though references to 'the Holocaust' in the manner which we now understand the term had appeared in a variety of forms in the years before Eichmann's capture – the Second World Congress of Jewish Studies had used the phrase in 1957, whilst the *New York Times Index* first listed it in 1960 – it was only in the aftermath of the trial that the Holocaust came to be widely recognised as a distinct event.[156] Particularly in the United States, but also in Britain and other parts of the Western world, this was a critical development in the wider understanding and appreciation of what had befallen the Jews, with Alan Mintz stating:

> The intensely public nature of the trial not only communicated an enormous amount of information; it also transformed the status of the Holocaust in the American mind. It became, in a sense, 'registered' in American collective memory as a key event in the modern age and as a watershed in the definition of what humanity is capable of.[157]

Essentially, then, the Eichmann trial clarified and contextualised Jewish suffering after earlier works, including *The Diary of Anne Frank*, had first introduced the Anglo–American world to the concept. Specific details of the extermination program emerged as a result of the proceedings, providing a greater appreciation of the level of organisation that had gone into the Holocaust. In turn, scholarly and popular engagement with the subject subsequently increased, with the Library of Congress finally creating a class of work entitled 'Holocaust: Jewish 1939–1945' in 1968. It was not until the late 1970s however, with the broadcast of the television mini-series *Holocaust*, that specific participants, locations and events related to this catastrophe would be visually represented to a large Western audience.[158]

Holocaust

In many ways, *Holocaust* was – much as *The Diary of Anne Frank* had been decades earlier – what might be termed a 'culturally appropriate' product for its time. Especially in the United States, still reeling from both Vietnam and the Watergate scandal, reengaging with the Holocaust in such a medium was in part an attempt to address the 'need for a public ritual involving clear-cut moral issues.'[159] Added to this, but no less important, was the fact that an increasing number of survivors were becoming more willing to share their own experiences – meaning that the cultural foundation, if one may call it that, had been already laid before *Holocaust* was ever put into production. Indeed, as Raul Hilberg notes, 'here was a television play that the author, Gerald Green, could not have sold to any network five or ten years earlier.'[160]

Although it is not a production which has aged particularly well, the broadcast of *Holocaust* was a watershed moment in terms of general Holocaust awareness. Described as the Jewish equivalent of 1977's slavery epic, *Roots*, the 9 ½-hour mini-series – which starred both James Woods and Meryl Streep in pivotal roles – managed to condense the enormity of the Holocaust into a workable narrative which was suitable for a mass audience.[161] Focusing on the fictional Weiss family from Berlin, the mini-series documented the trials of the various members of the family from 1935 until the war's end, with most major anti-Jewish measures – including

Kristallnacht, Babi-Yar and the gas chambers of Auschwitz – becoming central to the story at different times. Crucial to the story was also the parallel narrative of the fictional *SS* recruit, Erik Dorf – a role which won Michael Moriarty a Golden Globe. Dorf's story – which allowed the production to introduce real Nazi figures such as Eichmann, Heydrich and Himmler – was hugely important in terms of revealing the true nature of the Nazi extermination program, and illustrated and solidified the idea of the desk-killer, which had begun with Adolf Eichmann, in the Western consciousness.[162] Combined, the fusion of these two narratives allowed for a great deal of information about the Holocaust to be presented, and it is for this reason that *Holocaust* was such an influential broadcast in relation to raising awareness and understanding of this event. Whilst the production may indeed be, in the words of Annette Insdorf, 'simplistic and emotionally manipulative', Judith Doneson is correct in asserting that '*Holocaust*, an uncomplicated vision of the events in question but a morally honest one, served as the catalyst for a mass awakening of public awareness of the destruction of Europe's Jews'.[163]

To maximise audience figures, NBC also launched an awareness campaign to ensure that *Holocaust* was properly publicised in the weeks running up to its first broadcast. Advanced screenings were provided for interested parties, with special consideration given to providing for those from both the Christian and Jewish religious press. To highlight that the production was based predominantly on actual events, there was also a concentrated effort to circulate educational tie-ins with the broadcast, with study guides made available for viewers and various learning aids being provided for schools.[164] The timing of the broadcast of the last of the four episodes, which ran across consecutive nights from 16–19 April 1978, was also deliberately chosen to coincide with the 35th anniversary of the Warsaw Ghetto Uprising, which would later lead to the date being labelled 'Holocaust Sunday'. Certainly, given such concentrated and varied publicity, Doneson is not exaggerating in declaring that '*Holocaust*'s pre-broadcast promotion was probably unprecedented in history'.[165] With advanced publicity on this scale, it is perhaps unsurprising that *Holocaust* would go on to record enormous viewing figures, first in the US and then in Europe. An estimated 120 million people tuned in to watch the original broadcast, and by 1979 – when the production was re-aired on both sides of the Atlantic – the series had been viewed by somewhere in the region of 220 million.[166] Figures such as these are evidence of the growing awareness of the Holocaust by the late 1970s, whilst also showing the degree to which a large proportion of the Anglo–American public were given further exposure to the event through this important broadcast.

Holocaust was generally well reviewed, and went on to collect eight Emmy Awards and two Golden Globes – both considered among the most prestigious accolades in the realm of television. The days and weeks following the original broadcast also witnessed a great deal of opinion being generated which discussed the production. Media critics were quick to praise *Holocaust* and commentators in other formats debated the various strengths and weaknesses of the mini-series at length. One particular aspect of the show which gained considerable praise was the fact that it had brought the story of the Holocaust – and by extension more universal issues of intolerance and hatred – to a wider audience than ever before.[167] Many saw it as an accessible history through which the Western public could become familiarised with the Holocaust without being overwhelmed by it, with Rabbi Marc Tannenbaum arguing that:

> NBC-TV's 'Holocaust' has brought that message – as nothing else has, neither books, nor lectures, nor documentaries – to some 220 million people in 50 countries throughout the world. It is a message on which the very survival of the human family depends in a nuclear missile age, an age which for the first time is able to conceive of a global Auschwitz.[168]

This is not to say, however, that *Holocaust* did not also receive its share of criticism. Whilst some criticised the fact that most of the main characters were fictional (despite being based on the collective experiences of real people), others saw the very fact that the Holocaust had been utilised in order to make a prime-time drama as somewhat disrespectful.[169] The use of advertisement breaks (during one of which there was an unfortunate commercial for Lysol, a germ-killing agent) was commented upon in this regard, being viewed as a symptom of a commoditisation of the Holocaust. The harshest criticism, however, came from those who saw the production as a dramatic invasion into something which ultimately did not lend itself to television, with Elie Wiesel asserting that *Holocaust* was 'untrue, offensive, cheap [...] an insult to those who perished and to those who survived [...] It transforms an ontological event into soap opera.'[170]

In much the same manner in which Hannah Arendt's thesis on the Eichmann trial had broadened the discussion beyond the proceedings itself, the controversy and debate surrounding *Holocaust* also helped to ensure both its short-term impact and its position in posterity.[171] To many scholars, *Holocaust* would be the catalyst for a wider understanding and recognition of the genocide of the Jews and what it had actually involved. Though it had been represented in various mediums in the three decades since the end of the war, it was arguably this prime-time production which ultimately turned the word 'Holocaust' into a household term, first in the US and then the wider world. Novick describes the broadcast as 'without doubt the most important moment in the entry of the Holocaust into general American consciousness,' with Shandler echoing this point with the declaration that *Holocaust* was a 'threshold event in the dynamics of Holocaust consciousness in America.'[172] The Holocaust thus became more firmly established as an event which people were readily familiar with, and so *Holocaust* essentially built upon a process which had been slowly accumulating since the end of World War II. *Holocaust* also had a longer-term impact by virtue of the fact that it became a catalyst for further dramatic productions relating to the Holocaust. Though none of them would gain the viewing figures or critical accolades of Gerald Green's mini-series, productions such as *The Wall* (1982), *Wallenberg: A Hero's Story* (1985) and *War and Remembrance* (1988–9) would continue to reveal aspects of the destruction of the Jews to a mass audience, and in doing so helped to keep the Holocaust in the public eye.

There was also a notable upsurge in wider cultural developments related to the Holocaust in the wake of *Holocaust*'s original broadcast.[173] Lobbying for state laws in the US mandating the teaching of the Holocaust was 'revitalised' – beginning a process that now sees this event as an established part of the curriculum in both Britain and America. An important milestone in this phase of increased public engagement came in 1979, when President Jimmy Carter sanctioned a commission to consider the construction of a United States Holocaust Museum. Invoking what would soon become a familiar and oft-repeated sentiment, Carter linked this development to wider US foreign policy aims by proclaiming: 'we must forge an unshakable oath with all civilised people that never again will the world stand silent, never again will the world fail to act in time to prevent this terrible crime of genocide.'[174] Evidently then, the 1978 production helped not only to publicise the Holocaust as never before, but also succeeded in provoking a resurgent engagement with the subject in both public and academic spheres 'where scholarly dissertations and artistic interpretations [had] not.'[175]

Holocaust and other popular representations of this event would not be the only occurrences which would continue to draw attention to the Holocaust through the 1970s and 1980s, however. A number of cultural and political controversies, each of which had at least some basis in the memorialisation of the Holocaust, would also continue this public illumination at various times. One of the most important of these, at least in terms of the general discussion it provoked, was the rise in Holocaust denial. Beginning in the 1960s, in part due to the Eichmann trial and also the 1967 'Six-Day War', Holocaust denial was an established (but largely discredited) movement by the mid-1970s, involving both recognised scholars and pseudo-historians.[176] Publications such as Austin J. App's *The Six Million Swindle: Blackmailing the German People for Hard Marks with Fabricated Corpses* (1973) and Richard Verrall's *Did Six Million Really Die?* (1974) generated debate and discussion in several parts of the Western world. In the United States, these claims often evolved into wider debates regarding the value of freedom of speech and other matters of personal expression.[177] Though the arguments of the deniers were generally rebutted by other historians and given little widespread acceptance, the fact that the *question* of the veracity of Jewish suffering had been raised ensured that the event remained in the public eye, albeit in a manner which was not conducive to further understanding.

Another scandal which once again brought the Holocaust into the public domain was President Ronald Reagan's 1985 visit to Bitburg Cemetery. Originally planned as part of a reconciliatory gesture with West German Chancellor Helmut Kohl, the decision to lay a wreath at this particular site caused a great deal of controversy when it emerged that 49 *SS* officers were among those buried there. The issue was compounded by the fact that Reagan, in response to this criticism, argued that these men were themselves also 'victims of Nazism.'[178] The President's decision to go ahead with the event, despite serious misgivings from various quarters, led to comment and protest both in Germany and in the United States. A *New York Times* article urged the visit to be cancelled, describing it as 'one of the most embarrassing and politically damaging episodes of the administration,' whilst protestors from 21 countries clashed with police at the site itself.[179] Given Reagan's Cold-War position as 'leader of the free world', the media attention devoted to this episode was considerable. Though it did not shed any new light on the details of the Holocaust, or even contribute to a greater understanding of existing information, the sheer level of controversy surrounding the visit demonstrated the growing importance attached to properly memorialising the event.

A further development which contributed to the Holocaust becoming accepted as an integral part of Anglo–American culture was the establishment of museums and study centres which focused specifically on the Nazi atrocities. This process began to gain serious momentum in the United States in the mid-1980s, and there are now more than 100 such centres across the country. Some of these were unveiled amid intense media publicity, with the Simon Wiesenthal Museum of Tolerance – which opened in 1993 – seeing mainstream celebrities such as Arnold Schwarzenegger in attendance to mark its opening.[180] Though not as prolific or as numerous, there were also similar developments in the United Kingdom. A permanent exhibit – 'Belsen 1945' – was opened at the Imperial War Museum in 1991, the success of which prompted the establishment of a larger exhibition in 2000, which received £12.5 million in National Lottery funding and was officially opened by the Queen.[181] The undoubted pinnacle of this process of officially recognising the Holocaust, however, was with the opening of the United States Holocaust Memorial Museum (USHMM) in 1993.

The process of establishing a national memorial museum to the Holocaust began with President Carter's 1979 Commission on the Holocaust – a development which, as mentioned, may well have been influenced by the broadcast of *Holocaust* the previous year. This project was ultimately taken on by subsequent administrations, with Ronald Reagan's chief arms negotiator, Max Kampelman, declaring that the 'decision to build such a museum says something about our commitment to human rights and to the kind of nation we want to be.'[182] Built on federal land, and with a budget of $168 million, the USHMM was officially opened in a ceremony – attended by President Clinton, Elie Wiesel and, notably given the ongoing violence in the Balkans at this time, Croatian President Franjo Tudjman – on 22 April 1993.[183]

Described by Bill Clinton at the inaugural ceremony as 'an investment in a secure future against whatever insanity lurks ahead,' the USHMM was not simply regarded as a collection of artefacts but as a 'tribute to American willingness to remember this event.'[184] In many ways this establishment represented the official assimilation of the Holocaust into American culture, particularly when one remembers that it was situated on the Mall, alongside a number of other prominent national memorials that were all dedicated to *American* events. The museum has also proven exceedingly popular with the public, with one million visitors passing through its doors in the first year alone – a figure which would have been greater if not for restrictions on maximum attendance put in place by the curators themselves.[185] In spite of its popularity and official support however, like most major public engagements with the Holocaust that had preceded it the USHMM received criticism from a number of quarters. Though the museum was praised by many for enabling a 'personal and emotional' response to an event which hadn't even taken place in the same continent as it was situated, others decried the overall presentation of the various exhibits.[186] Dismissed as essentially a Holocaust theme park, others pointed to what they regarded as style-over-substance, with Shalmi Bar-Mor – Director of the Department of Education at Yad Vashem, Israel's own Holocaust memorial museum – describing it as being 'just a collection of gimmicks [...] I'm sure you come out with nothing.'[187]

Following these developments over previous decades then, it could be argued that by the early 1990s the Holocaust was more firmly established in Anglo–American culture than at any other time. Indeed, this trend was illustrated by the research of James Carroll, which showed that major newspapers in the US printed more stories on the Holocaust in the period between 1990 and 1997 than during the previous 45 years combined.[188] Such was the concentrated coverage in 1993 that it was dubbed 'the year of the Holocaust,' the greatest driver of this popularisation being the release of *Schindler's List* – a motion picture which, more than any other, brought the Holocaust into the realm of mainstream cinema.[189]

Schindler's List

Of course, whilst being undoubtedly the most influential, *Schindler's List* was not the first major studio-backed cinematic production which utilised the Holocaust as a plot device. Following on from *Judgement at Nuremburg*, a 1961 release which was notable due to its inclusion of actual documentary footage of the camps, films such as *The Pawnbroker* (1964) and *Sophie's Choice* (1982), both of which dealt with issues relating to survivors, received moderate acclaim and respectable viewing figures.[190] Nothing prior (or indeed since), however, would compare to the impact of Steven Spielberg's 1993 epic, which Alan Mintz described as 'an event of an entirely different order of magnitude.'[191]

Though many were at first sceptical about whether Steven Spielberg – a director at that time best known for 'chronicling dinosaurs and extraterrestrials' – could tackle such a serious subject, his three-hour cinematic journey ultimately surpassed even the most optimistic expectations. Whilst *Schindler's List* focused on the actions of industrialist Oskar Schindler and his attempts to save his Jewish workforce from the Nazi killing machine, the film also highlighted other aspects of the Holocaust, including graphic depictions of life in the ghettoes and conditions within the concentration camps themselves. Filmed almost entirely in black-and-white and using angles and editing which were common during the 1940s, aspects of the film had something of a documentary quality to them, prompting one critic to argue that it resembled 'a newsreel unearthed after more than half a century.'[192] Though a tale of survival, there were nonetheless several graphic depictions of violence, with Ralph Fiennes' portrayal of Amon Goeth – now recognised as 'one of the screen's most unforgettable villains' – personifying the evil of the Nazi regime. Given the serious and often traumatic nature of the film's main themes it was perhaps expected that *Schindler's List* would struggle to make a notable impact at the box office. On the contrary though, Spielberg's tale was not only a commercial success, but also went on to establish a place within Western culture arguably unlike anything which had preceded it.[193]

The viewing figures for *Schindler's List* surpassed any previous cinematic representation of the Holocaust, reaching a wide audience in both Britain and America. Approximately 25 million Americans saw the film when it was first released, with a further 42 million seeing it upon its video release and a record 65 million tuning in for its television premiere in 1997. *Schindler's List* was also seen by 'a quarter' of the British population, and went on to gross between $317.1 million and $321.2 million worldwide. This ensured that the influence of the movie went beyond specialist audiences, a factor illustrated by Bartov's assertion that 'more people saw *Schindler's List* in the first month of screening than have watched [Claude Lanzmann's] *Shoah* since it was first released.[194]' Like *Holocaust* some 15 years before, a huge effort was made to publicise *Schindler's List*, particularly to younger people. Study guides were distributed to schools upon its release and adults were strongly encouraged to see the film. Public officials in the US declared it a 'civic duty', whilst one notable column in *The Times* suggested that free Odeon tickets be distributed to 'the unwaged at DSS offices.' This is a trend that continued in the years following the film's release, with *Schindler's List* often being used to familiarise young adults with the horror of the Holocaust.[195]

Spielberg's epic, which as of March 2017 occupied seventh place on the imdb.com all-time list as voted for by users, also benefitted from an unprecedented degree of public support from a number of highly influential individuals. US President Bill Clinton urged all Americans to see the film, recommending *Schindler's List* as a moral lesson and asserting that it had helped him 'understand the nature of human suffering and its appropriate response.' This theme – of emphasising the redemptive qualities of *Schindler's List* – was common in other endorsements, in a manner which is rare for a motion-picture made for a mass audience. The chat-show host Oprah Winfrey stated that watching the film had made her 'a better person,' and like Clinton urged her viewers to attend their nearest screening.[196]

Perhaps the most emotive and hyperbolic support for the film however came from Walt Disney studio-boss Jeffrey Katzenberg, who argued:

> I think *Schindler's List* will wind up being so much more important than a movie. It will affect how people on this planet think and act. At a moment in time, it is going to remind us about the dark side, and do it in a way in which, whenever that little green monster is lurking somewhere, this movie is going to press it down again. I don't want to burden the movie too much, but I think it will bring peace on earth, good will to men. Enough of the right people will see it that it will actually set the course of world affairs.[197]

Schindler's List also benefitted from a notable level of critical success, to a degree unmatched by any previous Holocaust-related film. Among a variety of other awards and nominations, *Schindler's List* went on to claim seven Academy Awards – including Best Director and Best Picture. Given that the film was American-produced but featured a predominantly British cast, this combination of critical, popular and political endorsement ensured that the film cemented a prominent place in Anglo–American culture, prompting Mintz to argue that it had 'signalled the crossover of the Holocaust into a new prominence and acceptability.'[198] Miriam Hansen, writing three years after the original release, went further still, asserting that:

> If there were a Richter scale to measure the extent to which commercial films cause reverberations in the traditional public sphere, the effect of *Schindler's List* might be equal or come close to that of D.W. Griffith's racist blockbuster of 1915, *The Birth of a Nation*.[199]

Of course, like most engagements with the Holocaust which have entered the public consciousness, *Schindler's List* also generated debate and controversy.[200] One of the main criticisms of the movie was that its somewhat sentimental tone and uplifting ending bordered on 'kitchiness,' making such a depiction untypical of the destruction of the Holocaust. The unrepresentative nature of *Schindler's List* has also been remarked upon in relation to the chief villain of the piece, Amon Goeth. The success of *Schindler's List* has arguably ensured that this psychotic and sadistic character – the portrayal of whom gained Ralph Fiennes an Oscar nomination in the Best Supporting Actor Category – has since become the typical perpetrator in the minds of much of the public audience, despite the fact that most individuals involved in the destruction of the Jews did not embark on their crimes with such pleasure or vigour.[201] Again then, this could be used as an argument that the film is somewhat unrepresentative of the *reality* of the Holocaust – a position which is further compounded by the fact that no Jewish character in the film with more than 15 lines of dialogue dies. A final, and perhaps crucial, complaint about the film was that its graphic violence and epic scale had somehow trivialised the Holocaust, by trying to portray on screen what, in the eyes of some, is unimaginable.[202]

Ultimately though, both at the time and in the two decades since its original release, *Schindler's List* has generally been praised for bringing the Holocaust once again to the forefront of Western consciousness, and in doing so helped to ensure that the memory of this event would not fade. In an age where mass media representations can spark renewed interest in historical events, *Schindler's List* is perhaps the most persuasive of all.[203] Referenced in the years since in myriad other popular mediums – including *South Park*, *Seinfeld* and *Family Guy* – it is certainly true that the film has 'affected our society.' Indeed, such is the importance of Spielberg's film in bringing the Holocaust into mainstream Western culture that it is hard to argue with Loshitzky's claim that, '*Schindler's List* has penetrated historical consciousness on a global scale and has transformed the image of the Holocaust as perceived by millions of people all over the world.'[204]

Conclusion

By the early to mid-1990s then, it could be argued that Holocaust awareness had reached its peak in the Anglo–American world. As revealed in several polls and studies, by this period the Holocaust – as both an overall concept and in relation to certain details of the event – was increasingly well understood, particularly in the United States. Between 90–95 per cent of those polled in various surveys in the mid-1990s affirmed that they had heard of the Holocaust and knew what it was, with an earlier poll in 1992 revealing that 35.1 and 49.1 per cent of those questioned could give a correct definition of Adolf Eichmann and Anne Frank, respectively. The manner in which the Holocaust had become integrated into American consciousness was further emphasised by the fact that 'substantially' more people could identify the Holocaust than they could Pearl Harbor or the fact that the US and the Soviets were allies during World War II.[205] Although such widespread acknowledgment was not replicated to the same degree in the United Kingdom, the fact that most major pop-culture developments invariably find their way across the Atlantic ensured that Holocaust awareness was nonetheless also at notably high levels in Britain in this same period. Later described by Cole as 'probably the most talked about and oft-represented event of the twentieth century', the Holocaust had been gaining greater prominence in the UK throughout the 1980s and by the time that Bosnia and Rwanda were being reported on it could be regarded as having achieved 'great relevance in British society.'[206]

An unintended consequence of this revived and expanded interest in the Holocaust, and one which ensured the event's place in the public domain, was the usage of related terms for political and ideological purposes. From animal-testing sites being described as 'Buchenwald for animals' to the anti-abortion movement talking of a 'holocaust of babies', there are few issues, particularly those which might be considered as highly controversial, which have not invoked Holocaust analogies in some fashion.[207] This trend has also been repeated in official statements by those in a position of power, gaining notable prominence during matters of foreign policy. As Hume has noted, the 'most effective way to demonise anybody [...] is to link them somehow to the Nazi experience,' and this has been invoked to justify policy in, amongst others, Iraq and Kosovo. A futher result of this 'Holocaustising', one which has been commented upon for several years and is linked to later observations within the chapters on Bosnia and Rwanda, is that such flippant use of the memory of the event may have weakened the overall impact of the term – and therefore genocide as a concept itself.[208] Whilst this final point may be debated, this does not detract from the fact that Holocaust awareness had reached something of a peak by the early 1990s, predominantly as a result of the cumulative process influenced by the events and developments detailed in this chapter. This did not necessarily mean, however, that increased awareness would lead to a more robust response to subsequent cases of genocide; a central concern of the chapters which follow that deal with media responses to Bosnia and Rwanda.

3

Inconveniently Close

Anglo–American Coverage of the Bosnian War

Although the 1990s were marked by the eruption of multiple, but remote, conflicts across the globe, the 'illusion of harmony' which had swept the Western world after the defeat of Communism was truly shattered only when a crisis loomed in Europe itself, in what at that time was still being referred to as the former Yugoslavia.[1] The conflict which ignited the Balkans in the last decade of the twentieth century brought mass war crimes back to European soil for the first time in two generations, and introduced the term 'ethnic cleansing' into common usage in the English-speaking world.[2]

David Rieff once described the carnage of Bosnia as being 'the third great genocide of a small European minority to take place in the twentieth century', though it should be clarified here that only certain aspects of the conflict were what might be termed *intentionally* genocidal.[3] Debate concerning how best to accurately describe the violence in Bosnia, and whether or not the atrocities (particularly the more sporadic outbursts in rural regions) should be labelled as genocide, continues to this day. Whilst it is widely accepted that the mass slaughter of Srebrenica constituted an act of genocide, such a consensus in regards to wider patterns of violence within Bosnia has not been reached. With particular reference to the suffering of Bosnian Muslims during the war, it may be more accurate to talk of a deliberate policy of the systematic removal of populations (that is, ethnic cleansing), rather than describing the crimes in Bosnia as all part of a program of extermination. However, it should be noted that, in Bosnia itself, 'ethnic cleansing' is widely regarded as 'a euphemism employed to minimise or deny genocide by putting a pleasant face on mass atrocities.'[4] Ethnic cleansing can manifest in a variety of forms – many of which do not necessarily involve mass-killing – with Barbie Zelizer defining it as 'the mass expulsion of population from coveted areas by the deliberate use of terror.'[5] In Bosnia, this most commonly involved the use of tactics by Serb units – including burning of homes, mass rape and summary executions – to compel Muslim or Croat populations to flee. Humiliation of targeted groups, Muslims in particular, was also a crucial goal for the Serbs in several of these actions. This led to the burning of entire villages and the destruction of cultural monuments in a number of regions, with some reporting 'wanton, sadistic cruelty so base that [the victims] found themselves accused of fabrication to discredit the enemy.'[6] A notable aspect of these ethnic cleansing operations was the fact that a number of the worst atrocities were undertaken by irregular forces and paramilitary squads, the most infamous of these being Arkan's Tigers.[7] None of this is to say, however, that particular episodes during this conflict could not be regarded as genocidal – the most obvious example being the atrocities which followed the fall of Srebrenica to Serb forces in July 1995. In any case, and however one wishes to define the violence during this period, the destruction and suffering unleashed by this conflict nonetheless contributed to the deaths of tens of thousands of people in the region – the majority of whom were civilians. Estimates varied for several years, but until recently it was widely accepted that between 150,000 and 200,000 were killed in Bosnia from 1992–5; and as such this figure is cited when appropriate due to the fact that this was the general consensus in the years immediately surrounding the violence. In recent years, this total has been revised down, based on studies by the Research and Documentation Centre in Sarajevo. A more accurate total is now believed to be around 97,000. Nonetheless, this made the Bosnian conflict more destructive than any which has befallen Europe since World War II.[8]

Due to advances in telecommunications, several of these horrors were given exposure throughout the war, with many atrocities being reported on almost immediately after their initial disclosure. Norman Cigar alluded to this when he described Bosnia as being 'the first case of genocide being televised as it was actually taking place,' and the war engulfing the Balkans certainly did gain a great deal of coverage.[9] As will be highlighted throughout this chapter, whilst the reporting may have often been shallow and lacking in context, its sheer repetition ensured that it was difficult for the Western media audience to be completely ignorant of what was unfolding in Bosnia. This level of coverage, however, despite ensuring that 'ethnic cleansing' became part of the English vocabulary, did not lead to determined calls for action in the region, or even a persistent interest in the atrocities themselves.[10] This chapter will seek to develop and substantiate these observations, whilst also linking notable trends to a wider analysis of twentieth-century engagement with genocide and mass human rights abuses.

Western Discourse Regarding the Balkans

Prior to the early 1990s, when the conflict in Bosnia deteriorated to the point of ethnic cleansing, war and genocide, there was already an established Western discourse regarding the Balkans and its inhabitants. Whilst most of these assumptions and ideas were based on stereotypes or mythologies that were in some cases hundreds of years old, certain Western perceptions of the Balkans proved difficult to dislodge. This, in turn, inevitably had an impact on how the Anglo–American press subsequently characterised and explained the violence as it unfolded from 1992–5. The following section will look at the most dominant and persistent aspects of what might loosely be termed the Western discourse regarding the Balkans, and in doing so will help to situate and contextualise some of the later findings of this research as existing within an already-established Anglo–American framework.

Even before media coverage of the Balkan turmoil of the 1990s had cemented the idea in Western consciousness that the region was a hotbed of centuries-old, intractable ethnic tensions, there was already an established narrative in the West which regarded the Balkans as being somewhat apart from Europe itself. This separateness was not constructed in a strictly geographical sense either, with the people of the Balkans often depicted as backward, unrefined and uncivilised; at least compared to Western norms and customs. Speaking of his experience in the region in the 1970s – in what was then still regarded as Yugoslavia – *Sunday Telegraph* writer Simon Winchester echoed such a belief, claiming that 'there was something intractably wild and backward about the people in [those] parts.'[11]

Such depictions of the inhabitants of the Balkans would continue into the 1990s and ultimately influenced the overall framing of the conflict itself. This is perhaps unsurprising, however, as the idea of a brutish and generally uncivilised Balkans was given credence in a variety of sources over the course of the twentieth century. For example, one academic, writing in the 1930s, echoed this Western stereotype by commenting upon what he termed 'the proverbial Balkan mentality [...] the inability to give and take.'[12] Seen as inherently backwards when contrasted with Western standards, a discourse emerged in which, Todorova notes, 'the standard Balkan male is uncivilised, primitive, crude, cruel, and, without exception, disheveled.'[13] The violence in the Balkans – with its images of swaggering paramilitaries in camouflage fatigues and balaclavas – did little more than to establish this discourse further; a point which could be seen in cartoons from the time, which often depicted Serbs as ape-like creatures in combat gear. Certainly, this level of acceptable racism is further evidence of how entrenched this conception of the Balkans was by the 1990s. Indeed, as would be highlighted by Lene Hansen, this negative discourse surrounding the inhabitants of the region would continue throughout the duration of the conflict. Even though intermittent discourse regarding genocide and its proper response would occasionally confuse the use of such stereotyping, anti-interventionist positions would often be explained via explicit reference to the perceived barbarity and incivility of the Balkans; ensuring that it continued to be an influential frame in the reporting from the early 1990s.[14]

This stereotype of the Balkans tended to be supplemented by the belief that the region was not simply uncivilised, but also inherently violent. Historically tainted by the role of Serbia in the outbreak of World War I, the idea that violence came naturally to the people of the Balkans was a concept which greatly influenced Western perceptions of the region. Of this trait, Mary Edith Durham wrote in 1920, 'as for the Balkan Slav and his haunted Christianity, it seemed to me all civilisation should rise and restrain him from further brutality', with Roger Cohen later arguing that 'the notion of killing people [...] because of something that may have happened in 1495 is unthinkable in the Western world. Not so in the Balkans.'[15] What is most telling about these remarks is not merely the similarity of the ideas expressed, but that they were published more than 75 years apart – a further illustration of how persistent such myths can be within Western discourse, once allowed to take root.[16]

The perceived incivility and violence of the region also helped to encourage the previously mentioned notion that the Balkans were somehow distinct from Europe – '"the other" within', to use Maria Todorova's phrasing.[17] The geographical placement of the Balkans was a contributing factor in this particular construction of the region, with its location causing it to often be seen as 'the crossroads between two different worlds – the West and the East.'[18] Indeed, despite being written in 1940, the description of the Balkans as being 'a region of transition between Asia and Europe – between "East" and "West" – with their incompatible political, social, religious and social ideals', illustrates a generalised belief that whilst the Balkans may have been geographically attached *to* Europe, it was by no means common discourse that the region was a part *of* Europe. As will be shown in later sections, this discourse was occasionally challenged in relation to the inhabitants of Sarajevo, but in general the people of the Balkans were framed as being somehow separate from Europe itself. Accepting this idea can help to explain how the Anglo–American press were often able to frame the later atrocities in such a manner as to distance their respective nations from the unfolding conflict, in spite of its physical location[19]

The general perception of the 'otherness' of the region no doubt influenced the acceptance of a further aspect of what Todorova has termed 'a persistent hegemonic discourse from the West, continuously disparaging of the Balkans' – the oft-cited argument that the violence which erupted in the early 1990s was somewhat inevitable, given a perceived history of *ancient hatreds* and *ethnic tensions*.[20] Describing the war in terms of 'ancient ethnic hatreds' – later dismissed by Malcolm as 'the false analysis which had poisoned European policy since the start of the war' – was an established narrative frame within the Western reporting of several post-Cold War conflicts.[21] This persistent narrative largely ignored the fact that there were other reasons – not least economic pressures from outside the Balkans – which could help to explain and contextualise the violence. Indeed, the allusion to ancestral ethnic grievances as being the major cause of the violence was even propagated by Serbian nationalists and others for whom such a classification was politically beneficial, which in turn gave this pseudo-explanation further credibility among several Western observers. Noel Malcolm sees this as a vitally important aspect regarding discussions of the war in Bosnia, arguing that:

> The biggest obstacle to all understanding of the conflict is the assumption that what happened in that country is the product – natural, spontaneous and at the same time necessary – of forces lying within Bosnia's own internal history. This is the myth which was carefully propagated by those who caused the conflict, who wanted the world to believe that what they and their gunmen were doing was not done by them, but by impersonal historical forces beyond anyone's control.[22]

Given the proposition in some theories of news framing that 'causal interpretation is one of the key elements used by media to communicate the understanding of social issues to the public', the dominance of the *ethnic conflict frame* is one of the central themes which ultimately emerges from this research.[23]

A direct corollary to the ethnic conflict concept was the more generalised argument that violence in the Balkans had resulted from *ancient hatreds* – that is, that the conflict was simply the latest conflagration in a centuries-old cycle of tension and war between the peoples of the region. One of the most explicit contemporary proponents of this explanation was George Kennan, who provided a new foreword to a 1913 publication (concerning the Balkans) which was re-released in 1993. A noted commentator on matters of American foreign policy, Kennan saw few variations in the general explanations for the two Balkan wars that erupted at either end of the twentieth century, stressing that the main contributing factor in both instances was 'not religion but aggressive nationalism. But that national-ism, as it manifested itself on the field of battle, drew on deeper traits of character inherited, presumably, from a distant tribal past.'[24] Ultimately, framing the conflict in the Balkans as being the repetition of a pattern of inter-generational violence that had existed for centuries helped to dis-courage debate about whether anything worthwhile could be done to end the violence. Certainly, by consistently explaining the violence by reverting to the idea of ancient hatreds – and thus painting the situation as utterly intractable – it is little wonder that calls for intervention in the region were only ever discussed in the wake of the most horrific atrocities. This stereo-typing of the violence in such a manner thus allowed for a rationale to be built with regards to non-intervention, with Kennan stressing that:

> [N]o one – no particular country and no group of countries –
> wants, or should be expected, to occupy the entire distracted
> Balkan region, to subdue its excited peoples, or to hold them in
> order until they calm down and begin to look at their problems
> in a more orderly way.[25]

Taken together then, the persistent depiction of the Balkans and its inhab-itants in the negative terms listed above (e.g., uncivilised; brutish; inher-ently violent; somewhat separate from Europe; and mired in ancient ethnic hatreds) contributed to a Western discourse through which a number of myths and generalised assumptions were disseminated. This led to a stere-otyped, and largely stigmatised, image of the Balkans emerging in Western quarters – a consequence of the formation of what are termed 'mental communities', a reference to the generalised concepts that humans tend to construct about others.[26] Another manner of describing this mental con-struction of other peoples and cultures is through the concept of 'pluralis-tic ignorance', which O'Gorman defines as:

> [N]ot ignorance in the ordinary sense of not knowing. On the
> contrary, it is knowledge of others that is mistakenly considered
> to be correct [...] Pluralistic ignorance refers to shared cogni-
> tive patterns, that is, socially accepted but false propositions
> about the social world.[27]

This general acceptance of a series of related 'myths' – which Jack Lule defines as 'archetypal stories that play crucial social roles' – thus led to a naturalised and widely accepted conceptualisation of the Balkans within Western discourse.[28] Building on existing notions of the region, some of which were more than a century old, newspaper coverage of Bosnia in the early 1990s was therefore not only influenced by an already firmly established discourse, but also did much itself to reinforce, through repetition and adaptation, these same mythologies. This 'frozen image' of the Balkans – to cite Todorova – was thus an important factor in the manner in which the Anglo–American press subsequently framed the conflict in the early 1990s.[29]

Quantitative Analysis: Overall Findings of Bosnia Data Set

What follows are the overall findings resulting from a quantitative analysis of the entire 114-day sample – in essence, the statistics which present themselves when the entire body of coverage is analysed. Individual statistical observations and in-depth analysis are reserved for the sections dealing with specific periods, and relevant comparisons are highlighted as required. Given that the analysis concerns the coverage devoted to Bosnia from eight Anglo–American newspapers (details of which are provided in the introductory section of the book) across 114 days, this equates to 912 separate days of coverage analysed. As a result, the statistics produced are rather more extensive than those cited in other, more focused studies (selected tables are also provided in the Appendix).[30]

News Article Coverage

A total of 3,028 news articles directly related to the crisis in the Balkans (not counting comment pieces, editorials or letters, which will be quantified separately) were produced over the 114-day period of analysis. Of this total, 1,819 (60 per cent) were found in British newspapers and 1209 (40 per cent) in American. The individual newspapers which devoted the highest number of articles to the Bosnian crisis were *The Times* and the *Independent*, publishing 482 and 466 articles respectively. The lowest figures in this regard were recorded in the *Chicago Tribune*, with a total of 238, and the *Los Angeles Times*, which published 246. It is worth noting that all UK titles in the study printed *at least* 427 articles regarding the conflict in Bosnia, whereas the *most* ever produced by an individual US title was 381 (the *New York Times*). Across the entire period of analysis, British newspapers published a daily average of 3.99 news articles per day, a number which easily surpassed the US average of 2.65 over the same period. The publication with the highest daily average was *The Times* (4.23), which was more than double the average of the title with the lowest recorded average, the *Chicago Tribune* (2.09). This noticeable discrepancy between overall coverage in British and American outlets may be partially explained in terms of geographic proximity, with London's comparative location in relation to Bosnia therefore influencing the degree of coverage which the conflict was to receive.

Front Page Coverage

Another focal point in analysing press coverage of Bosnia is the number of front page mentions that the conflict prompted. The front pages of any newspaper are generally reserved for the main stories of the day, and therefore the quantity of articles being given such coveted space can be considered a useful indicator of the degree to which the war in Bosnia was considered worthy of the public's attention. Across the four periods analysed, a total of 853 articles devoted to Bosnia appeared, at least in part, on page one of their respective outlet. This equates to 28.2 per cent of all news articles produced, and demonstrates the degree to which this conflict – in comparison with Rwanda, where 16.7 per cent of articles began on page one – was regularly given prominent exposure. In terms of comparing the number of front page articles produced on a collective national basis, there is a degree of statistical difference, with British publications producing a total of 379 front page articles to an American total of 474. When calculated as a percentage of the total number of articles, however, more direct contrasts become apparent. For UK-based sources, 379 front page articles equates to 20.8 per cent of *all* British news articles produced. In comparison, the US total of 474 front page articles accounted for 39.2 per cent of American news article output. It is debatable how revealing this contrast is, however, as it must be remembered that American publications tend to cram a greater number of stories onto page one than their British counterparts do. This position is given further credibility by the observation that three of the four American titles selected published a greater number of front page articles than *any* of the four British titles chosen – this, despite the fact that each of the chosen British titles produced a greater *total* number of news articles (anywhere in the newspaper). In addition to this, the American data set has something of an outlier, by way of the *Los Angeles Times* positioning 109 of its 246 (44.3 per cent) news articles at least partially on page one. Figures for UK-based newspapers, on other hand, were more consistent, with between 19.9 and 21.9 per cent of all articles produced in the respective British titles appearing on the front page. In any case, as will be highlighted later through comparison with press coverage of the Rwandan genocide, these figures still represent a notably high level of press interest – especially for a humanitarian situation, in a foreign country, which unfolded over a period of years.

Editorial, Comment and Letters Coverage

One of the main reasons for utilising newspapers as a source is that certain constituent parts of these publications – namely the editorial, comment and letters sections – allow more explicitly subjective views and opinions to be expressed, in a manner which is not as frequent in the 'standard' news as reported by the likes of broadcast media (or, for that matter, standard news articles, such as those discussed in the previous section). Whilst opinions and biases, however subtle, can of course be determined through an analysis of all forms of media, the sub-sections covered in this section are nonetheless illuminating, in that the articulation of explicit opinions is, in many ways, their 'expected' function.

Within the 114-day period around which this analysis of Bosnia is based, a total of 183 editorials (lead articles) were published that engaged with at least some aspect of the conflict in Bosnia. Of these, 105 were found in British publications and 78 in American – that is to say, that almost three-fifths (57 per cent) of all editorials were produced by British sources. The most prolific single title in this regard was *The Times*, whose editors discussed Bosnia on 31 separate occasions. The least productive title was the *Los Angeles Times*, which published 12 lead articles in this same period. Several comment pieces were also published regarding Bosnia, with a total of 384 being produced. British newspapers published a slightly greater share of these with a total of 205 (53.3 per cent) such articles, with American titles publishing 179 (46.7 per cent). *The Times* and the *Guardian* were the most proactive in discussing the crisis in the Balkans, with 68 and 61 comment articles, respectively. These totals easily surpassed those tallied by the least productive outlets, the *Chicago Tribune* and the *Daily Telegraph*, which published 29 and 34 such opinion pieces across the entire period of research. The most obvious contrast of any of the variables quantified, however, was among letters to the editor. Out of a combined total of 457 letters published, 367 were in British newspapers and 90 in American. This equates to slightly over 80.3 per cent of all letters concerning the Bosnian conflict being printed in British outlets, meaning that less than one-fifth of such correspondence appeared in US dailies. The title which was the most proactive in terms of publishing such letters was the *Guardian*, whose 112 letters accounted for a remarkable 24.5 per cent of the entire total from eight newspapers. At the other end of the scale, the *Washington Post* accounted for only 3.5 per cent of this total by publishing 16 letters. When considered alongside many of the other statistical observations listed, the fact that British coverage of Bosnia from 1992–5 generally surpassed that of the American news media can be provided as evidence in support of the importance of 'proximity' in relation to influencing the news agenda. Essentially, Bosnia was closer to the United Kingdom than it was to the United States, and this was reflected in the statistics.

Though the above findings may be somewhat revelatory in themselves – in that they indicate a notable level of interest in the Balkans whilst also highlighting a contrast between overall levels of British and American press attention – they do not become truly illuminating until compared with the same relevant figures recorded with regards to press coverage of the Rwandan genocide of 1994. This will be examined and commented upon in later chapters where relevant, with the remainder of this chapter devoted to an analysis of those specific, individual events which form the key case studies of this research.

Period One: 1–28 August 1992

By August 1992, more than three years before a permanent peace agreement was forged, the conflict in Bosnia was already being described as 'the most fully reported in history.'[31] Advances in electronic communications ensured that major events could be transmitted almost instantaneously to audiences around the world and the proximity of the violence to various major European cities made Bosnia, and Sarajevo in particular, something of a magnet for ambitious reporters. Televised images of flak-jacketed journalists became a regular sight on television news bulletins, and satellite link-ups enabled many of them (from both broadcast and print media) to submit their reports remarkably quickly – an advance which would have been the envy of the generation of reporters preceding them. Certainly, Daniel Kofman was not far wrong when he stated that 'the Holocaust was high-tech genocide with low-tech coverage, genocide in Bosnia is just the opposite.'[32]

The technological advantages that were available to Western journalists in Bosnia did not, however, mean that such an assignment was necessarily easy. Reporters were assailed by a plethora of practical concerns on a routine basis; one of which was the prevalence of warlords and racketeers, who would frequently prove a hindrance to journalists seeking to report from the region. In Sarajevo, for example, some areas were notorious for journalists being stopped and forcibly stripped of their money and other personal possessions.[33] Transport was also a problem as the UN were not allowed to carry members of the press, and competing journalists – those working for rival publications – would often refuse to assist one another.[34] Of far more immediate concern to most than basic amenities or transportation, however, was the fact that being a member of the foreign press in Bosnia was to essentially make oneself a target, sometimes for all sides involved in the conflict. The Bosnian crisis was, throughout its duration, one of the most dangerous places in modern history for those reporting it. Unlike in some other conflict zones, press affiliation – and the accompanying symbols on personnel and vehicles – was not to provide any meaningful protection from opportunistic snipers and the like. Certainly, as was voiced at the time, such affiliation could often invite journalists to be specifically targeted.[35] To illustrate this point, more photojournalists were killed in a three-year period of the Bosnian war than in the decade-long US involvement in Vietnam – with 27 journalists killed in 1992 alone. The danger to members of the press was vividly apparent to a British audience in particular, following the coverage of reporter Martin Bell being wounded during a mortar attack in late August 1992, an event which gathered extensive attention in the British news media.[36] All things considered then, the violence in the Balkans during this period ensured that reporting the conflict – at least at ground level – came with a number of challenges and considerations, both practical and personal.

Despite such immediate dangers and difficulties, however, a number of journalists did actively search out stories, often placing themselves at risk in doing so. Indeed, it was through such diligent journalism that the concentration camps in Bosnia were first exposed in the summer of 1992. Although it would be the first week of August before pictures of the camps reached Western living rooms, the first journalistic article on the subject was published on 19 July, by Roy Gutman of the American daily *Newsday*.[37] With a focus on the soon-to-be-notorious Omarska, Gutman's early reporting prompted a brief flood of publicity in the weeks to follow. Concentration camps, and the suffering of those incarcerated in them, had been discussed in the media in the immediate aftermath of Gutman's revelations, but it was a 6 August television bulletin – on British network *ITN* – which prompted a period of consistently focused interest in the Balkans. Capturing the first television images of such an institution, Penny Marshall's report on the camp at Trnopolje – with images of malnourished prisoners behind barbed-wire fences, reminiscent of the Holocaust – was crucial in reviving media coverage of Bosnia, and was later described as 'probably the most memorable single piece of journalism of the entire conflict.'[38] Given the nature of these revelations – a 'world scoop', in the words of one contemporary – a number of other journalists subsequently sought out other such institutions looking for evidence of further atrocities, though several of them later turned out to have been abandoned.[39] Nonetheless, the response to the disclosure that concentration camps were once again operating in Europe was immediate, and there was a renewed interest in the situation unfolding in the Balkans. Whilst describing the reaction to this new information as causing an 'international uproar' is perhaps over-emphasising the reality of the time, these revelations nonetheless led to this aspect of the Bosnian war becoming one of the biggest stories of 1992.[40] The quantitative findings related to this period will now be presented, both in order to substantiate this claim, and to demonstrate the degree to which this particular aspect of the Bosnian conflict gained a total degree of coverage which was beyond most subsequent developments.

Quantitative Findings: 1–28 August 1992

Across the eight titles analysed, from the period 1–28 August 1992, a total of 857 news articles were devoted to Bosnia. This accounted for 28.3 per cent of *all* news articles concerning Bosnia across the four separate periods being studied, and represented the most prolific single period in terms of overall article production. British publications, in particular, paid a great deal of attention to Bosnia during this time, with only the *Independent* not seeing this specific period as its most productive. Of the 857 articles produced, 538 (62.7 per cent) were from British sources and 319 (37.3 per cent) from American. The title with the highest number of articles was the *Guardian*, which published 149 in total; a stark contrast to the 62 published by the title which produced the fewest articles in this period, the *Los Angeles Times*. These examples, however, were by no means outliers in terms of coverage. British titles consistently devoted more column inches to Bosnia during this period, with the *Daily Telegraph* – the title with the lowest count among British publications, with 126 – still outmatching the 100 articles published by the most productive American title, the *New York Times*. Also of note, and indicative of the level of coverage generated by the discovery of the camps, this individual 28-day period was the only one within the research where a daily average exceeding five articles was recorded (the *Guardian* – 5.32, and *The Times* – 5.0). The only other period within this research in which an average like this was recorded was during later coverage following the fall of Srebrenica, and was, in any case, far greater than anything recorded during the reporting of the Rwandan genocide.

Perhaps resulting from its geographical proximity to the West, in addition to its aesthetic similarity to the Holocaust, Bosnia was also afforded an impressive degree of front page coverage during August 1992. A total of 212 relevant articles appeared on page one, a figure which represents 28 per cent of all articles published in this period. 130 of these articles appeared on British front pages, with the remaining 82 appearing in American titles. The *Independent* was the most prolific in this regard – with 38 articles being at least partially on page one – whilst the *Chicago Tribune* printed the least overall, with 13. Notably, this was the only 28/29 day period of the four analysed in which British titles produced *at least* 25 front pages each, with three of the four UK publications printing a minimum of 31 from 1–28 August 1992. In addition to these observations, this was also the *only* single period where the average number of front page mentions, among British titles, equated to more than one per day. Conversely, three of the four US titles produced their lowest total of front page mentions, for a single period of analysis, in August 1992. This contrast can perhaps be explained, partially, by the fact that with the UNPROFOR deployments in November and December of that year, British military involvement in the region was more developed than American at this point. This observation helps to further underline the notion (expanded upon in subsequent sections) that suffering of civilians is generally of secondary importance to Western interests in terms of Anglo–American press coverage.

When this period is further analysed, it soon becomes apparent that 1–28 August 1992 also saw far more opinion pieces produced (including editorials, comment and letters) than any other with in the study. Though this can again be explained, to some degree, by the fact that the Bosnian conflict was still somewhat in its infancy (and thus still 'fresh' as a news story) and occurring in a region which was in close proximity to Western interests, it is also highly probable that the discovery of concentration camps in this month was also a crucial determining factor. This will be discussed in greater detail in the sections to follow but, for now, relevant statistics shall be highlighted in order to further illustrate the fact that combined coverage during this single period was generally in excess of anything which came subsequently.

In terms of editorial coverage, 55 lead articles were produced within this 28-day time frame – a number which in itself was greater than the 54 editorials devoted to Rwanda, by the same sources, over its *entire* 114-day period of analysis. This contrast of Bosnia generating more editorial coverage in four weeks than Rwanda did in four months, clearly illustrates the argunent that genocide is rarely judged only on its relative severity. Of these 55 editorials, which represented 30 per cent of all those produced across the four periods analysed during the Bosnian conflict, 37 were British in origin whilst 18 appeared in American titles. This discrepancy between US and UK editorial comment – in that two-thirds were produced in Britain – can, again, perhaps be explained by the fact that British military involvement in the region, at this point, was more developed. This aspect is further highlighted by the observation that for *all* UK sources, this period saw more editorials produced than in any other 28/29 period, whilst each US title, by contrast, had at least one other period in which the number of editorials produced exceeded the total for 1–28 August 1992. The greatest number of editorials published in a single title were in the *Daily Telegraph* (12) and *The Times* (10); each of which produced more than three times as many as the title with the lowest count, the *Los Angeles Times*, which published only three. When one considers that editorial space is generally reserved for what are constructed as the most important issues of the day, it is clear from these findings that the conflict in Balkans, especially in the United Kingdom, was constructed as being temporarily worthy of the public's attention.

A similar pattern emerges in relation to the number of comment articles produced during this time. Across all eight sources selected, a total of 119 comment pieces directly related to Bosnia were published – which represents 31 per cent of op-ed pieces produced in the entire sample. 71 of these were to be found in British publications, with the remaining 48 appearing in American newspapers. The *Guardian* and *The Times* devoted the greatest number of comment pieces to the Balkans with 25 and 26, respectively, whilst the *Chicago Tribune* published a mere eight. Though the British/American divide which was immediately obvious in terms of editorial coverage was partially repeated in relation to comment pieces (a ratio of essentially 60/40 in favour of British coverage), individual differences between titles were more apparent. the *Daily Telegraph* and the *Independent*, for example, which each produced ten comment pieces, were outmatched by three of the four US titles selected. Nonetheless, it is worth noting that no American title recorded their highest one-month total during this period, whilst three of the four British titles had a total number of comment pieces in August 1992 which was equal to or higher than the total recorded in the three periods which subsequently followed. Given these observations, a tentative way of reading the overall commentary on Bosnia (1992–5) may be to see British interest peaking early and then receding, whilst discussion in American sources progressed as the conflict wore on – an observation which would again corroborate the notion that American press interest was generally correlated with the likelihood of NATO action. In terms of total letters printed, August 1992 also outmatched all other periods analysed. 170 were published during this time which had at least some focus on Bosnia, a number which represented 40 more than were devoted to the period surrounding the massacre at Srebrenica. Of these, 132 (77.6 per cent) were from British sources, with the remaining 38 (22.4 per cent) appearing in the American press. The most productive in this regard was *The Times*, which printed 47 letters, whilst the *Washington Post* and the *New York Times* each published eight – the joint-lowest recorded in this particular period.

As a final means of further illustrating the degree to which total coverage of Bosnia during this time was of a notably high level, it is revealing to compare the respective commentary dedicated to Bosnia and Rwanda. When all opinion contributions (that is, editorials, comment and letters) produced from 1–28 August 1992 are added together, across all eight titles, a total of 344 is recorded. The total for Rwanda, across the *entire* 114-day period of comparable analysis, is only 185. Put another way, almost double the number of opinion articles were produced in regards to Bosnia in just 28 days than was the case for Rwanda over 114. This in spite of the fact that by most estimates the Rwandan genocide of 1994 claimed between four and ten times as many victims in just over three months than were killed in the entire four-year Bosnian conflict. Despite claims to the contrary then, it is clear from these statistics that the cumulative death toll of those killed in genocidal acts is not, in itself, the most important factor in determining levels of press coverage. In terms of newsworthiness, human lives are valued – if at all – in a markedly different manner across the globe; with race, proximity to the West, geo-political interests and the nature of such violence all being seen to be a greater determining factor in influencing the degree to which such events will be given attention by Anglo–American media outlets. In the section(s) to follow, with a particular focus on the discovery of concentration camps and its influence on levels of reporting at this time, it will be shown that the *form* which violence and atrocities take, rather than their objective scale, can be crucial in determining the types of suffering which are granted a place in the Western media spotlight. Further to this, however, it will also be shown that, even when a given event *is* considered worthy of Western attention, there still remains a tendency to frame the story in such a way as to minimise the suffering of the victims themselves.

The Importance of Concentration Camp Imagery

Unsurprisingly, the revelations of concentration camps operating in Bosnia aroused considerable interest within the Western news media, and were a critical factor in explaining the levels of coverage recorded during this period. In addition to their proximity to the West, the fact that many of the atrocities being associated with the camps were reminiscent of the Nazi methods of World War II provoked a level of interest and discussion which was unlike anything that was to subsequently be seen in Bosnia (or Rwanda) – at least in the sense that the focus of the reporting, rather than being determined by the potential for outside intervention or the like, was largely on the perceived atrocities themselves.

Though there were difficulties in verifying and substantiating early reports, details started to emerge regarding what had been taking place in locations like Omarska (which was quick to become regarded as the most notorious of these camps), by late July and early August 1992.[41] As Karnik states, the 'greatest felony in the news business today is to be behind,' and so a number of journalists were quick to file reports detailing the atrocities that were being endured by the inmates of the concentration camps.[42] Though some of these were more sensationalist than would normally be expected of a quality publication, they nonetheless highlighted a number of horrific crimes that were taking place. Several articles described the process of systematic torture that was rife in some locations, complete with lurid details of summary executions, random beatings and even the use of dogs to savage inmates.[43] In a manner similar to reports from the likes of Buchenwald and Belsen in 1945, accounts of the material conditions in some of the worst camps – which had turned captives into 'filthy, emaciated shadows of the persons they had once been' – were regularly invoked, often taken from first-person testimony.[44] Also, in reference to a crime which would later become an emblematic feature of the entire conflict in Bosnia, reports also drew attention to the prevalance of rape and other sexual torture being used to inflict terror on local populations.[45] It is worth noting that in a number of these instances such claims were presented in quotation marks, indicating that in many cases such testimony could not be verified at the time. Such grotesque human rights abuses took place both before and after the discovery of the camps, however, and yet it was only when such atrocities directly contributed to a wider narrative that drew on Holocaust imagery and language that they gained formidable placing and commentary within the Anglo–American press.

One of the most commonly discussed components of the ethnic cleansing process which fit with this particular (Holocaust) narrative was the process of transporting people, including women and children, to the camps in sealed railway carriages.[46] That this feature of the violence in Bosnia was regularly remarked upon was, partly, due to the fact that accessing the sites of mass transportation was generally easier than infiltrating the camps themselves. This, and the fact that the transporting of civilians in such a manner was an 'all too vivid [reminder] of the suffering and fate of the Jews during the Holocaust', also helped to ensure that it received Western media attention.[47] As further details emerged of the camps, particularly when accompanied by photographs which were aesthetically similar to the horrors of Nazi Germany's camp system, the 'painful familiarity' aroused by such reports in turn led to one of the first concentrated debates surrounding the Bosnian conflict – regarding the degree to which such sites were indeed concentration camps.[48] A lack of complete information led to a variety of terms being used to characterise these installations, with some having far more immediate connotations than others. From the reserved *prison* and *detention* camps, to the more evocative *torture* and *death* camps, a variety of different terms were used in the weeks following the broadcast of Penny Marshall's landmark *ITN* report.[49] Initially, however, the most commonly used term was 'death camp', though it was generally published in quotation marks. Whether this was because of a genuine belief that this was the main function of the camps or due to a realisation that such a term was a dramatic means of grabbing the attention of the reader is unclear, but its consistent use in the first weeks of August soon contributed to a discussion regarding the most appropriate term to use. Though some commentators would debate the most appropriate description for these locations, and others still would remark that such definitions were immaterial in the face of such atrocities, the most vocal and persistent voices were those which were raised in order to *challenge* the notion that these sites were indeed 'concentration' or 'death' camps at all.[50] A number of prominent contemporaries weighed in on this side of the debate, including then-Liberal Democrat leader Paddy Ashdown, who stated after a visit to the region that the detention centres could not be properly described as concentration camps in the historical sense of the term. That Ashdown would be as assertive in this distinction is of note, given that he was, in general, a strong supporter of intervention in the region. Simon Wiesenthal, the famous 'Nazi hunter', also rejected such comparisons, arguing that they trivialised the Nazi camps.[51] This contrast – between the media's use of imagery (camps, trains etc.) which drew its cultural 'relevance' from the crimes of the Nazis, and the accompanying debates that often rejected the validity of such comparisons – is interesting in that it demonstrates the means by which the suffering of a given people can be both highlighted *and* marginalised at the same time.

Whilst the exact term for the Serb-run camps was often disputed, there was little argument within the press over how important their initial disclosure remained. Soon after the claims of former inmates and other witnesses had been verified, several articles then started to question whether, in official channels, more had been known about these camps before this sudden wave of publicity. Essentially, following the first disclosures, journalists from outlets on both sides of the Atlantic began to investigate whether knowledge of such atrocities was available to government intelligence sources in the weeks and months prior. The details of previous memorandums, some of which explicitly invoked the term 'concentration camp', were publicised and questions were put to both British and American intelligence agencies.[52] Others noted that the conditions revealed in Roy Gutman's early *Newsday* articles, first published in mid- to late July, had only become a topic of global interest once the camps had actually been photographed and filmed.[53] Certainly, there are echoes here of the response to the liberation of the camps in 1945, where pictorial evidence was seen to generate a greater reaction than simple written testimony. Though no clear consensus was ever reached in the press as to *when* knowledge of the camps had first emerged, the fact that this was being debated is interesting in itself. Levels of prior knowledge of ongoing catastrophes are rarely debated in the Anglo–American press, not least when the story is based in a foreign country. However, the fact that the atrocities in Bosnia were considered to be sufficiently similar to aspects of the Holocaust – at least at face value – meant that a lack of earlier publicity was seen by many to be unacceptable, with one commentator arguing that the 'response to this new Holocaust has been as timid as [the] reaction to the beginnings of Hitler's genocide.'[54] Indeed, it is plausible to argue that it was their aesthetic similarity to the Holocaust which led to the camps (in contrast to, for example, the massacres in Rwanda) being discussed in such a wide range of forums. Whilst the Bosnian conflict had certainly been covered in considerable detail up to this point, at least in comparison to most other overseas wars, it was not until the existence of camps was established that the story took on a whole new level of (temporary) importance. The coverage of conditions which were, at least in part, reminiscent of the likes of Belsen and Buchenwald (though on a much less catastrophic scale) sparked an interest in the Western press which was unmatched throughout the duration of the war, particularly in British outlets. Not even the organised massacre at Srebrenica, coverage of which will be discussed later, could match the intense level of overall interest sparked by Omarksa, Manjaca and others. Certainly, Con Coughlin was not far wrong in describing the days following the camp revelations as 'the week the world woke up.'[55]

That the concentration camps in Bosnia should have sparked such press interest is understandable, since the Holocaust is one of the most documented events in modern history.[56] Though the similarities between the Nazi genocide of the Jews and the atrocities in Bosnia were actually rather few in number, the fact that some key occurrences and observations mirrored the crimes of World War II was enough to prompt several commentators to frame their coverage of the conflict in this manner. One of the important similarities, as previously mentioned, was the practice of the Serbs utilising rolling stock to transport potential detainees – the vast majority of whom were civilians – away from those areas which they sought to 'cleanse.' Indeed, the brutal transportation of these individuals gained several prominent mentions even before Penny Marshall's emotive report on the camps themselves, with the extract below, from Anthony Lewis, representative of a variety of such accounts from August 1992:

> The men were taken from the village at gunpoint and forced into freight cars. As many as 180 were jammed, standing, into boxcars measuring 39 by 6 feet. They were kept that way for three days, without water or food, as the train moved slowly across the countryside. Nazis transporting Jews in 1942? No, Serbs transporting Muslim Bosnians in 1992: one glimpse of the worst racial and religious bestiality Europe has known since World War II.[57]

The type of language used in this report was not restricted to a few crusading journalists, however – Holocaust analogies often helped to frame the description of such transports (and conditions in the camps), with several people highlighting such similarities as a reason for the Western world to take a greater interest in the Balkans. Again though, it must be reiterated that a key reason for such focus on Bosnia was *not* due to the fact that civilians were being treated in such a brutal manner – ethnic cleansing had, after all, already claimed thousands of lives up to this point – but because these images and reports were seen to be revealing something which was in some respects reminiscent of the Holocaust. Through various forms of representation in the media in the decades prior (as was discussed in the previous chapter), the Holocaust had by the 1990s become, as Rubinstein would describe it, 'a universally internalised symbol of evil.'[58] More importantly, however, it could also be argued that such familiarity with the crimes of the Nazis also led to *genocide*, as understood outside legal and academic circles, to be intrinsically linked to the form it took under Hitler's regime. By the 1990s, therefore, the Holocaust was essentially the 'model' for what constituted genocide in the minds of many in the Anglo–American world; and Bosnia, at least for a brief period in 1992, was seen to fit this ideal. This helps to explain why this particular period of the Bosnian conflict whilst not being the worst in terms of loss of life, nonetheless commanded the greatest degree of attention in the Anglo–American press. The words of Mike Bamborn, a Bosnian-American, help illustrate this point:

> I have sympathy for the Jewish people at the time of World War
> II. The Bosnian people are going through the same thing. When
> I see the trains full of women and children crying, it reminds
> me of World War II Nazi movies. The Bosnian Holocaust.[59]

Whilst the 'Holocaust frame' was first invoked in response to the transportations, the quantity of such comparisons inevitably increased once the destination of these same human shipments was ascertained.[60] The reports and (in particular) images that were soon emerging from Bosnia concerning the camps bore a sufficient resemblance to the crimes of World War II that they prompted a fresh wave of comparisons with the worst of Nazi brutality.[61] It was soon a rarity for the camps to be discussed in comment pieces and editorials *without* some allusion being made to the World War II era, and several articles invoked this comparison for the purposes of illustration or context. One such editorial piece described the ethnic cleansing process as being 'horribly reminiscent of the *Judenfrei* policies of the Third Reich', whilst a letter printed in *The Times* asserted that the stories emanating from Bosnia bore 'an uncanny resemblance in manner, if not in scale, to those which disfigured humanity half a century ago.'[62] The pictures of terrified prisoners behind barbed-wire fences, heads-shaved and obviously suffering from exposure and malnutrition, echoed the images of the likes of Auschwitz, with which the Western public had become familiarised with over preceding decades. To cite an editorial from the time, the 'scars of memory' were suddenly re-opened, and in turn the press was quick to devote considerable attention to this development.[63] A number of commentators were subsequently compelled to discuss the implications of such a discovery within Europe's borders, with Robert Jay Lifton's assertion that the revelations had provoked 'a symbolic reactivation of Holocaust images that [had] long been inside us' helping to explain a key reason for this resurgent, though temporary, interest in the Balkans.[64]

All of this is not to say, however, that every journalist was automatically inclined to describe the atrocities in the Balkans as being comparable to those that took place during the Nazi regime. Indeed, many found the comparison to be both premature and inappropriate – the result of an impulse that David Rieff attributed to 'an age mired in rhetorical excess which has to insist that anything good is the best and anything bad the worst.'[65] Others passed comment on the fact that such a spike in coverage at this specific time was solely down to the influence that using such Holocaust imagery had been seen to have, often implying that debate regarding potential intervention and the like had been disproportionally influenced by such comparisons. For example, seeking to explain this sudden interest in Bosnia, Coughlin and Sherwell argued: 'This is all because the emotive phrase "concentration camps" has returned to haunt all those "good Europeans" who believed that the new Europe of the Maastricht Treaty and the ERM would be safe from the horrors of 50 years ago.'[66] Similarly, in his diplomatic memoirs regarding his involvement in the eventual peace settlement, Richard Holbrooke recounted the words of a senior aid worker, Tony Land, who also commented on the camp revelations gaining more press attention than the various other atrocities in Bosnia: 'We are absolutely amazed at the press and public reaction to this. For six months we have seen Sarajevo systematically being destroyed without the world getting very upset. Now a few pictures of people being held behind barbed wire, and the world goes crazy. We have seen more deaths in Sarajevo than in the prisons.'[67] This argument – that Bosnia was only receiving attention due to the notion that concentration camps were once again operating on European soil, mere hours from its major capitals – is convincing when combined with the statistics listed earlier, in that this particular period was seen to gather more journalistic attention than any other.

All things considered then, it seems that the perceived similarity of the atrocities in Bosnia to those of the Holocaust were indeed the main catalyst for the notable increase in coverage recorded during this period. As will be discussed in later sections, this is a key observation in seeking to explain why only certain instances of mass violence in the case studies selected were seen to provoke concentrated attention from the press, and challenges the wider notion that body-counts, in themselves, are the most crucial factor in determining Anglo–American media responses to genocide.

Calls for Intervention

Evidently then, the concentration camps sparked a fresh wave of interest in Bosnia, which in turn prompted a range of comment and discussion from myriad media outlets. With such emotive coverage of the humanitarian crisis in the Balkans, it was perhaps inevitable that calls for intervention would be debated in the wake of such disclosures. This is not to say, however, that intervention had been a non-issue in the months preceding August 1992, but the revelations surrounding the camp system and their subsequent framing in terms of their similarity to the Holocaust gave these calls a new sense of urgency and immediacy. In the days following the first pictorial verification that the Serbs were operating concentration camps, demands for outside intervention quickly gathered pace. Although several of these were somewhat vague as to how such an intervention should proceed, they nonetheless argued that these revelations demanded at least some kind of response from the Western powers. Leaders were urged to 'harness the public mood and seize the initiative' with regards to the use of air strikes, which was supported by the fact that some polls had shown that a majority of the public were in favour of such a course of action.[68] As has been noted since by various scholars, the Holocaust language and imagery generated by Bosnia undoubtedly contributed to these demands for a stronger response. Terms like *genocide* and *concentration camps*, in the words of Mick Hume, 'invoke modern moral absolutes,' and so it is perhaps unsurprising that the press should have reacted in the manner in which they did.[69] To illustrate this point, consider the following statement by Alan Deshowitz, who supplemented his pro-intervention stance by arguing that,

'Not to act on the face of what we know is a crime and sin, *especially after the Holocaust*.'[70] It would, of course, be misleading to state that there was a pro-interventionist stance across the board. Certainly, even those who were in favour of some form of action were cautious as to how such a plan should be undertaken. Various commentators were wary of getting involved in the Balkans from the beginning of the conflict, citing various factors such as a lack of Western interests in the region or the political ramifications for the US during what was approaching election season.[71] What is seen developing here is a dynamic whereby certain forms of violence, due to their historical resonance, can be seen to generate comment and debate *without* necessarily leading to anything by way of concrete response. David Campbell eloquently highlighted this contrast between words and actions:

> Here, then, we have a conundrum – the images are read in a way that appears to make a particular response likely if not inevitable, yet that predicted response fails to occur and is instead actively avoided. How might we begin to explain the way in which images taken to be so powerful and historically resonant do not result in the expected outcomes?[72]

Whilst the existence of the camps, and the continuing violence in Bosnia, led to outcry from some quarters, this did not lead to a notable increase in calls for intervention. Of the various reasons given, more prevalent than any other cited to support non-intervention, was the notion that violence was somehow endemic to the region. This was a belief which would persist, in various guises, over the duration of the conflict, and it is to this concept that this chapter will now turn.

The Framing of Violence in the Balkans

An oft-cited explanation for the war in Bosnia was that it was the almost inevitable result of ancient hatreds that had long been festering in the region; a dominant frame echoing a discourse long established in the West. Even those commentators who were cautious advocates of intervention would often describe the conflict in such terms, though the notion that 'ancestral' or 'ancient' grievances were behind the slaughter was far more prevalent in the writings of those contributors who did *not* wish for the Western powers to get involved.[73] As the conflict wore on, this belief – that Bosnia was somehow pre-destined to erupt into violence – continued to remain prevalent within the Anglo–American press. Commentators, most of whom it is clear had no real understanding of Balkan history, would speak of Bosnia returning to 'its old traditions', whilst one particular contribution asserted that the Balkans was a 'region that cannot handle freedom for more than five minutes'.[74] In a similar trend to how the media would oversimplify the reasons for the Rwandan genocide of 1994, these stereotypes and mistaken explanations also instilled a sense of inevitability around the violence in Bosnia.

Perhaps it was purely down to a lack of knowledge regarding the region, or as a result of a tactical decision to deliberately cloud the nature of the conflict in order to stave off further calls for intervention, but throughout the war it was repeatedly argued that what was going on in Bosnia was simply unavoidable. British Prime Minister, John Major would describe the conflict as 'a product of impersonal and inevitable forces beyond anyone's control', whilst President George Bush actively tried to distance himself from the atrocities occurring in what he mistakenly labelled the *Baltic* situation.[75] Further highlighted in these discussions was the perceived idea that all parties in the conflict were equally guilty, and that there was some kind of innate lust for war written into the DNA of the people of the Balkans. Despite the fact that the region had been largely peaceful under Tito's reign, many were quick to highlight the 'irrational hatreds' that had ensured that these 'warrior races' would be forever locked in a cycle of ethnic violence.[76] Yugoslavia was, in the words of Conor Cruise O'Brien, 'full of people who enjoy killing people, and don't mind risking their own lives in pursuit of their favourite pastime'.[77] Though this last example is one of the more direct and extreme generalisations about Bosnia, it is nonetheless representative of a trend which was common throughout the reporting of the conflict. There is always the argument though that the prevalence of such claims was simply a reflection of the general manner in which the Anglo–American world viewed the different groups in Bosnia. This was commented upon in early August 1992 by Dr Cornella Sorabji, who argued that 'people are all too ready to accept a crude, stereotypical version which simply notes past conflicts and concludes that the Balkans are an alien and barbaric place whose inhabitants are programmed to exterminate each other.'[78]

Other voices were also raised in defiance of these claims. Often in the 'Letters to the Editor' section, the dominant view of Bosnia was occasionally challenged, with some highlighting the fact that such distortions were probably being used a means to justify inaction. Contributors would point to the fact that historical violence in the region was normally a result of wider geopolitical conflicts, whilst others would challenge the assertion that the people of the Balkans were somehow destined to be in eternal conflict with one another.[79] Overall, however, such challenges were limited and most outlets continued to voice such stereotypes throughout the conflict. This then brings one to the rather paradoxical conclusion that the concentrated coverage devoted to Bosnia in August 1992 would have also ensured that many people were exposed to this mistaken 'explanation' of the situation there. Whilst the intense coverage introduced the atrocities in Bosnia to the wider world, the language used to explain these same atrocities may have, inadvertently, led various people to the conclusion that very little could be done to salvage the region. Indeed, this initial reporting – dense, though full of inaccuracies and generalisations regarding the conflict – may have contributed to the notable reduction in the overall coverage of later atrocities. This is an important consideration in relation to the broad focus of this research, given Robert Entman's observation that dominant frames, especially when invoked early in the reporting of a news event, can be difficult to challenge and dislodge in later coverage.[80]

Period Two: 29 January – 26 February 1994

By early 1994, Sarajevo was a city which was under a near-constant state of siege.[81] Artillery from the surrounding hillsides could rain down destructive shells at any time and large areas of the city were notorious for indiscriminate snipers. Although the 5 February bombing of Markale marketplace was to prove the single most lethal attack on the city, the death toll had been consistently rising in the preceding several months due to these siege tactics. This persistent threat was illustrated by the story of one Sarajevo resident, who stated he had seen 56 new graves appear in the three days since burying his own father.[82] It was not only physical assault which was to threaten the lives of most Sarajevans, however. In what would later be described as 'an attempt to destroy not just the material fabric of the city but its soul,' the Serb-led siege of Sarajevo also involved restricting the flow of vital supplies – such as food, fuel and medical aid.[83] Many daily essentials often proved difficult to procure, despite attempts by the UN and other agencies to resupply the city. Starvation became an issue in some areas, particularly those on the outskirts of the city, and much of the food which *was* available in Sarajevo was controlled by black-marketeers who formed informal cartels in order to keep prices deliberately high.[84] The winter months were to prove especially difficult for the residents of Sarajevo, with the bitter cold forcing many to improvise in order to keep warm. In the absence of proper supplies of fuel, books and furniture were often used as an inefficient substitute – with the destruction of the former being remarked upon by several of those who had spent time in what had once been recognised as a cultural hub of south-east Europe.[85] Many of those worst affected by the intolerable conditions in Sarajevo were children, some 1,500 of whom had been killed in the Bosnian capital by early 1994. Due to the constant threat of shelling – which a contemporary survey revealed that 97.3 per cent of Sarajevan children had lived through – and the familiarity with seeing dead and dying people on the city's streets, many adolescents were described as becoming 'numb to danger' and demonstrating suicidal tendencies.[86] This further illustrates the ultimate goal of the Serb militias who surrounded Sarajevo – the destruction of both the physical and psychological life of the city.

The shelling of 5 February 1994, which slammed into the Markale marketplace, was to surpass anything which had preceded it; and as such the news coverage of this particular incident can be partially explained when the attack is understood as representing an *intensity increase* in the shelling of the city. Literally hundreds of thousands of mortar shells had been fired into Sarajevo since the beginning of the conflict, but the one which exploded on that particular day caused unprecedented devastation – described at the time as 'staggering, sickening, numbing' by one contemporary – for a number of reasons.[87] One of these, ironically, was that it was during what would be described, by Sarajevo standards, as a quiet day – citizens often braved the marketplaces when they perceived a lull in the shelling.[88] In many cases, this was seen as a form of resistance in the city; the meagre goods providing a basic means by which Sarajevans could pursue something which resembled normal life. As a result, Markale was particularly busy on this day, and this contributed to the carnage which unfolded. The layout of the marketplace also maximised the level of destruction – Markale was surrounded by high walls, a fact which ensured that the mortar blast was contained within the condensed crowd.[89] Though Markale was not an inevitable 'tragedy waiting to happen' – to cite one editorial from the time – the conditions on this specific date combined to produce a perfect-storm scenario, in terms of destructive potential, for those in the immediate vicinity.[90] The chaos which erupted in the midst of the shelling left even the most hardened journalists stunned and appalled. Contemporary news reports gave vivid descriptions of arms, legs and unidentifiable pieces of flesh clinging to the surrounding buildings, and of pavements dyed red with pools of blood. The death toll eventually reached 68 – with another 200 wounded – making it the single deadliest attack by this point in the war, leading John Sweeney of the *Guardian* to describe the scene as a 'slaughterhouse.'[91] The attack prompted a national day of mourning within Bosnia, and dominated Anglo–American news coverage in the days which immediately followed.

It should be remembered, however, that the shelling of Markale was not a unique incident. As was described previously, intense shelling had affected Sarajevo since the very beginning of the conflict and had killed or wounded thousands of the city's inhabitants.[92] Shelling had become so commonplace in the Bosnian conflict by this point, and in Sarajevo in particular, that such incidents rarely warranted in-depth coverage or comment from the press. To illustrate this point, one need only look at the newspaper coverage of a shelling which was reported the day *before* the Markale story broke. In what the *Los Angeles Times* described as 'Sarajevo's Bloodiest Day in a Month', ten people were killed whilst queuing for food aid. Despite it being the highest death toll for a shelling in Sarajevo for a month, this event was sparsely covered by the Anglo–American press, with only the *Daily Telegraph* affording it a (box-sized) front page mention.[93] By comparison, the Markale marketplace bombing commanded prominent front page attention across a range of titles, in addition to prompting indignant editorial and comment pieces.

What set Markale apart from previous mortar attacks was the quantitative change in the number of those killed – in the words of one editorial, it was 'a mortar too far […] it killed too many people.'[94] Whilst Sontag is correct in stating that the modern world has seen that the 'excruciations of war' have 'devolved into a nightly banality,' the sheer destruction unleashed by this single shelling caused a number of people to once again focus their attention on the Bosnian situation, even if for only a brief time.[95] Certainly, the fact that it was only the *scale* of the slaughter which had changed, and not its specific form, was noted by a number of contemporary commentators. Many lamented the lack of adequate reporting on previous incidences of shelling, whilst others argued that such an atrocity warranted a strong military response from the Western powers. Though there are myriad examples of such comment, the following extract from a piece by Andrew Marr is representative of a number of these discussions:

> Why this nervy sabre-rattling? Because a Serbian mortar crew got lucky. Had the Serbian soldiers behaved sensibly and carried on just blowing apart two or three small children a day, contenting themselves with a moderate and humane rate of decapitations and maimings, then there would have been no problem. Western television viewers have become hardened to shots of white-faced Sarajevans being operated on without anaesthetic. But Milovan and Zarco felt greedy last Saturday, just couldn't help themselves, copped too many in one go. And here we are.[96]

Indeed, it could be argued that the Markale bombing temporarily reinvigorated media interest in Bosnia – at least to some degree. Before looking at the themes and trends which dominated press coverage during this period in early 1994, the statistical observations for this case study will first be presented.

Quantitative Findings: 29 January – 26 February 1994

In terms of the number of news articles produced across the period 29 January – 26 February 1994, a total of 749 were recorded in the eight selected titles, a number which represents 24.7 per cent of all articles related to Bosnia within this study. Of this total, 423 (56.5 per cent) were from British publications whilst the remaining 326 (43.5 per cent) were from American sources. The most prolific titles in this regard were the *Daily Telegraph* and *The Times*, producing 118 and 115 news articles respectively. At the other end of this scale were the *Chicago Tribune*, which published 51, and the *Los Angeles Times*, with 64. It should be noted, however, that the obvious UK/US divide which was seen in Period One was not replicated in Period Two. Whilst the British coverage had surpassed *all* American titles in August 1992, two British sources were bettered by their American counterparts during this period of analysis.[97]

In terms of front page coverage, a total of 171 articles (22.8 per cent of the total) were produced between the selected dates. There was little in terms of variation when compared on a national basis, with UK sources publishing 88 and American outlets 83. The *Washington Post* devoted the greatest number of front page articles to the Bosnian crisis, producing 25 within this period. The *Chicago Tribune*, on the other hand, published a comparatively few 13 – the joint-lowest number recorded across the entire project during a single 'month'. This last figure is something of an outlier though, when one considers that the seven remaining titles all produced between 20 and 25 front page articles between 29 January and 26 February 1994.

Although the total number of editorial pieces dedicated to the Bosnian crisis during this period was less than that recorded during August 1992 – the period in which concrete evidence of the existence of concentration camps was first established – there was still a substantial number of leading articles produced during this time. For the entire sample of eight newspapers, a total of 45 editorial pieces were produced, with 24 of these appearing in British publications and the remaining 21 in American outlets. The *Times* was the most prolific in this regard, with eight such pieces, whilst the *Chicago Tribune* was the least productive, with three. One notable difference between British and American titles is that, collectively, the latter actually produced more editorial pieces during January–February 1994 than they did during the previous period (1–28 August 1992). Indeed, the 21 leading articles published in American sources at this time represent the joint-highest total recorded in a single period – the most likely reason for this being the possible consequences, for NATO and American forces, of an escalation of military involvement.

In terms of comment pieces concerning the Bosnian conflict, a total of 97 such articles were produced, with a ratio of 44 British to 53 American – the only period of the four analysed in which American publications out-matched their British counterparts. *The Times* and the *New York Times* were the most productive in this regard, with 16 and 17 comment pieces respectively, whilst the *Daily Telegraph* published a comparatively few eight articles. Though the total of 97 comment pieces is lower than the 119 recorded during August 1992, it still far surpasses the total of 70 which was produced during the entire 114-day period for the Rwandan genocide. This provides further evidence to support the importance of race and proxim-ity in determining the Anglo–American news agenda; given that devel-opments in or on the periphery of Europe will generally take precedence over events in Central Africa. Though a number of comment pieces during January and February 1994 focused on the possibility of outside interven-tion in Bosnia (as opposed to the crimes themselves), the fact that a single shelling in Sarajevo could generate greater coverage than the systematic destruction of perhaps one million people in Africa certainly demonstrates some geographic and/or racial bias within Anglo–American reporting.

88 letters were published in this second period – 65 British and 23 American – which was an almost 50 per cent decrease on the 170 pro-duced in August 1992. Some individual titles showed even greater changes between both periods, with *The Times* publishing 15 letters to their previ-ous 47 (a drop of around 68 per cent). This is of note when one remembers that the siege of Sarajevo ultimately claimed more lives than the camps did earlier in the war. Once again, however, this demonstrates that cer-tain *types* of violence (in this instance, the appearance of camps and sealed trains) will generally trump the more drawn-out processes – such as that witnessed in Sarajevo – in terms of general press interest.

Themes within Coverage

Though there was a noticeable quantitative decline in how Bosnia was covered within the pages of these various Anglo–American newspaper outlets, at least when compared to the previous period (August 1992), the conflict in Bosnia nonetheless generated considerable discussion. A number of commentators were clearly horrified by the shelling of Markale, an event which was soon described as 'the worst single atrocity of the war in Bosnia,' and calls for stronger intervention quickly gained vocal support.[98] Demands for military action had been lukewarm at best in the months prior to Markale, rarely surpassing 25 per cent from the American public, but the reports and images following the carnage of 5 February stiffened resolve to a level previously unseen, with 48 per cent of people interviewed in an *ABC* poll approving of President Clinton's decision to offer an ultimatum to the Serbs regarding the removal of heavy weapons around Sarajevo.[99] Public support for intervention in the United Kingdom was generally higher – a *Gallup* poll conducted one week before Markale finding that 68 per cent of Brits would support military action which could lead to peace. It was likely, as commented on at the time, that the marketplace massacre would have hardened such support. Several world leaders also became more vocal in their calls for action, with even Pope John Paul II urging the international community to 'try every means to stop the fighting.'[100]

The prospect of intervention, however, soon over-shadowed the attacks on Markale, and the ongoing atrocities in other regions of Bosnia, almost entirely. Once it was established that NATO were likely to intervene in at least some capacity, this angle quickly dominated both news and comment – though with this being potentially the first armed intervention in NATO's history, this was perhaps to be expected. Continuing a pattern which is frequently observed in media responses to mass violence, the in-depth coverage of the slaughter, which had led to the deaths of 68 people and wounded 200, soon diminished to the point of an afterthought – often only being mentioned, if at all, to properly frame the much larger discussion regarding NATO action.[101] A number of comment pieces were clearly partisan in their support for the proposed deployment, with one *Los Angeles Times* editorial arguing that to not act would be 'to turn one's back on genocide.'[102] Upon further analysis of the relevant sources, it becomes apparent that one of the main reasons for this sudden upsurge in interest in Bosnia was due to the manner in which Sarajevo, specifically, came to be identified with the West. Though atrocities, described by one commentator as 'an obvious affront to the values on which civilisation is based,' were taking place throughout Bosnia – often surpassing the barbarity and poverty which afflicted the Bosnian capital – Sarajevo was the focal point of a clear majority of newspaper coverage.[103]

With the exception of the brief period in 1992 during which the camps, which were predominantly in Eastern Bosnia, were revealed, this Sarajevo-centric trend was consistent throughout the conflict. One of the main reasons for this was that the city provided a comparatively secure base for those reporters covering the Bosnian conflict for Western press outlets. Though difficulties remained regarding supplies of electricity and gas, many hotels remained open throughout the war, and despite being within range of Serb mortar rounds they were still a safer option than risking abduction or worse in the more remote regions of the country. Sarajevo was also a 'dependable' option for journalists, in the rather macabre sense that the frequency of sniper fire and mortar attacks guaranteed that a story of some description would present itself on a regular basis. Indeed, it was common for reporters to wait near those areas that were notorious for sniper attacks in the hope of such an occurrence, though as has been shown earlier in this section it often required destruction of some magnitude for such a report to be elevated to the status of a main story.[104] Aside from the 'convenience' which Sarajevo afforded those wishing to report on the developing conflict in the region, there is evidence that another factor was greatly influential – the perception of Sarajevo as a civilised, Western city. This selective framing – which was temporarily at odds with the established discourse characterising the Balkans as uncivilised and violent – was surely influenced by the fact that the majority of the city's inhabitants were white. In several reports, Sarajevo was described in terms which were rarely mentioned in relation to cities in less-developed regions of the globe – particularly those in Africa or Asia. The 'multicultural' nature of the city was often remarked upon, and the sophistication of its people and culture was highlighted regularly, particularly in those articles which were clearly pro-intervention.[105] One notable headline declared that 'The spirit of Europe lives and dies in Sarajevo', with the city described elsewhere as 'a once cosmopolitan jewel, an Olympic-class city.' In addition to the Western way of life in Sarajevo, however, was the assertion that the people living there were like us – 'white people to whose predicament we can relate,' in the words of one editorial.[106] Though short-lived, this identification within the press with the victims of mass violence was rarely, if ever, replicated in relation to African victims in Rwanda.

This solidarity, or at least empathy, with the people of Sarajevo was greatly enhanced by the fact that the stories of specific individuals were occasionally highlighted. Though stories about individuals are generally over-represented within the news – as opposed to those focusing on issues – this is a rarity during times of war and genocide, for the simple fact that the numbers involved have a tendency to become somewhat abstract and so individuals are lost in the overall suffering.[107] Occasionally, however, an aspect of an individual's story would grab the attention of the press in a manner which the wider conflict was unable. One such tale, which was judged to be suitably unique to warrant coverage, was that of Zeyneba Hardaga – a Sarajevo resident who found refuge in Israel, decades after helping Jews during the Holocaust.[108] The most well-known individual during this period, however, was Zlata Filipovic, a 13-year-old Bosnian girl who had lived in Sarajevo until fleeing with her parents to Paris in 1993. During her time in the Bosnian capital, she had witnessed the violence and poverty afflicting the city, and since 1991 had recorded her experiences in her diary. The English publication of her diary in late February 1994 gained widespread coverage in the Anglo–American press, particularly in Britain. Media appearances followed on the likes of *Blue Peter* and her picture graced the front cover of *Newsweek*. Predictable similarities were drawn with Anne Frank, the twentieth century's most famous diarist, though this was not a comparison that the author herself was comfortable with.[109] Perhaps most crucial, in regards to this section, was the fact that a number of aspects of Zlata's life mirrored those of similarly-aged children in the West – 'She watched MTV and raved about Madonna and Michael Jackson, read *Adrian Mole* and Enid Blyton.'[110]

Certainly, the civilians of the Bosnian capital were now regularly described as being similar to those in the West in most regards, but for the fact that their country was in the midst of a brutal conflict. The following extract from Peter Preston is a good example of this style of empathetic journalism, which tended to increase in the aftermath of a particularly bloody occurrence:

> The real chill of Bosnia, as you watch those endless television bulletins, is that they feature people like us. People in jeans and T-shirts. People with CDs and Top Tens and double espressos. People Bill Gates would like to sell the new Windows to. Because these are people like us [...] The wreck of Sarajevo haunts us because it is our wreck.[111]

Such sentiments were rarely voiced when similar violence flared in other regions of the world, and most certainly not in relation to Africa. The likes of Kigali had not been a favoured tourist destination for Americans before the outbreak of violence in Rwanda, nor had it imprinted itself onto the popular conscience of the British people by providing the backdrop for a Torville and Dean-esque show of sporting triumph.[112] This factor may also, therefore, go some way to explaining the discrepancy in the level of coverage afforded to Rwanda in comparison with Bosnia. Not only was Bosnia geographically closer to the West than Rwanda, it was also closer *socially* – a belief which probably influenced the author of a letter to the *Independent* when they argued that 'Every day's indifference diminishes the humanity in all of us.'[113] These references to Sarajevo's cultural status, and the emphasis on its inhabitants' common bonds with the West, are notable in that they contradict much of the established discourse regarding the Balkans (e.g., as being uncivilised and at the mercy of irrational ethnic hatreds) which influenced the framing of the conflict at various other times. There is, of course, also an undeniable racial element to the media employing such comparatively empathetic framing in their coverage of Bosnia. The victims of Sarajevo could be portrayed as 'like us' because they were white, and seen to have similar cultural and commercial habits to the 'civilised' West. In the reporting of Rwanda, however, where the victims were mostly impoverished black Africans, allusions to such common humanity were rarely articulated in such emotive terms, if ever.

Though the Markale bombing led to an indignant reaction from various contemporaries on both sides of the Atlantic, an equal number of voices were soon raised which urged caution regarding any possible response.

One of the more obvious trends when analysing the selected titles is that even the most shocking crimes were soon relegated to secondary status once the possibility of military intervention was advanced. Indeed, the Markale bombing itself was supplanted by this shift in focus within only a few days of the actual event, and the reporting of interventionist measures soon dominated coverage for the remainder of the period. In the weeks following the marketplace massacre, it was rare to find an edition of any of the selected titles which did *not* focus on intervention and the forms it could take. The most interesting discussions, however, took place within the comment sections of these various publications, with the arguments for and against intervention often taking precedence.

One of the most persistent observations, particularly by those in the US, was that the demand for further action had been heavily influenced by television coverage of Markale – seen as a knee-jerk reaction which had little in the way of a solid footing in any workable objectives. Charles Krauthammer of the *Chicago Tribune* stated this in clear terms by asserting that the decision to intervene was 'made on the basis of TV pictures,' a belief which was seconded by Walter Goodman, who argued that little change in foreign policy would have been pursued by the Clinton administration had it not been for the television coverage of the 5 February attack.[114] More important – or perhaps ominous – to some was the potential escalation of the conflict to other regions outside of the Balkans, a fact which was made increasingly plausible in the eyes of many by the increasing role which Russia was to take in diplomatic negotiations. Certainly, Russian political maneuvers in the Balkan arena were soon front page news, with the victims of Markale losing prominence.[115]

In a geopolitical climate which was only a few short years detached from the fall of Communism and the end of the Cold War, Russian involvement in the negotiating process was soon viewed as something with the potential to renew military tension with the West. Indeed, in many instances, policy options were explicitly framed in such terms, with the potential for wider conflict being cited as a reason to steer clear of military involvement in the region. The term 'World War III' was not uncommon at this time when commentators were discussing the potential fallout from a NATO/Russian stand-off over Bosnia, and there was a genuine belief in some quarters that the Bosnian crisis could lead to a global conflict. This fact was rendered more plausible by a declaration to the UN, by Russian Foreign Minister Andrei Kozyrev, that 'Already once in 1914 a provocation was staged in Sarajevo when a similar horrible act of terror became the cause of a global tragedy.'[116] American commentators were particularly wary of Russian antagonism, with one editorial piece describing the 'Sarajevo artillery crisis' as becoming 'the Cuban Missile Crisis of the 1990s,' a historical analogy which would have struck a chord with many readers.[117] The main consequence of this greater focus on outside involvement in the Balkans was that it led to the suffering of civilians within Bosnia being relegated further down the list of journalistic priorities, to the point where, by the end of February 1994, they were rarely mentioned except to frame the coverage of diplomatic considerations.

Confusing Victims and Perpetrators

When looking at the framing of the Bosnian conflict in the Anglo–American press, one cannot help but detect a determined bias on the part of a number of contributors to lay at least some of the blame for the atrocities committed on the Bosnian Muslims themselves. Whilst it is entirely probable that these individuals deliberately forwarded this line of argument in an attempt to counter the increasing calls for intervention, it is also apparent that this belief may have been part of the reason as to why it took an event on the scale of Markale to establish Sarajevo on the front pages once more. Indeed, it was in the wake of Markale that the greatest concentration of this 'distrust' of Muslims was recorded (within this research).

The blood on the walls surrounding the Markale marketplace was barely dry before the identity of the perpetrators was brought into question. Though it would stand to reason that it had been the work of the Serb units stationed in the hills surrounding Sarajevo, who had already launched tens of thousands of mortar rounds into the Bosnian capital in the several months prior, explanations contrary to this were expressed almost immediately. The most vocal proponent of Serb innocence – and therefore Muslim guilt – was Bosnian Serb leader, Radovan Karadzic, who stated that the massacre had been the result of an operation by Bosnia's own government. By way of further 'explanation', Karadzic argued that the shelling had been falsely blamed on the Serbs in an attempt by the Bosnian government to force NATO intervention – going as far as to claim that mannequins, actors and cadavers supplied by Croatian forces had been used to maximise the carnage witnessed at the scene.[118] Though the idea that the shelling had been 'staged' to look worse than it actually had been was rejected almost immediately, a number of observers remained unconvinced of Serb guilt. This position was clouded further by the fact that the UN itself was unable to determine the exact trajectory of the shell which destroyed the marketplace, and often implicated the Muslims in the event of ambiguous evidence.[119] It is perhaps worth highlighting that the 'disbelief' aspect at play here is distinct from that witnessed in responses to the liberation of the camps in 1945. The crimes of the Nazis were questioned because their *scale* and *barbarity* were beyond what many could readily accept or understand at the time; whereas, in Bosnia, the disbelief or skepticism was generated by a distrust of the *victims* themselves.

A distrust of Muslim claims was persistent throughout the conflict – Silber and Little later describing this as a 'whispering campaign' – with some commentators arguing that the Western press was too readily reporting atrocity stories without verification of the facts.[120] Letters, in particular, often voiced this opinion, with one example, printed in the *Los Angeles Times* in the immediate aftermath of Markale, stating that: 'The latest massacre in Sarajevo is blamed on Serbs, even though the United Nations cannot confirm who did it. The media will not speculate whether Muslims could have done such a thing.'[121] This assertion was simply a continuation of an opinion which had been prevalent since the very start of the conflict, as seen in the following letter excerpt from 1992:

> Horror stories pour out of Bosnia daily and you print them. You do not ask for corroboration, or even warn your readers that stories come from only one side of this cruel civil war. Does it never occur to you that you are being manipulated by Bosnian Muslims? Evidently not.[122]

Whilst it should be mentioned that some of the 'anti-Muslim' rhetoric which appeared in the press was voiced by those who had some sort of vested interest in the conflict – sometimes due to their own ethnic background – there is evidence that several such 'sceptics' expressed such views in an attempt to bring greater balance to the reporting. This position was later reiterated by Ed Vulliamy, when he stated that newspapers 'loved the idea of the Muslims slaughtering their own people [...] It was perfect for neutrality.'[123] Although neutrality and objectivity are two of the principles upon which good journalism is based, analysis of the sources within this study shows evidence of a determined attempt by many contributors to depict all parties within the conflict as being equally at fault, despite evidence to the contrary. Whilst some may have argued that the Anglo–American press were too willing to print stories which painted the Serbs in a bad light, the benefit of hindsight allows one to realise that, in relation to the atrocities committed in the war, such a position would have been justifiable. It has been estimated that the Serbs were responsible for close to 90 per cent of the atrocities committed during the Bosnian conflict, and it should be remembered that Serb forces were behind the attack on Srebrenica – now recognised as the most brutal war crime to take place in postwar Europe.[124] Describing the situation in Bosnia, Cushman and Mestrovic illustrate the point effectively: 'All sides may have committed atrocities and war crimes, but all sides have not committed genocide.'[125]

Regardless of the fact that Serb forces were behind the majority of war crimes committed during the Bosnian conflict, many newspapers attempted to stress the equality of all sides in this regard. This was a trend which persisted throughout the conflict, to varying degrees, with one such argument coming from Jonathan Eyal, who asserted that 'Whatever ethnic paradise Bosnia may have been in the past,' the reality was that 'most of its people would love to slit each other's throats.'[126] Even by 1995, in the midst of a renewed wave of Serb assaults – which climaxed in the now infamous slaughter of Srebrenica – commentators continued to voice the opinion that 'all parties' within the Balkans were 'on a par for atrocities.'[127] One journalist, Eve-Ann Prentice, sought to further this notion, in addition to perhaps attempting to excuse Serbian excesses, by commenting that:

> Television coverage of Bosnian Serb 'death camps', Muslim refugees, and shell-pocked villages has been largely responsible

for conjuring the impression that almost the only victims are Muslims. This, in turn, has deeply influenced American policy. The Serbs have committed the majority of atrocities in the war because they have been the best-equipped. But it has become apparent that elements on all sides have been as vile *as they have had the capacity to be* [emphasis added].[128]

The assertion, if not the genuine belief, that all parties in the Bosnian conflict were equally guilty was also voiced by those outside of the press. Arguably the most influential of these was President Bill Clinton, who declared in the aftermath of Markale that, 'Until those folks get tired of killing each other, bad things will continue to happen.'[129] This was probably expressed in this manner to dampen further calls for US airstrikes to be used against the Serbs, but it is not unlikely that this was a genuinely held opinion of the people of the Balkans. With regards to the possibility of intervention, it is fair to argue that the persistent emphasis on 'guilt on all sides' in the civil war was often deliberately used in order to complicate calls for outside engagement. This view is illustrated by the words of Canadian General Lewis MacKenzie, who commanded the Sarajevo contingent of the UNPROFOR mission between 1992 and 1993. Testifying before Congress in 1993, he argued that 'dealing with Bosnia is a little like dealing with three serial killers – one has killed fifteen, one has killed ten, one has killed five. Do we help the one that's only killed 5?'[130] MacKenzie's analogy implied that the Serbs were responsible for 50 per cent of the atrocities committed in Bosnia – a dramatic underestimate – but it nonetheless demonstrates the deeply rooted belief that identifying clear victims and perpetrators in the war was next to impossible. Though there were regular assertions to the contrary – with one respondent describing the writings of another as being similar to accusing Jews of burning their own synagogues during Kristallnacht – these rarely had any impact on the tone of the overall coverage.[131]

Whilst it is difficult to ascertain with any degree of certainty, the 'everyone is guilty' position – described in a later publication as a 'moral obfuscation' – continued to predominate throughout reporting on the Balkans for two reasons.[132] First of all, it could be used as a means for those who did not support intervention to strengthen their argument. Calls for US airstrikes or the deployment of British troops were more likely to gain public support if it could be established for certain that one side in the conflict were the aggressors. This was made all the more plausible during the reporting of events in the Balkans due to the fact that there was, indeed, a multi-sided war being waged. In spite of the fact that the vast majority of victims were civilians – the majority of them being Muslims – any act of aggression against the Serbs, or Croats, could be held up as proof of the equal guilt of all sides.[133] In their quest to be seen as neutral and impartial, a number of newspaper outlets would therefore highlight Muslim-led attacks to a degree not repeated for any but the worst Serb atrocities, a style of reporting which must surely have influenced a large section of their readerships. Certainly, in the words of Ed Vulliamy, 'it takes very little to poison the groundwater of truth.'[134] This notion was further illustrated by columnist Meg Greenfield, who wrote in 1993:

> You'd think that with only a few years left to go in this genocidal century, we'd have at least by now have figured out some rudimentary way to confirm the recurring horror. But we haven't. We have only gotten better – more subtle – at looking the other way.[135]

The other, more sinister, reason for this prevalence of what might be termed 'disproportionate emphasis' on Muslim atrocities (self-targeted or otherwise) was the simple fact that several people in the West were clearly distrustful of Muslims in general. Though by no means reaching the levels of Islamophobia which followed in the years following 9/11, analysis of this newspaper sample reveals a persistent trend in which several commentators were openly apprehensive about weighing in completely on the side of the Bosnian Muslims – despite the obvious suffering to which they were being subjected. Generally, as mentioned earlier, this would take the form of attempting to downplay the severity of reported atrocities, such as the siege of Sarajevo. Commentators argued that to focus solely on atrocities *against* Muslims was misguided, and that this was in part as a result of the Muslims learning 'how to exploit their victim status and play the Western press.'[136] Such articles, which attempted to minimise the particular sufferings of the Muslim population in comparison to other groups in the Balkans, were most likely driven by a desire for NATO countries to steer clear of military intervention and so were fairly common throughout the conflict. Many other commentators, however, voiced concerns over what aiding the Muslim population might lead to, with many exaggerating a fundamentalist element which could threaten the rest of the Western world. In a manner which would later be replicated in post-9/11 anti-Islamic rhetoric, the Crusades were often invoked in order to emphasise the scale of this perceived threat, with one letter warning that a 'Pandora's Box' might be opened which could 'bring into play an Islamic world which stretches across every continent on earth.'[137]

By the latter stages of the conflict, including the immediate aftermath of Srebrenica, such beliefs continued to find vocal support. One commentator, writing in *The Times*, went as far as to state: 'If you enlist against the Serbs, you are to some extent fighting for Germany and for Islam. I don't know about you, but that's one combination that gives me the creeps.'[138] Whilst it is true that there were fundamentalist elements within the Muslim population of Bosnia, to apply such a label to the entire people was a gross misinterpretation. By the early 1990s, the Bosnian Muslims were 'among the most secularised Muslim populations in the world,' though this was a fact which was lost on many observers.[139] In relation to this research, this trend highlights the fact that there are methods by which even the suffering of a European people – which in some instances could be categorically classed as genocide – can be evaded or minimised by its framing in the Anglo–American press.

Period Three: 7 July – 3 August 1995

By the summer of 1995, the conflict in Bosnia had presented the world with more than its share of notable human rights violations. With the ethnic cleansing of entire regions, the existence of prison camps and the slow but brutal strangulation of Sarajevo all being covered in some way or another by the Anglo–American press, few members of the public could be mistaken as to the volatile nature of the Balkans at this time. However, it was the Serb attack on the town of Srebrenica – which saw the death of some 7,000 men and boys – that would ultimately become the symbolic atrocity of the war.

Accounts of the exact timeline of the massacres which took place following the fall of Srebrenica vary, but they are generally accepted to have taken place over a period of several days between 12 July and 19 July 1995. As Jacques Semelin once noted, 'since the dawn of time [...] war and massacre have married well,' and what happened at Srebrenica was a clear example of their matrimony.[140] The military assault, and the massacre that followed, were both organised and implemented on the orders of Ratko Mladic, the Serb general whose subsequent infamy was illustrated by the intense coverage which followed his eventual capture in May 2011.[141] Described by one contemporary UN negotiator as 'a psychopath – highly intelligent and profoundly violent,' Mladic would be involved in all aspects of what took place at Srebrenica and his ruthless, calculating nature was evident from the beginning.[142] Working to a carefully constructed plan, the Serbs first set about separating all men of military age – including boys not yet in their teen years – from the rest of the population and corralling them in factories, warehouses and sports fields. In the carnage that followed, more than 7,000 of these male captives were executed and buried in mass graves, making this, in the words of Brendan Simms, 'by a considerable margin the biggest single war crime in Europe since 1945.'[143] This latter description was by no means hyperbole, and is made all the more potent when one considers that the vast majority of the victims were civilians, with most of those considered to be of political or military importance successfully evading capture.[144]

What took place in Srebrenica in mid-July 1995 can be regarded unquestionably as genocide. With the Serb actions being 'committed with intent to destroy, in whole or in part, a national, ethnical, racial or religious group, as such,' they clearly fell within the definitional parameters of what constitutes this monumental crime.[145] This concept was also invoked at the time, with Haris Silajdzic, the Bosnian Prime Minister, asserting that 'those who are against the lifting of the embargo [...] are guilty of genocide.'[146] Few of these claims can be disputed – Srebrenica was indeed the single largest massacre in Europe since World War II – but, as shall be demonstrated in the following sections, this did not necessarily ensure that this particular crime would dominate newspaper coverage in the weeks that followed.[147]

Quantitative Findings: 7 July – 3 August 1995

During the period analysed, between 7 July – 3 August 1995, a total of 764 news articles were printed in relation to the crisis in the Balkans, making this period only marginally more productive than the 749 recorded in the period surrounding the attack on Markale. Of this total, 475 articles were published in British titles, with 289 appearing in US publications. The *Independent* was the single most productive in this regard, publishing 135 articles on its pages during this period. At the other end of the scale was the *Chicago Tribune*, which published only 57 articles in the period surrounding the destruction of Srebrenica. In an interesting contrast to the numbers recorded for The *Independent*, this total of 57 articles in this period is the joint-second *lowest* for any one publication in a 28/29 day period – once again illustrating the large differences between various publications.

In relation to one of the key themes which has emerged from this research – that it is not mass violence per se which commands attention, but rather the *nature* of that same violence – a comparison between the number of articles produced in Period One (1–28 August 1992) and Period Three (7 July – 3 August 1995) is revealing. Across all eight selected titles in August 1992, a total of 857 articles were produced, almost 100 more than the 764 which would be recorded for the period between 7 July – 3 August, 1995. Indeed, it is conceivable that these statistics are further evidence of the important role that the *perception* of genocide and mass violence has in relation to depth of press coverage. Put another way, the discovery of camps like Omarska echoed memories of the Holocaust, and thus allowed the conflict to be framed in those terms, to a degree which was never the case with Srebrenica. Though the destruction of the 'safe haven,' with the subsequent use of organised mass shootings and mass burials, to an extent mirrored the crimes perpetrated by the Nazis during the first stages of the advance into the Soviet Union, this was not enough to challenge the discovery of 'concentration camps' in terms of perceived cultural significance. With the exception of the mass killing at Bleiburg/Maribor in May 1945, Srebrenica was indeed the worst massacre to take place in Europe since the end of World War II; but as the aforementioned statistics attest, something about the nature of the violence that took place there was insufficient for it to warrant a place as the most intensely covered story of the Bosnian war.[148]

Of the 764 articles produced in this period, 199 would ultimately begin on the front page of their respective publication. 91 of these were on the front pages of British titles, with 108 appearing in American publications – a notable observation when one remembers that there were far more British articles in total (475) than there was American (289). Again, this can be most readily explained by the fact that American newspapers, in general comparison to UK titles, include a greater number of stories on their front page. the *New York Times* was the most prolific in this regard, giving front page status to 35 articles during this period, with the *Chicago Tribune* producing the lowest amount with 14. Indeed, this period saw the highest total number of American front page articles in a single month, with 108 being produced. Whilst this could be interpreted as an indication of an intensification of American interest in the region as a result of the crimes of Srebrenica, it should be noted that the majority of coverage was in fact focused primarily on diplomatic considerations resulting from the attack and *not* on the crimes themselves – a trend that shall be further highlighted in later sections.

When measuring editorial coverage, a total of 41 lead articles were produced during this period; with 23 appearing in British publications and 18 in American. *The Times* printed the greatest number of editorials, registering a total of eight – coincidentally the same number which was produced by *all* titles during April 1994, the first month of the Rwandan genocide (a further example of the racial dynamic at play in terms of Western media interest in mass violence). The *Los Angeles Times*, on the other hand, published only one such lead article in this same period. This particular total is of note as it is the only occasion in which a given title devoted a solitary editorial to the events in Bosnia during a given 28/29 day period. A further observation can be made in this regard when compared to the coverage of Rwanda during April–July 1994 – where there were fifteen separate occasions in which an individual title posted a 'one month' total of one editorial or fewer.

In terms of comment pieces which engaged with the Balkan conflict, 101 were published in this period. Of these, 55 were from British outlets and 46 from American – revealing statistics when compared with the focus given to the Rwandan genocide; which prompted only 70 comment pieces *in total* from 7 April to 29 July 1994. These numbers are highlighted not simply for means of illustration, but to demonstrate that even though Srebrenica was not the most intensive period in terms of press interest in Bosnia, it still dwarfed what little coverage was afforded to a small African state which ultimately saw at least 800,000 people die in 100 days. In relation to individual titles, the *Guardian* and the *Washington Post* were the most prolific in discussing Bosnia, producing 19 and 16 comment articles, respectively. The titles which printed the least amount of comment articles were the *Los Angeles Times*, with eight, and the *Chicago Tribune*, which published seven.

During this same period 130 letters to the editor were published, with 114 appearing in British titles and 16 in American. Both *The Times* and the *Guardian* printed 35 letters, whilst the *Washington Post* printed none whatsoever. Combining both the American and British totals, the period in question was the second most prolific in terms of letters produced, with only 1–28 August 1992 (with 170 letters printed) surpassing it. Also of note is that the period surrounding the fall of the Srebrenica enclave saw the greatest disparity, proportionally, between national origin of letters, with some 87.7 per cent of letters published between 7 July – 3 August 1995 appearing in one of the four selected British publications.

Themes within Coverage

After several months of focus on Sarajevo, the fall of Srebrenica quickly became an established news story in the Anglo–American press. However, an analysis of the reporting from the time reveals that there was a general lack of appreciation for what had occurred there in the days following its capture. Details of the massacres at Srebrenica are now well understood, and the organised nature of the killings glaringly obvious with the benefit of hindsight.[149] As it was unfolding though, testimony was often hard to verify, and Srebrenica's position as the 'worst civilian genocide to occur on European soil' in the postwar world was not immediately apparent.[150] As shall be highlighted, the crimes themselves were often regarded as exaggerations or, in other instances, relegated to a position of secondary importance behind considerations which were more closely linked to the interests of the Western powers.

Although it was clear to some commentators early on that Srebrenica had witnessed scenes of atrocity worse than anything which had preceded them in the Bosnian war – one journalist described the scenes as constituting 'the worst crime against humanity in Europe since Auschwitz' – it took several weeks for the exact details to gain a general level of acceptance in the press.[151] An understandable reason for this, at least in the days immediately following the massacre, was the deliberate policy of the Serbs of trying to cover up what had taken place after the fall of the enclave itself. In a manner which echoed the 'night and fog' policies of the Nazi extermination program, Mladic wanted to seal a great victory for the Serbs without having their military glory tarnished by the senseless butchery which accompanied it. At the time, this took the form of depositing the victims in 'clandestine mass graves', whilst also restricting access to the media. Indeed, denial and obfuscation regarding the massacre continues to this day, as part of what Wagner and Nettelfield describe as an attempt to 'articulate a different narrative arc of the war.'[152]

In line with this, humanitarian organisations and members of the press were denied access to the enclave for weeks after the initial assault, with even Bosnian Serb journalists being kept far from the scene.[153] This ensured that many early dispatches relied on the testimony of those refugees who were fleeing from the region, with even UN personnel, out of fear of 'jeopardising' their comrades, at first hesitant to discuss anything that they had witnessed.[154] Certainly, this is part of the reason as to why the intentions of the Serbs were often misconstrued in early reports from the region. When read with the benefit of hindsight, it is clear that Srebrenica was not, at first, seen as a particularly notable departure from the accepted *model* of the Bosnian conflict up to that point. Rather than speaking of an organised venture which ultimately claimed the lives of at least 7,000 (mostly civilian) men, a number of dispatches framed what was taking place as 'evacuations' or as captives being 'screened for war crimes', with little intimation that genocide was being ruthlessly committed.[155] Although the earliest reports did mention summary executions and instances of mass rape, it is evident that the overall understanding of Srebrenica was that it was another violent *expulsion* of people by the Serbs, and not a prelude to a massacre.[156] At the time, however, this was in some ways understandable – a variety of war crimes had accompanied Serb advances in the past, but a descent into localised genocide was not something which would have been immediately conceivable to many. There are of course echoes here of the initial difficulty experienced in 1945 over the revelations of Nazi genocide, which were themselves beyond expectations up to that point. This is not to say though that there was a general belief that Mladic's forces would treat their prisoners with dignity and respect. One editorial, published only days after the initial fall of the safe haven, asserted that, 'Given the region's history of ethnic cleansing and torture camps, these captives [...] must be considered at grave danger.'[157] It was only with the increased availability of first-hand testimony from refugees, however, that the grim reality of Srebrenica emerged.

The defining horror of Srebrenica, the organised annihilation of men and boys of military age, gradually came to light in the days and weeks following the capture of the town by Mladic's forces. Reports of males having 'disappeared,' along with allusions to full-scale massacre, appeared quickly, but the grisly details only emerged once refugees from the region were able to make it to relative safety.[158] Vivid accounts soon emerged that revealed Srebrenica to be a break from the usual methodology of Serb expulsion, with a number of refugees testifying to what they had seen in the period before they had been expelled from the enclave. Ajkuna Alic, a 50-year-old Bosnian mother, described how the bodies 'were mutilated, all men,' whilst the elderly Haka Nukic asserted that the Serbs had taken 'the women away and did bad things to them, and killed the men the way you slaughter cattle.'[159] These were just two examples from a number of similar accounts, all of which stressed the male-targeted nature of the bulk of the killing. Only after several days would the *scale* of the destruction begin to become apparent, with initial (under)estimates stating that hundreds had been killed. By 21 July, the true figure of those murdered at Srebrenica gradually revealed itself, with one unidentified woman, speaking more than a week after the first assault, arguing that 'about 4,000' men had been slaughtered.[160]

These emerging details, however, did not lead to a general consensus, or appreciation, of what had actually taken place. Several early accounts stressed that most reports could not be confirmed, with one article, written almost two weeks after the initial assault, reporting that the United Nations had 'not found any first-hand witnesses of atrocities.'[161] Other stories were more neutral in their reporting, clearly seeking to avoid labelling Srebrenica as a massacre whilst still maintaining that *something* awful had taken place. As Boris Johnson opined, on the question of how best to deal with Serb war criminals: 'If only a *tenth*, a *twentieth*, of these *alleged* atrocities have *genuinely* occurred, then the perpetrators must be brought to justice, no matter how long it takes.'[162]

This approach – of accepting that crimes had been committed, but reserving judgement on their actual scale and ferocity – was employed by several journalists at the time. Indeed, this style of journalism had already been seen years before in the initial disclosures of the camps, with several correspondents clearly not wishing to report something so terrible without verification. Once again, in the context of the Bosnian war *to that point*, this hesitation was understandable; the mass killing of men, and especially young boys, on such a scale was unheard of at this juncture and so these same journalists can perhaps be excused for not immediately believing the most graphic descriptions of what was taking place.[163]

Others would explicitly state that though there was difficulty in finding out the truth of the atrocities – one spoke of a 'Balkan mist' descending – the number of similar reports indeed pointed to some gruesome reality.[164] The following extract, written only days after the fall of Srebrenica, is an illustration of this approach:

> Their stories cannot be corroborated and could be the fantasies of people driven to the extremes of despair. But there is a terrible ring of plausibility in the insistent accounts of the women and old men of Srebrenica about the atrocities they saw in the days after the fall of their town.[165]

The veracity of these accounts could not, however, be questioned indefinitely. As July wore on more first-hand accounts emerged and, even though doubts remained, the Anglo–American press slowly began to give credence to the fact that something truly horrible had unfolded at Srebrenica. What would ultimately be the catalyst for this new-found acceptance was the degree of consistency in the accounts which soon emerged from those, mostly women, who had escaped from the safe haven. As Tim Butcher would assert in a 15 July article, 'the consistent stories tend to be the truth,' and this belief was echoed in the dispatches of a number of contemporary journalists early on.[166]

That war crimes had been committed in and around Srebrenica was rarely a matter for debate, but the exact scale of the disaster continued to cause confusion for several weeks.[167] By 22 July, tentative though often confused estimates were being offered as to the true number of victims at Srebrenica, but there was little by way of an established figure. Those at the lower end of the scale tended to cite a figure of 'many hundreds,' with one report – also notable due to its position as the smallest article on a page which was dominated by an advert for improving one's foreign language skills – citing the Dutch defence-minister, Joris Voorhoeve, who stated: 'We still do not have a complete picture but I fear that hundreds, if not thousands of people have died [...] I believe that grave war crimes occurred.'[168] Even those reports which did give a larger estimate of the numbers killed were often forced, due to lack of information, to give wholly uncertain figures. One example of this came from Raymond Bonner, whose estimate of between 2,000 and 10,000 was supplemented by an admission that 'the range of the estimate underscores the confusion that reigns.'[169] The lack of a more precise figure would continue into August, with several articles continuing to cite estimates of between 5,000 and 9,000 *missing* – though few would make any assertion as to what had happened to these same 'missing' men.[170]

Whilst the exact details of Srebrenica were slow to emerge, one might assume that the idea that a war crime of such magnitude had occurred on European soil would have prompted the Anglo–American press to devote further attention to the atrocities themselves. On the contrary, however, an examination of newspapers from the time reveals that Western strategic considerations quickly dominated coverage. As will be highlighted, whilst the issue of genocide was indeed discussed by various journalists, this was generally a side-issue to topics such as damage to Western prestige, or the dangers of becoming too heavily involved in the region.[171]

Indeed, one of the first themes to emerge following the assault on the enclave was the perceived weakness of the UN, a topic which would soon replace focus on the atrocities themselves in both the 'news' and 'comment' pages. The fall of Srebrenica, once described as 'the darkest moment in international involvement in Bosnia,' was viewed as symptomatic of a larger process which had seen the international community fail to challenge Serb aggression on numerous previous occasions.[172] The NATO airstrikes which had followed in the wake of the Markale market bombing had achieved little in the long term – shelling of Sarajevo continued, and war crimes of various descriptions were still being reported throughout the region. What was particularly notable about Srebrenica though, at least in the context of Western involvement, was that it was the first time that a designated UN 'safe haven' had been overrun.[173] Whilst by no means a foregone conclusion, attacks on these safe havens – the 'Achilles heel of the UN peacekeeping mission' – demonstrated the weakness of the UN in the region, and many took this to be an illustration of wider issues facing the organisation in the post-Cold War world.[174]

Though some commentators had previously argued that military setbacks in Bosnia were simply a 'failure to achieve the impossible,' in that an underfunded force with a weak mandate could not be expected to bring peace to a region that had been at war for more than three years, others would use the example of Srebrenica to launch a scathing attack on the UN and its key member states.[175] Certainly, the manner in which Srebrenica had fallen was one of the key reasons why the reputation of the UN took such a hammering at this time. Pictures of UN peacekeepers standing idly by as a civilian population was left to the mercy of military forces provoked an angry response from some, with the pinnacle of this embarrassment coming with the release of images showing UN forces being forced to share a toast with Ratko Mladic as part of his victory celebrations.[176] During this time the UN was described in a variety of negative terms, but 'impotent' was one of the most frequently used.[177] The peacekeepers in the region were seen as an irrelevance, a token force symbolising the lack of will to help even those directly under their care and supervision. Indeed, for the UN, the fall of the Srebrenica 'safe haven' was viewed, at least in terms of the *purpose* of the Western role in Bosnia, as being 'the worst day in the war.'[178] Unable, or unwilling, to offer any meaningful resistance to Serbian aggression, the role of the UN in the region was seen as becoming increasingly untenable, with Patrick Bishop remarking: 'A simple way of looking at the UN role in eastern Bosnia is to see it as a sort of cowboy movie – but a movie in which the bad guys always win.'[179]

More than simply the role of the UN was at stake, though – the very fabric of the Western alliance was regarded as being in serious jeopardy. The bonds that had tied Western states together throughout the uncertain decades of the Cold War were seen as becoming little more than an outdated sentiment, in danger of collapsing entirely. Richard Holbrooke – one of the key negotiators at the Dayton Peace Accords – later recalled that in mid-1995 it had 'become commonplace to say that Washington's relations with [their] European allies were worse than at any time since the 1956 Suez crisis.'[180] Indeed, some had already resigned themselves to the fact that the Bosnian conflict had caused irreversible damage to transatlantic relations, as illustrated by the following extract from Charles Kupchan:

> [I]t is too late to prevent what could prove to be one of the most devastating legacies of the slaughter in Bosnia: the rot of the West. Since the beginning of the breakup of Yugoslavia, the Western democracies have exhibited such strategic myopia, moral weakness and political paralysis that their behaviour calls into question the very existence of a Western community of civil states.[181]

One of the reasons as to why the 'Western alliance' was at the forefront of many an article at this time was the fact that the fall of Srebrenica came only weeks after the 50th anniversary of VE-Day had been celebrated with a flurry of media attention and grand political gestures.[182] Amidst the memorialisation of what could be termed the greatest collective triumph of the Western democracies, the mounting slaughter in eastern Bosnia proved to be a most unfortunate, and unwelcome, coincidence of timing. Perhaps expectedly, analogies were drawn between the 'strength' of this past alliance and the perceived 'weakness' of the current system – the same system that had, in part, been formed in an effort to ensure that the aggression which had blighted Europe in the 1930s and 1940s would never return. Christopher Brooker, writing only days after the fall of Srebrenica, underscored this perceived contrast:

On VE-Day we play sentimental pop songs to bask in the inherited glory of having had the courage and vision to stand up to rare evil. Yet when the same evil arises in our own time, we run away in clouds of humbug.[183]

Allusions to historical precedent did not simply focus on the triumph of World War II, however, with many commentators invoking the collective failures of the 1930s to highlight what was at stake in Bosnia. Though by no means a new development – comparisons between Milosevic and Hitler, and to Bosnia as 'our Czechoslovakia,' had been made since the very beginning of the conflict – the spectre of the 1930s hung over a number of comment pieces up to and including the period which saw the fall of Srebrenica.[184] The most frequent equation was with the lack of will in challenging Serb aggression and the consequences of allowing Hitler free rein to expand his early empire unopposed. Essentially warning that unopposed violence simply begets more violence, there was a genuine belief that the horror of Srebrenica could have been a prelude to wider-ranging and more destructive Serb policies in the region. Stressing that 'a repeat of the thirties awaits,' Will Hutton of the *Guardian* warned that Bosnia would be held up as an example to other regimes that individual acts of aggression would not be challenged, whilst Andrew Neil lamented that 'Appeasement echoes once more through the corridors of power.'[185] The shadow of appeasement would also be highlighted, somewhat interestingly given that the US was not historically associated with this same policy in the manner which Chamberlain's Britain was, in the American press, with Richard Holbrooke cited as arguing that the situation in Bosnia represented 'the greatest collective failure of the West since the 1930s.'[186] In each of the examples cited, it is clear that the primary focus of debate was not the crimes themselves, but instead the danger of the West being perceived as weak.

Particularly for those who were against any increase in Western involvement, similar appeals to history were made throughout the Balkan crisis – with the Vietnam conflict being one of the most frequently invoked. One of the main reasons for citing Vietnam was to highlight the risks of entering into a potentially long-term engagement; or 'quagmire,' to use a common phrase from the time.[187] Regardless of the extent of human rights abuses in the Balkans, the risk of another failed foreign intervention was a political cost which was considered by many to be unacceptably high – certainly, in the words of Peter Novick, 'the lessons of Vietnam [...] easily trumped the lessons of the Holocaust.'[188] Contrary to what might be expected, it should be noted that such allusions to Vietnam were frequent on both sides of the Atlantic, and not simply within the country that had such a troubled recent past there. What did set some American comment apart, however, was the fact that the potential for a Vietnam-type scenario in Bosnia was not viewed simply in terms of military risk. In a post-Cold War environment in which the US was still attempting to adjust to its new role as the world's only superpower, the very fabric of American society was seen as being threatened by intervention in European affairs. Published only two days after the fall of Srebrenica, the following extract articulates this concern well:

> A quick success in Bosnia might serve US interests by enhancing NATO's credibility, maintaining alliance unity and marginally bolstering European stability – at least until the next ethnic war. But failure or even a costly success could mortally wound our fragile, fractious polity – and finish the job Vietnam started of destroying the American Dream.[189]

Though some editorials did try to draw attention to the fact that the Vietnam analogy was being utilised to deflect and dissuade stronger calls for action, the dangers of full-scale intervention in the Balkans continued to be framed through this prism throughout the conflict.[190] This was perhaps understandable, given the relatively recent nature of the South East Asian campaign and its established place in various pop-culture mediums, though it was not the only historical precedent that was invoked during this period.

Another precedent cited, often mistakenly, was the supposed experience of the German Army fighting partisans in the Balkans during the 1940s. The fact that 'Adolf Hitler couldn't beat Serbian guerrillas; Josef Stalin couldn't bend them to his will' was highlighted from the very beginning of the conflict, and estimates as to exactly how many German divisions were engaged in this fighting ranged from between 20 and 37.[191] It was suggested that 'some of Germany's toughest and most cruel divisions [had been] hopelessly tied down in a losing guerrilla war,' and the following extract from Paul Johnson even went as far as to draw a direct analogy with the aforementioned American failure in Southeast Asia:

> Germany is full of old soldiers who vividly recall fighting Yugoslav guerrillas in impossible terrain between 1941 and 1945. At one time the Germans had 750,000 men there, and it brought them nothing but blood, sweat, tears and eventual defeat, a Teutonic Vietnam.[192]

Generally utilised to the same effect as Vietnam – as a warning of the dangers of getting too heavily involved in the region – this assertion of German failure in the Balkans was voiced throughout the conflict, despite the fact that very little of what was being said was actually true. Though the German Army had indeed engaged in bloody fighting with the Serbs, the number and capabilities of these same divisions were nowhere close to those frequently cited. In fact, commentators in both British and American newspapers actually stated as much, challenging these myths as early as 1992. Norman Stone highlighted how many of the divisions were in fact manned by elderly territorials, whilst a letter from Timothy Francis argued that those fighting in the region had a 'level of training, morale and motivation' which was 'nowhere close to a professional force.'[193] These challenges did little in the long run, however, to dislodge the established belief that not even the Nazi war machine could tame the Balkans. This myth continued to be cited into 1995, with a letter to the *Daily Telegraph* arguing that those who would send Western troops into Bosnia 'should take a long hard look at what happened to the German Army in their Yugoslav campaign.'[194]

The framing of policy options in this manner – that is, citing specific examples and thus emphasising the risks that were expected to follow any form of heightened intervention – is likely to have had an impact on many Anglo–American readers' opinions concerning intervention. As Price & Tewksbury note: 'The way in which choices are presented to people [...] the way in which choices are framed – will affect the likelihood that particular options will be selected', meaning therefore that the references in the press to the potential for long-term, large-scale military commitments ('quagmires') can be interpreted as an attempt by the media to influence opinion/policy.[195] This position is also supported by studies that have shown that 'framing in terms of negative consequences appears to have greater persuasive impact than framing that emphasises consequences or gains.'[196] In essence, by highlighting the *quagmire frame* during discussions of policy, the Anglo–American media established a discourse that disproportionately emphasised the negative aspects of intervention; which in turn can be inferred as evidence of an overall lack of concern for the civilian suffering in the region when weighted against post-Cold War foreign policy priorities.

Given the opinions discussed so far, one could be forgiven for assuming that the Anglo–American press was rather partisan in its general view of Bosnia. But to imply that a non-interventionist consensus had been reached would be an oversimplification. Though Srebrenica would not prompt a sizable shift in the way in which the Balkan conflict was interpreted, there *were* increased attempts to draw attention to the region and to offer suggestions for a change in Western policy. Calls for stronger action against Serb aggression – as would be the case, with varying degrees of insistence, following virtually every major atrocity which was publicised – would begin almost immediately following the assault on Srebrenica. Partly due to the fact that Mladic's forces were now viewed as being in direct defiance of the UN, myriad suggestions were forwarded in the weeks following the fall of the enclave, reaching something of a peak between 20–26 July 1995. Whilst the most frequent calls were for airstrikes – a move which received 59 per cent approval in one UK poll – and a lifting of the arms embargo on the region, some of the suggestions provided in letters from the public were slightly more creative.[197] One such example was that from P.J.W. Raine, who argued for the creation of an international brigade under the same model as that which had fought in the Spanish Civil War.[198] Another proposal, again in a letter, highlighted the following:

> We build monuments to military heroes and leaders of nations; we lay out long solemn walls to silently honor those who died for no good reason in Vietnam, and we reserve sidewalks for impressions of the feet and palms of Hollywood stars. Why not

build a museum to expose the identities of those people who have participated in this great war crime? Journalists, victims, survivors and witnesses can collect the names and photographs of those responsible for the Bosnian horror. Name after name and misdeed after misdeed can be added to this museum of shame, engraved into stone, memorialized into a form telling the perpetrators we know who you are and we will not let future generations forget what you are doing.[199]

Within the bounds of this research, this particular suggestion is notable – since it presupposes that knowledge, and recording, of war crimes and other atrocities would act as some sort of deterrent for would-be genocidaires of the future. As this research seeks to illustrate, however, there is little evidence that increased knowledge of such atrocities will have any such desirable effect. *Knowledge* of past genocide does not necessarily lead to a *response* to unfolding genocide.

Even though exact details of what had taken place at Srebrenica were only clarified after several weeks, the number of reports from the region, both in the press and on television, provided enough information for a number of journalists to affirm that genocide had occurred in the fallen safe haven. Pictures of refugee columns, ominously devoid of all men of military age, turned Bosnia into a 'living room killing field' and it is perhaps unsurprising, especially given the greater recognition of the Holocaust by the 1990s, some people drew this conclusion about what had befallen the doomed enclave.[200] In the most concentrated manner since the discovery of the concentration camps in 1992, the label of 'genocide' was regularly applied to Srebrenica, invariably in those articles which were critical of what was seen as Western inaction. Although many were keen to stress that the Serb-led massacre should not be compared to the Nazi crimes, this analogy was nonetheless invoked several times in the days and weeks following the fall of Srebrenica, with a letter printed in the *Guardian* arguing that 'For the second time this century, Europe is passive as a non-Christian minority in its midst is being destroyed.'[201] Others would avoid invoking the model of the Holocaust, but would stick to their convictions in detailing the scale of the slaughter in Bosnia. The following extract from Robin Harris of the *Daily Telegraph* is one such illustrative example:

With some 200,000 Bosnians dead or missing, and almost two million forced to flee; with voluminous evidence of Serb prison camps, systematic torture and organised mass ethnic cleansing; and now with the 'safe areas' being eliminated one by one by the Serbs, and civilians led into captivity or expelled, there is no excuse for describing what is happening as other than genocide.[202]

In the same article, Harris also asserted that there had been 'in the moral sense at least, some complicity with genocide,' and this was a common theme at the time. Other articles were rarely as specific or coherent in their characterisation of Serb atrocities, but *invoking* genocide was an influential tool in attempting to frame the event in a certain manner – particularly for those commentators who were pro-intervention. In a manner which was rarely recorded during comment on the genocide which had engulfed Rwanda a year earlier, the fact that Srebrenica could be positively identified as a war crime, and yet prompt little response from the Western powers, was held up as an example of the failure of Britain and America to offer any effective deterrent to mass violence against civilian populations. A letter from Francis Brown, printed in both the *Daily Telegraph* and the *Independent*, warned that 'If we fail to act now, history will condemn us with that terrifying accusation: you knew, but you did nothing.' Continuing this theme, a comment piece from Holly Burkhalter suggested that all those Americans who left the US Holocaust Memorial Museum wishing that they 'could have helped before so many died' were now in a position to do so.[203] Also utilised was the established sentiment of 'Never Again,' with a Charles Gati piece challenging President Clinton to 'go see the people of Srebrenica' and to tell them that Never Again was only 'meant for domestic consumption.'[204] These not infrequent invocations in the wake of Srebrenica illustrate the fact that a small number of observers viewed the carnage as genocidal in nature and, in turn, saw this as an issue which warranted a more robust response. What they also show, however, is a mistaken faith in the general importance which was afforded to genocide as an issue of international concern.

Perhaps the clearest indication of this lies in the fact that, in several instances, the focus of comment was on the potential damage which could be done to the liberal democratic identity of the West, and not on the plight of the victims themselves. Reaching a peak in the weeks following Srebrenica, continuing a pattern which had been seen throughout the conflict, the human cost of genocide was essentially removed from comment, with the abstract notion of Western identity being regarded as the real *victim* of such crimes. The 'moral impact' that Britain and America were in danger of suffering proved to be the focal point of several articles, many of which discussed such problems with only fleeting mentions of the actual suffering of Bosnian civilians.[205] An editorial in the *Independent* questioned the 'moral basis of our own society' for resisting further intervention in the Balkans, echoing a similar piece from 1992 which argued that it was not difficult 'to imagine hypothetical cases where the moral damage done to a nation by standing idly by might become so profound as to undermine the noble myths by which that nation lived.'[206] Whilst these particular quotes may imply that the suffering in the Balkans was regarded as important, an overall reading of coverage from this period – which generally gave only a brief mention to the crimes themselves – leads one to the conclusion that potential damage to Western prestige was in fact the more important issue. By way of a further illustration of this tendency, the following extract from Robin Harris is particularly revealing:

> Many things have died or been seriously compromised in Bosnia. The optimism of the cold war's end. The credibility of NATO. The American commitment to European security. That the notion that a Europe no longer divided shares a commitment to basic human dignity. But perhaps the death of Western honor has been the most devastating [...] This defeat – for the mixed society of Bosnia is now in shreds – has its political and military implications; but in themselves they are perhaps not overwhelming. Bosnia is a small country of no compelling strategic significance or wealth. It is defeat of Western values in this ill-born state that may prove most costly.[207]

In November 1946 a *Washington Post* editorial, perhaps influenced by the still-recent optimism of victory over fascism, argued that 'Genocide can never be the exclusive concern of a country. Wherever it occurs, it must concern the entire civilised world.'[208] As demonstrated 50 years later by the general response to the massacre of Srebrenica, this sentiment persisted, but for very different reasons. Barring a few exceptions, 'genocide' in Bosnia was framed predominantly in terms of what it could mean for the perception and strength of Western values, with the victims themselves invoked only to supplement this point. An article from earlier in the conflict, written amidst the camp revelations, questioned whether 'in time people [would] simply become resigned to the horror' – by the late summer of 1995, one could argue that this question had been answered. The barbarity of Srebrenica was the greatest war crime to have taken place in Europe since the defeat of Nazism, but the violence itself would generally assume secondary importance within Anglo–American coverage.[209] To say that this event was marginalised in the same manner as Rwanda would be an overstatement, but the overall response to Srebrenica was not in line the supposedly revitalised interest in genocide which had accompanied the renewed focus on the Holocaust in the years immediately prior.

Period Four: 21 August – 18 September 1995

The late summer and early autumn of 1995 represented, for many, the 'end game' in terms of Western involvement in Bosnia. Diplomatic considerations came to the fore during this period to a degree unmatched in the previous three years, and as a result the political maneuvering in London, Washington, Moscow and elsewhere once again came to dominate press coverage of the conflict.[210] Most trends which presented themselves through an analysis of Anglo–American newspapers from this particular period have been highlighted and discussed in previous sections, but some other notable themes that emerge will be examined in the pages that follow.

Quantitative Findings: 21 August – 18 September 1995

In the period from 21 August – 18 September 1995, a total of 658 articles regarding Bosnia were produced across the eight selected titles. As was the case with each of the other periods, a greater number (383) of these articles were to be found in British sources, with 275 appearing in American publications. The highest number of articles appeared in the *Guardian*, which published

111 during the period analysed – a figure which, it should be noted, surpasses any 'one-month' total recorded in a US daily across all four periods. The least prolific in this regard was the *Los Angeles Times*, which published 57 articles related to the Balkans.

Of the 658 articles devoted to the Balkans during this period, 172 were situated on the front page of their respective publication, with 70 of these appearing on page one of British newspapers and 102 appearing on US front pages. The newspaper with the highest number of articles appearing on the front page was the *Washington Post*, with 30, whilst the *Los Angeles Times* was close behind with 29. This second total is rather interesting in that it shows that the *Los Angeles Times*, despite producing the lowest over-all number of articles with 57, afforded more than 50 per cent of them front page placement. Of course, as was noted earlier, this can in part be explained by the fact that US newspapers tend to cram far more stories onto a front page than their British counterparts. Nonetheless, though they produced more articles in general, British newspapers (with the exception of *The Times*, which bettered the *Chicago Tribune*'s front page tally of 19 with a total of 21) were far less prolific in devoting front page status than American publications during this period. The least productive overall in this regard was the *Guardian*, which gave such priority to 14 articles – the second-lowest number recorded in any one period.

In terms of editorial coverage, the continuing crisis in the Balkans prompted 42 lead articles from the selected newspapers during this period. Of these, 21 were found in American newspapers, and 21 were from British titles. The *Chicago Tribune* published the greatest number of editorials, with seven, whilst the *Los Angeles Times* – devoting three editorials to Bosnia from 21 August – 18 September 1995 – was the least productive in this regard. In reference to combined comment pieces, this period was the least productive of the four by a considerable margin. A total of 67 comment articles were published during this time, with 35 originating in American newspapers and 32 in British. Fourteen of these were produced by the *Guardian*, which was the most proactive overall in this regard, with the five printed by the *Chicago Tribune* being the smallest amount in this particular sample. When compared with the figures from the pre-vious periods of analysis, it is apparent that there was notable decrease in comment during August and September 1995. Indeed, seven of the eight selected titles published their lowest one-month total during this period, with only the *Guardian* being the exception to this trend.

The period between 21 August – 18 September 1995 was also the least productive single period in terms of the combined number of letters published. The total of 69 (56 of which were found in British newspapers and 143 in American) was lower than anything previously recorded, though was still greater than the 63 letters published in relation to the Rwandan genocide between the dates of 7 April – 29 July 1994; a further illustration of the importance of race and proximity in determining Anglo–American interest. *The Times* was the most proactive in this regard, publishing 28 letters related to developments in the Balkans, whilst the *Los Angeles Times* failed to print a single letter during this specific period.

Themes within Coverage

One of the trends which presents itself during this period is the persistent, though marginalised, focus on Srebrenica. Despite the original reporting of the massacre being quickly superseded by diplomatic developments – as was highlighted in the previous section of this analysis – details of what had taken place in the fallen safe haven continued to emerge, although rarely were these revelations given extensive coverage or important placing within the Anglo–American press.

A close reading of reports from this period indicate a continuing confusion over the extent of the violence which had ravaged Srebrenica, with the final death toll often being wildly underestimated. The figure of 2,700 – around a third of what is now accepted as the actual death toll – was quoted well into September 1995 and demonstrates the initial difficulties of contemporary reporters in forming an accurate account of the massacre in early July. Certainly, the failure of the Western powers to properly divulge the details of Srebrenica was commented upon by journalists at the time, with the American response to the tragedy often being singled out for criticism. One of the most common themes in this regard, at least in those few articles which continued to regard Srebrenica as a relevant story, was the assertion that both the UN and the United States had deliberately sought to *avoid* publicising details of the Srebrenica massacre in the weeks that followed. Citing the fact that US spy planes had photographed tire tracks and signs of disturbed earth in areas in and around the enclave – both of which alluded to the existence of mass graves, which would have further corroborated the accounts given by a number of witnesses several weeks before – the UN was accused of attempting to 'cover up' the extent of the atrocities committed in Srebrenica. Indeed, one contemporary advanced this accusation by arguing that 'it had taken longer for the Americans to release this evidence than it did for William Russell's dispatches to reach London from the Crimean War by messenger horse and steam packet.'[211] These allegations, however, did not lead to a renewed interest in Srebrenica from the Anglo–American press, and the marginalisation of what is now regarded as one of the worst massacres to take place in Europe since the end of World War II continued much in the same manner as it had in the days and weeks immediately following the initial attack.

Though Srebrenica continued to be referenced irregularly, one violent occurrence did manage to secure notable, though short-lived, attention from British and American newspapers during this period – the 28 August attack on Sarajevo, which would be the most destructive single incidence of shelling since the Markale market bombing of early 1994. The assault – described by one contemporary as 'entirely in character with the Serbs' previous conduct' – caused huge destruction and would be a major cata-lyst for the airstrikes unleashed by NATO forces on 5 September. As with the February 1994 attack, there was initial confusion regarding who had been responsible, but it was quickly established that it had been the work of Serb forces surrounding Sarajevo.[212] Although the attack did not claim as many victims as had been killed at Markale, it was still the worst assault on the city in 18 months. Estimates varied during the first reports of the carnage, but it is now accepted that the shelling – which took place only 50 yards away from that which had caused such destruction in early 1994 – claimed 37 lives and saw around 90 wounded.[213] Early coverage described a viciously brutal scene in the aftermath, with one front page article describing how 'Limbs and flesh were splattered on storefronts, and bodies fell to pieces as they were lifted into cars.' Another cited the attack as being 'one of Sarajevo's blackest days since the Bosnian war erupted in April 1992,' reflecting the manner in which this tragedy was quickly regarded as notable even amongst the score of other atrocities which had come before.[214]

Though this particular attack on Sarajevo did provoke front page attention in the days which immediately followed, like the coverage of most previous atrocities the focus of the Anglo–American press quickly shifted to other developments in the region – most notably the prospect of a more proactive and forceful NATO response. What is telling, however, at least in relation to overall press engagements with Bosnia between 1992–5, is that the shelling was considered an important story at all. Whilst there had been a brief lull in the shelling of Sarajevo following the Markale attack of February 1994, the 18 months up to the end of August 1995 had seen the city under almost constant bombardment – the intensity of which could vary from day to day. In mid-May, for example, 1995, UN observers had counted in excess of 800 shells landing on Sarajevo in the space of just six hours – an indication that the 28 August attack was hardly out of the ordinary. Indeed, only days before this particular assault, there had been an attack which killed six people and wounded almost 40, though this was not given anywhere near the same press attention as the assault which took place less than a week later.[215] As was the case with Markale, this highlights the fact that the violence in Bosnia – targeted predominantly at civilians – was in itself only seen as worthy of coverage when there was some notable quantitative or qualitative change from what was by then *expected*. It was estimated at the time that some 10,500 people had been killed in Sarajevo by shelling or sniper fire by the autumn of 1995, with perhaps 50,000 more wounded, so it is revealing that this single instance was selected for intense, though brief, coverage.[216] Also of importance is the fact that it occurred in Sarajevo – where most of the media were based – given that an artillery strike on Tuzla on 25 May, which killed 71 people and injured around 240 more, was rarely even referenced.

The main reason for this temporary increase in the focus on Sarajevo was because the 28 August bombing killed far more people in a single attack than had been the norm during the attrition of the siege of the city. As Hartman states, 'terrible things, by continuing to be shown, begin to appear matter-of-fact, a natural rather than manmade catastrophe,' and the fact that by late 1995 only the most deadly instances of shelling were able to secure a dominant position within the news indicates that this same process was at work in relation to press interest in the Balkans.[217] In essence, the murder of 37 civilians in one attack was sufficiently horrific to briefly reignite the interest of the Anglo–American press – however, as with the previous incident at Markale, this did not lead to any notable increase in overall discussion and comment on the atrocities themselves.

A further observation – continuing a pattern which had been seen in previous periods – was that in late August and early September 1995 the attention of the Anglo–American press shifted once again away from the atrocities and instead focused on the response from Western military forces. The NATO retaliation, which began on 30 August, quickly came to be the dominant theme within Western press coverage of Bosnia and superseded the violence itself once more. Several newspapers made the airstrikes their main story for two and three days at a time, with many giving the story front page positioning and accompanying them with dramatic pictures.[218] It can be argued that this was to be expected – not simply because it had been seen to happen during most other periods of reporting in Bosnia, but also because the rapid escalation in Western involvement was now viewed as being part of the possible resolution to the conflict. Analysis of the press coverage of NATO's intervention, which would be the largest operation in the organisation's history up to that point, also shows that the prospect of intervention reinvigorated discussion and comment in the press.[219]

In many ways, the attack on Sarajevo prompted a fresh wave of press support for military intervention in the Balkans, to a degree exceeding that which had followed in the wake of Srebrenica not even two months before. The reason for this, of course, may be that the details of the massacre in Srebrenica were not yet fully realised; though another explanation could lie with the greater availability of vivid images which accompanied the 28 August attack. With these two atrocities happening in such a relatively short time period, many commentators argued that the conflict had continued for too long and that Western involvement had now reached, in the words of one contemporary, the 'diplomatic endgame.'[220] The wider conflict which had seemed destined to continue for several more years was finally viewed, by some at least, to be worth expending military resources on, with an editorial in the *Chicago Tribune* arguing that 'Four years of orchard-by-orchard destruction, mass murder and rape as a tool of warfare are enough.' Others contributed to the calls for intervention by stressing the 'moral' imperative to do something practical to stem the violence in the region – a sentiment shared by the author of a letter to the *Guardian*, who decried the inability of the newspaper to actively support such measures by simply stating: 'Get off the fence and be a little braver.'[221]

All this is not to say, however, that there was anything approaching a consensus in terms of support for the NATO intervention. On the contrary, a number of commentators actively discouraged such a course of action, with some even attempting to portray the Serbs as the victims in the conflict. The American-led assault, which would be the most robust response to genocide in the twentieth century, came to be criticised for several reasons. One of the more persistent arguments came from those who were again concerned with the possibility of such an action provoking Russian involvement in the region – a development which was regarded as having the potential to once again bring the former Cold War rivals into conflict. Another argument against intervention which was voiced during this time was that any outside interference in the region was bound to lead to further civilian casualties. This was a perfectly reasonable position, especially given that the NATO retaliation would ultimately claim the lives of several innocent people as *collateral damage* during assaults on Serb targets. Such a position was voiced by a group of British M.P.s who, writing only days after the 28 August attack on Sarajevo, warned of the consequences of outside military intervention:

> The massacre of civilians in Sarajevo must be utterly condemned along with every other outrage that has taken place in Bosnia. But the international community loses all moral authority when it adds to the many atrocities which have already taken place.[222]

What is most interesting, in terms of opinions voiced regarding the conflict, is that this anti-interventionist position led to several people expressing a belief that the *Serbs* were in fact the true victims of this conflict – a belief which had only ever been voiced fleetingly, if ever, in the periods previously analysed. Though, as discussed in previous sections, there had been several instances where those in the Anglo–American press had been somewhat 'anti-Muslim' in their sentiments, this shift to something of a 'pro-Serb' position was a notable development in the autumn of 1995.

The idea of an element of bias towards reporting only those atrocities which affected Muslims was a theme which had developed throughout the conflict, and tended to be commented upon more frequently on those occasions when Western involvement seemed likely. When one considers, however, that the majority of atrocities, particularly those targeted at civilians, were perpetrated by Serb forces, then it is deeply revealing that this would be mentioned at all. With the prospect of NATO airstrikes looming large by late August 1995, challenges to the idea that it was only Muslims who were suffering in this protracted conflict soon grew in number. One article in *The Times* argued that 'From the beginning much of the media has refused to provide any balance in reporting Bosnia, simply treating the Muslims as right and the Serbs as wrong,' whilst another stated that the 'blatant' use of photographs of grieving Bosnian women – and the lack of comparable footage of Serb suffering – was 'not news but propaganda designed to incite rather than to inform.'[223] Another letter to the *New York Times* further grappled with this perceived bias in Western reporting of Bosnia, with its author arguing:

> Throughout this war, if you are a Serb trying to keep your ancestral land, to keep your family together and your land intact, you are a 'rebel.' If you are a Croat or a Muslim doing the same thing, you are heroic [...] If you commit atrocities (despicable on all sides) as a Serb, you are considered a war criminal; if you commit atrocities as a Croat or Muslim, your atrocities are relegated to small news items.[224]

This swing towards something resembling support for Serb actions is even more noteworthy when one considers that the above statements were made in the aftermath of the Serb-led Srebrenica massacre – the details of which, whilst perhaps not being immediately clear, were nonetheless sufficiently crystallised for even the most casual observer to know that it had been Muslim civilians who had been killed in their thousands.

The notion that the Serbs had been somehow demonised by the Western powers became even more pronounced in the days and weeks following the NATO bombardment, and some commentators went as far as to claim that it was the Serbs themselves who were now the victims of genocide. Repeating the Russian government's claim that the Bosnian Serbs faced 'extermination', the argument that the Serbs were victims of genocide appeared in a number of press outlets – finding particular prominence within the letters-to-the-editor sections.[225] One such letter argued simply that 'The Nato attacks were targeted at Serbs because they are Serbs: that is genocide', whilst another described NATO as being an 'accomplice to genocide'.[226] Though it is clear that a number of these opinions were being expressed in response to what was conceived by some to be a misguided intervention by the West, it is nonetheless remarkable that one of the few times, barring Srebrenica, in which 'genocide' was mentioned in relation to the conflict was in an attempt to amplify the suffering of the group which had itself been responsible for the majority of the atrocities committed in the years prior.

Conclusion

When the four selected periods have been analysed, it is apparent that the Anglo–American press devoted considerable attention to the conflict in the Balkans. Newspapers on both sides of the Atlantic engaged with the developing crisis throughout its duration, especially when there was some notable development in the region – such as a particularly brutal shelling, for instance – often affording it front page status and publishing a great deal of comment and analysis. It is revealing, however, that the actual violence in the region – which throughout the conflict was aimed disproportionately at civilians – was only ever the main focus of reporting for short periods of time. Though the likes of Markale would be highlighted by a number of outlets, the journalistic focus would often shift away from this to the resulting diplomatic manoeuvres or wider matters of foreign policy options. This was a trend evident even after the massacre at Srebrenica, showing that genocide, even on European soil, cannot be automatically expected to receive concentrated or persistent coverage from the Anglo–American media.

The one arguable exception to this came in August 1992, with the discovery of the Serb-run concentration camps. As will be developed in the concluding chapter, however, it is likely that this was more as a result of the aesthetics of these specific crimes – in that they resembled the violent excesses of the Nazi regime which were, in themselves, widely recognised in the Western world by the early 1990s. Though there were indeed calls from some sections of the media for more to be done to stop the violence, these were fleeting at best, and were generally only voiced following the worst instances of atrocity. Such calls were, however, generally outnumbered by those voicing the opposite opinion, with the Balkans being regularly caricatured as out of control and burning with ancient hatreds.

Whatever the opinions expressed, the conflict in the Balkans was indeed considered a major story between 1992–5. However, the lack of focus on the violence itself indicates that the geographical location of the crisis – which eventually provoked NATO intervention – was a more critical catalyst for press coverage than the atrocities themselves. Certainly, it is likely that Bosnia may have suffered from the same lack of press attention as Rwanda – the case study which will be explored in the following chapter – had it not been only a few hours from London.

4

A Faraway People

Media Coverage of the Rwandan Genocide

Even if humanity's past amounts to little more than 'a history of hate and genocide,' there can be few examples which rival the speed and scale of what unfolded in Rwanda.[1] By some accounts, Hutu massacres of Tutsi began in 1990, when the predominantly Tutsi Rwandan Patriotic Front (RPF) commenced hostilities against the regime of then-President Juvenal Habyarimana. What is generally recognised as the 'Rwandan genocide', however, did not begin until 6 April 1994. Following the shooting-down of Habyarimana's presidential jet, extremist Hutu elements within the government implemented a deliberate campaign to destroy Rwanda's Tutsi minority. The killings began within an hour of the plane crash and, in the following 100 days, a slaughter of epic proportions engulfed the tiny African state.[2]

Although the death toll is impossible to accurately calculate, estimates range from a minimum of 507,000 to more than one million. The most widely cited estimate is around 800,000, of whom perhaps 300,000 were children.[3] Considering that Rwanda had a population of eight million in early 1994, these figure provides a clear indicator of the sheer scale of the massacres. To borrow an illustration from Samantha Power, this number equates to *more* than two World Trade Center attacks, every single day, for 100 days.[4] Whilst the genocide raged for more than three months, most of the killing took place in the first six weeks following the death of Habyarimana. It should be reiterated that several thousand Hutu were also murdered during this time, but it was Rwanda's Tutsi minority which bore the brunt of the violence. From a population of about 930,000 in early 1994, fewer than 130,000 Tutsi had survived by the time the RPF victory brought the genocide to an end. Between 75 and 77 per cent of Rwanda's Tutsi minority were annihilated, a proportion which mirrors the fate which befell Europe's Jews during the years of Nazi tyranny. Evidently, this was clearly a devastating level of violence; 'for every Tutsi remaining alive, seven had died'.[5]

It is estimated that between 175,000 and 210,000 individuals actively took part in the genocide – a level of participation which is remarkably high for a country with such a small population. What truly sets the Rwandan genocide apart, though, is the swiftness with which the killing took place.[6] Despite being portrayed by the press as chaotic – a frame which was used by a number of sources in the first weeks of the conflict, and which fitted well with established stereotypes about Africa – the Rwandan genocide may well rank as the most well-organised genocide in recorded history.[7] Whilst the figure of 800,000 dead is incredible in itself, its impact is increased when one remembers that this figure was reached in only 100 days. This equates to 8,000 people being murdered *every day* for the duration of the slaughter – some 333.3 deaths per hour, or 5.5 deaths per minute – demonstrating a degree of planning and control scarcely seen in modern times.[8] To contextualise this; the carnage of World War I – the conduct of which resulted in the deaths of millions of people through the attrition of trench warfare – saw a daily average of 5,600 killed deaths.[9]

Fettweis once remarked that war 'brings out the worst aspects of human nature to the surface,' and there has seldom been a more vivid example of this than in Rwanda.[10] Often fueled by the consumption of alcohol and drugs, a variety of methods were used by the Hutu to murder the Tutsi. Before researchers 'stopped counting,' 56 methods of killing were recorded, encompassing everything from shooting to clubbing.[11] Many thousands were also deliberately drowned, burned alive, made to commit suicide and even forced to murder their own families. It is the machete, however, which has become synonymous with the genocide. This simple farming tool, cheap to purchase in bulk, was responsible for 37.9 per cent of all fatalities and has since become symbolic of the genocide in contemporary representations.[12]

Despite the extraordinary swiftness and brutality of the Rwandan genocide, however, the crisis rarely received the level of focused reporting which it surely warranted. It was not ignored, necessarily, but instead often marginalised to the point of irrelevance, and frequently misrepresented on the occasions where it did make the pages of the Anglo–American press. As Susan Moeller argues, genocide is a news story that should always be covered; Rwanda would prove that is by no means a given. The latter sections of this chapter will seek to properly underline this apparent lack of interest in the genocide, whilst the sections below are intended to help situate the framing of the Rwandan genocide within a general Western discourse regarding Africa and to describe the cultural and political factors which contributed to the lack of overall interest in Rwanda during the spring and summer of 1994.

Western Discourse Regarding Africa

As was the case with Anglo–American coverage of the Balkans – indeed, even more so – the reporting of the Rwandan genocide largely conformed to a more generalised Western discourse regarding the African continent and its inhabitants. As will be detailed in the section to follow, Western perceptions of Africa were invariably negative – generally invoking established ideas concerning Africa's image as a savage and primitive continent, and explaining sub-Saharan conflict in terms of tribalism and other colonial-era designations. A crucial aspect of this discourse on Africa was the notion of Africans as 'savage' or 'brutal' – a conceptualisation which mirrors that which developed regarding the people of the Balkans. This reflects a discourse, strengthened and emphasised throughout the colonial period and beyond, that perceives Africa as being below the level of development achieved in the West. A central component of this idea is that the continent stagnated, both technologically and culturally, in the centuries before Western colonisation – a myth which Thomas Hodgkin describes as the 'Hobbesian picture of a pre-European Africa, in which there was no account of Time; no Arts; no Letters; no Society'.[13] The observation that Western discourse regarding Africa has commonly invoked the notion of brutality and incivility has been further noted by Heather Jean Brookes, who, in her study of British newspaper coverage of Africa, found that Western discourse largely framed the continent as somewhere that 'may try to emulate the West, but just below the surface the sorcery and savagery lurk.'[14]

To this we may add the tendency for Western sources to characterise African conflict as having its origins in tribalism, a perspective which framed Anglo–American reporting of the Rwandan genocide in several examples cited in this research. The use of the *tribal frame*, which one might argue can be compared to the *ancient hatreds* frame presented during reporting on Bosnia, permits Western journalists to connect all African atrocities to an oversimplified narrative; which in turn is seen to have a trivialising effect on further discussion of the causes of the respective conflict or issue. As W.A. Gamson notes, 'frames for a given story are frequently drawn from shared cultural narratives and myths,' meaning that the persistence of the Anglo–American news media in their use of this 'tribal' explanation has its basis in the prominence of this characterisation of Africa within wider Western society. Certainly, as Johnson-Cartee notes, 'Mythical narratives are comfortable much like old shoes, for the narrative forms are familiar, readily understood, and easily digested.'[15] Essentially, the persistent negative framing of African conflicts is rarely challenged by Western audiences, because such descriptions support an established narrative regarding the continent and its inhabitants.

The reason that these particular conceptualisations of Africa have become so well established is primarily due to the range of sources through which they have been propagated, in addition to decades (if not centuries) of repetition in Western discourse. Though Western conceptions of Africa pre-date the colonial period, the establishment of the entrenched beliefs which now dominate various discourses related to the continent did not gain momentum until the early nineteenth century.[16] The reports of explorers, emphasising images of exotic landscapes and 'beastly savages,' were one of the primary sources of such material, though the influence of the correspondence of missionaries was at least equally important. Certainly, V.Y. Mudimbe is not overstating their influence in his assertion that: 'It takes little imagination to realise that missionary discourses on Africans were powerful. They were both signs and symbols of a cultural model.'[17] This discourse, supplemented by the academic community, thus contributed to the cumulative construction of a particular Western perception of Africa and its people. Taking these influences into consideration, Brookes summarises the power of this discourse in the following terms:

> Perhaps the most archetypal metaphorical construction of Africa is in terms of darkness. The symbolic use of darkness suggests evil, sin, paganism and unenlightenment. Africans are primitive, savage, murderous and violent. Darkness gives a sense of anarchy and chaos that is beyond normal understanding. Since Africa is the heart of the core of this darkness, this is where these characteristics emanate from.[18]

Given this overall discourse, it is likely that this has been a contributing factor to Africa's subsequent portrayal in contemporary news media. The influence of this discourse is further extended by the observation that Africa is also a drastically marginalised region, in terms of coverage by Anglo–American media outlets. Research by Virgil Hawkins found that Africa was the least reported continent within the American news media; emphasising the point with the illustration that even though conflict in Africa had been responsible for '90 per cent of the world's total war dead' between the end of the Cold War and the turn of the millennium, it had suffered 'an almost complete media blackout.'[19] In the event of the continent actually receiving press coverage, it is invariably in a negative context. A limited number of occurrences in Africa are regarded as sufficiently newsworthy to warrant Anglo–American media attention, but these are generally humanitarian disasters or various forms of human suffering. 'War, disease, and famine symbolise Africa in news reports by the US media,' notes Ammina Kothari, whose suggestion is substantiated by Brookes' observation that 'Civil war, civil conflict, aid, human rights, politics, crime and disaster account for 92 and 96 per cent of all news about Africa in the [Daily Telegraph] and the [Guardian], respectively.'[20] A further influence of this tendency for the news media to focus only on *bad news* from Africa is on the framing of Africans themselves, who are often portrayed only as victims or otherwise passive participants. Often lacking any contextual explanation for their suffering, and 'frequently referred to in terms of numbers of people who have been killed', African civilians are generally depicted by the news media as both dependent and hopeless.[21] The pattern of negative reports and images concerning Africa, in a trend which is seen to have expanded from the 1980s, thus presents each new African crisis as part of an ongoing continental saga. According to Arnold S. de Beer, Africa has subsequently been portrayed by the news media 'in a predominantly negative fashion as a continent without hope at best, or as a basket case at worst.'[22]

What these factors indicate, then, is that Western discourse on Africa is both 'highly uniform and completely naturalise.'[23] Largely ignored or marginalised at the best of times, Africa's inclusion in the Anglo–American news media (invariably under negative circumstances) has tended to not only recycle colonial-era stereotypes regarding tribalism and savagery, but has also contributed to Africans themselves being persistently constructed as victims. This is an important consideration for this chapter, as recording low levels of news media coverage in response to the Rwandan genocide can therefore be viewed not as a deviation from the norm, but rather as a continuation of a discourse in which Africa 'is portrayed as a homogenous block with violence, helplessness, human rights abuses and lack of democracy as its main characteristics.'[24] The dominant frames and themes used by the Anglo–American media to report the genocide in Rwanda (along with the refugee crisis which followed), to be developed throughout this chapter, will therefore be presented within a framework that echoes the patterns of discourse described in this section.

Quantitative Findings

Linda Melvern once wrote that the Rwandan genocide should be the 'defining scandal' of Bill Clinton's presidency.[25] This same accusation could also be extended to a number of newspaper editors from 1994, for despite being one of the most horrifying episodes in African history, the genocide was not given the concentrated media coverage it might have been expected to command.[26] Although the crisis was by no means *ignored*, it certainly struggled to maintain a consistent level of reporting within the 'news' section of several newspapers. Of course, Rwanda was not the *only* news event occurring in the spring/summer of 1994, but it was surely the most significant. Indeed, given the fact that at least half a million people had perished by its conclusion, one could reasonably argue that it was among the most newsworthy global events to take place between the fall of Communism and the dawn of the new millennium. As will be highlighted in the following sections, however, the genocide often went through prolonged periods of media silence and, when it *was* extensively reported on, the violence itself was often of secondary importance within the framing of the coverage. In the mass circulation market of modern media it is arguably to be expected that news events will no longer have the same 'shelf life' which they once did, but for the coverage of a genocidal event to noticeably *decrease* as it unfolded, even as the death toll rose into the hundreds of thousands, is indicative that such violence was not considered a 'main story' in this period.[27]

News Article Coverage

Across the eight titles selected, the events in Rwanda were the subject of a total of 1,222 news articles between 7 April and 29 July 1994. There was a slight difference between the combined totals from American and British sources, with 630 articles (52 per cent) and 592 articles (48 per cent) being published, respectively. The total of 1,222 equates to an average of 152.8 articles per title, or 1.34 articles per title/per day. Whilst this last statistic may sound rather generous – essentially stating that the genocide received an average of four articles every three days, in each publication – this is misleading, as this total quantified even *box articles* (those reports, normally including 100 words or fewer, which can be easily missed by a casual reader). The *New York Times* devoted by far the greatest number of news articles to Rwanda, with a total of 188 over the four-month period. Those remaining all produced somewhere between 165 and 144 articles, except for *The Times* (136) and – the overall lowest in this regard – the *Los Angeles Times*, which published only 122 news articles on the crisis in Rwanda.

The least productive 'month' in total was the period from 7–30 April, which saw 238 articles published between the eight selected titles, with the *Washington Post* producing the most (37) and both *The Times* and the *Los Angeles Times* the fewest (27). May and June were an improvement on April, with a total of 314 and 270 articles published, in total, respectively. In May, the most prolific title was the *Chicago Tribune*, which produced 46 pieces, whilst the title with the fewest news reports was the *Washington Post*, which produced a total of 32. The *New York Times* published the most stories in June with 43, while the *Los Angeles Times* produced the smallest number of articles with 24. With the exception of the *Independent*, July was the most productive month for publication for each and every title selected. In total, 400 articles were produced during this period – 86 more than the next most productive individual month, May. The *New York Times* was by far the most prolific, with 69 articles published in July. In the same month, the *Los Angeles Times* gave Rwanda the least coverage, featuring only 34 articles on the crisis.

Comparing these totals to those recorded over the 114-day analysis of Bosnia indicates a notable difference in the relative press attention devoted to these comparable instances of mass violence. Whilst the Rwandan genocide prompted a total of 1,222 news articles, the Bosnian conflict saw 3028 published. Put another way, despite Rwanda seeing between four and ten as many victims in only a fraction of the time, the carnage was only able to command some 40.4 per cent of the coverage that was devoted to Bosnia over a comparable number of days. As was alluded to in the previous chapter, this contrast demonstrates clear evidence that the racial composition of victims is of paramount importance in determining levels of Anglo–American press attention. Put simply; the victims of the genocide in Rwanda – despite numbering in their hundreds of thousands – were (black) African, and so their deaths did not provoke anywhere near the same interest from Western media as did the suffering of (white) Europeans.

Front Page Coverage

The Rwanda crisis (which includes both the genocide and the subsequent refugee exodus) featured as a front page article on a total of

204 occasions – meaning that 16.7 per cent of articles dedicated to the Rwanda crisis appeared on page one. Overall, the *New York Times* and the *Washington Post* gave the genocide the most front page publicity, dedicating a front page article to the genocide on 47 and 40 occasions, respectively. Despite the fact that US newspapers tend to cram several different stories onto their front pages, this figure is still notable coverage for a situation in Africa. By far the least productive in this regard was the *Daily Telegraph*, which highlighted the Rwandan crisis on ten occasions – meaning that this newspaper only publicised the genocide in this manner on less than ten per cent of possible opportunities. Despite the magnitude and sheer ferocity of the violence, these numbers are indicative of the fact that the genocide was not considered to be worthy of consistent coverage.

There was 138 front page articles produced by US newspapers within the sample, with the *New York Times* accounting for almost a third of these, with 47. By far the least active reporter of the violence, from an American perspective, was the *Chicago Tribune,* which only gave Rwanda front page coverage on 23 occasions in four months. In the British titles analysed, the Rwandan genocide gained some form of front page coverage on 66 occasions – less than half of the number of such articles produced in US titles. Probably through the efforts of its Africa editor, Richard Dowden, the best-performing British title in this regard was the *Independent* – which highlighted the conflict in Rwanda on 24 occasions. As mentioned, by far the worst performer was the *Daily Telegraph,* which failed to give Rwanda significant front page coverage except on some ten dates within the entire 114-day sample. When one remembers that the *Telegraph* is a publication which is widely respected for its ability to report on foreign events, then this statistically low level of coverage over Rwanda is surely indicative of a lack of interest in the story.

Looking at the statistics regarding front page mentions on a month-by-month basis provides further evidence that the violence in Rwanda failed to retain the attention of the Western press. When the genocide first began in early April, it received fairly inconsistent publicity for the duration of the month. Articles related to the genocide appeared on the front page across all sources a total of 52 times in this period, with 32 of these being in American outlets and the remaining 20 in British titles. Between the selected dates in this month (7–30 April), the *New York Times* gave the unfolding violence a front page mention 12 times – a far cry from the worst-performing titles, the *Chicago Tribune* and *The Times*, both of which highlighted the suffering on four occasions.

The total number of front page articles for May numbered 43, of which 29 were from American newspapers and 14 from British. As in the previous month, the *New York Times* had the greatest total number of front page inclusions, with ten overall. By far the worst in this regard were the *Daily Telegraph* and the *Guardian*, both of which failed to afford front page positioning to even a single article discussing Rwanda during the month of May. On first inspection, these figures do not seem to be dramatically different from those recorded in April. 43 total mentions in May compared with 52 in April does not, at first, seem to be particularly noteworthy. However, when one considers that the period of analysis in April was only 24 days whilst the period of analysis for May included 31 days, then it becomes apparent that there actually *was* a significant reduction in the overall front page coverage.

Though May was an uneventful month in terms of coverage of the Rwandan genocide, it was nonetheless more productive than June, by which time front page focus on the Rwandan genocide had started to noticeably scale back. With the cumulative death toll undoubtedly surpassing half a million by this point then it might be assumed that newspaper coverage would *at least* continue on a similar level to that recorded in April and May. Overall, however, June was by far the least productive month in terms of covering the Rwandan genocide on the front page. In fact, when broken down between sources on a month-to-month basis, June was the worst-performing month for seven out of eight titles selected.[28] In June 1994, from a potential 240 front pages, the violence in Rwanda appeared on the front page on only 16 occasions. Eleven of these were to be found in American titles, with the remaining five appearing in British publications. Continuing the trend from the previous two months, the newspaper which highlighted the conflict most during this time was the *New York Times*, which ran the story on page one on five occasions. The newspaper which granted the fewest front page mentions to Rwanda was the *Daily Telegraph*, which failed to dedicate a single front page to Rwanda for the duration of

June. This was not an outlier, however; *The Times*, the *Guardian* and the *Los Angeles Times* all afforded front page status to Rwanda only once during this particular month.

What was hinted at in the levels of coverage during May was thus essentially verified by the reporting in June; as a story, the genocide simply did not have the staying power to command consistent front page attention. Considering that a front page headline is used to grab the attention of potential consumers, the decision to *not* provide the genocide with regular front page publicity can be seen as indicating that the violence was not considered a marketable story.[29] As further evidence of how the genocide was simply not seen as worthy of coverage, despite the numbers involved, consider the following sentence: 'Rwandan rebels say a million people may have been killed in two months of carnage.'[30] Whilst appearing on the front page of the *Independent on Sunday*, this was relegated to inclusion in an easily missed box-size article. Such a lack of prominence for as monumental a figure as one million is surely evidence of an apparent indifference to mass violence, as one would assume that slaughter of this magnitude would command prominence over most other news stories.

Following the slowly receding pattern of coverage over the initial three months of the genocide, one could be forgiven for making the assumption that this trend would continue into July 1994. On the contrary though, July proved to be by far the most prolific in terms of front page attention. In fact, all four American titles saw July as being their most productive in terms of producing front page articles, and within UK titles only the *Independent* achieved a higher 'one-month' total (in May) in a month other than July. July saw a total of 93 front page mentions during the period of analysis (1–29 July 1994), which was almost equal to the *combined* total for both April and May (95). 66 of these came from US sources, meaning that, for the only time during the entire crisis, Rwanda appeared on the American front pages, on average, more than half of the time during this month. Though the total for the UK was smaller, with a total of 27 articles across the four British titles in this month, this still represents an average of one 'lead' story every four days or so.

The newspaper with the most prolific front page record in July was the *Washington Post*, which dedicated 22 front page articles to Rwanda. The

141

Daily Telegraph and *The Times* were the least productive in this regard, publishing five and six front page articles, respectively. An interesting point to note here is that the *Guardian*, despite giving Rwanda front page coverage on only nine occasions in July, still produced more front page articles in this *single* month than in the previous three months *combined*. One may be tempted to think that this sudden and rapid increase in front page attention was as result of the genocide finally being appreciated for what it was, that various editors had suddenly woken up to what was happening in central Africa and had decided to make up for lost time. However, as will be discussed in greater detail below, the genocide itself had very little to do with the increase in front page publicity in July. What *did* make Rwanda suddenly newsworthy at this point (at least temporarily) was the refugee crisis which followed the rebel victory in the civil war – an event which seemed to strike a collective nerve which the genocide seldom had.

Opinion Coverage

Such was the prominence of the Holocaust within Western media in early 1994, with the USHMM already open and *Schindler's List* triumphing at the Academy Awards, one might assume that an 'unambiguous case' of genocide like Rwanda would have provided the Anglo–American press with an ideal context in which to propagate a committed stance against one of humanity's greatest crimes.[31] As will be highlighted in later sections, however, this was very rarely the case. On the few occasions in which Rwanda *did* receive editorial coverage, the focus of the piece was normally the justification of non-involvement, or framing the atrocities in terms of established stereotypes regarding Africa. Also, as was generally the case in the reporting of Bosnia, very seldom was the violence itself the issue which was being highlighted.

When looked at in terms of quantity alone, it becomes immediately obvious that the Rwandan genocide was simply not constructed by the Anglo–American press as a major story. Across all eight titles examined, only 54 editorial articles were published in response to the crisis in Rwanda – of which 28 were in US publications and 26 in British. Multiplying the number of titles (eight) by the duration of the period of analysis in days (114) gives a total of 912 potential editorial days. This equates to the

Rwandan genocide receiving prominent editorial inclusion only 5.9 per cent of the time – an alarmingly low figure when one considers the magnitude of the carnage. In an announcement on the infamous RTLM radio station, helping to direct the early violence, one extremist announcer encouraged viewers to 'Stand up, take action […] without worrying about international opinion.'[32] As the above figures demonstrate, *international opinion* should have been the least of their concerns.

In contrast to the wide variation observed in terms of front page coverage, there were few dramatic differences between titles in terms of editorial inclusion. The *New York Times* and the *Guardian* were the most proactive – each devoting eight editorial articles to developments in Rwanda between 7 April and 29 July 1994 – whilst the *Washington Post*, the *Los Angeles Times*, *The Times* and the *Independent* all contributed seven editorials during this same period. The publication which gave the least overall editorial space to Rwanda was the *Daily Telegraph*, which focused on Rwanda on four occasions – a single incidence in each month of the analysis. The *Chicago Tribune* was only marginally better, devoting a total of five editorial articles to this event.

April was the least productive month in this regard, with eight editorials engaging with the unfolding violence. This figure rose sharply to 17 in the month of May, and this can perhaps be explained by the fact that there may have still been some confusion over the *true* nature of the violence during the first few weeks of the crisis.[33] Eleven editorials appeared in June, by which time the genocidal aspect of the civil war was clear for all to see, though the *Independent* did not include a single editorial to Rwanda during this month. July was the most productive month in terms of editorial coverage, with a combined total of 18 lead articles published in this period which were directly related to Rwanda (again, the focus was by this point on the refugee crisis, as opposed to the violence).

With the above statistical observations in mind, it becomes apparent that the editorial coverage devoted to Rwanda was not consistent with prevailing Western notions concerning the protection of human rights. Exclusion of any particular news item is a legitimate control in the world of news media and therefore such editorial decisions can be seen as an indication of a belief that a story is not worth covering.[34] The fact that the

Rwandan genocide had only 54 editorial articles dedicated to it, across eight titles over four months, is evidence that the crisis was not considered to be a major story. Moreover, this level of attention can also suggest that there is a racial dynamic at play in press coverage of genocidal events. By contrast; over 114 days, the conflict in Bosnia provoked some 183 editorial articles. This means that there were more than three times as many lead articles devoted to the crisis in (white) Europe, despite the fact that the genocide in (black) Africa claimed the lives of up to ten times as many people in only a fraction of the time. As Melvern has noted, the genocide should have been condemned in the strongest possible terms, but it was not until the mass refugee crisis in July that editorials began to draw prominent attention to the suffering.[35] This shows how genocide, whilst perhaps not becoming *accepted*, had become infinitely more tolerable come 1994 – particularly when occurring in those regions of the world which were not strategically or culturally important to the West.

In terms of comment pieces, the Rwandan genocide did not feature prominently within the op-ed pages of any of the titles selected within this study. The carnage was by no means ignored, as has been asserted in several discussions of the media response to the genocide, but it was undoubtedly marginalised when one considers the ferocity of the violence. Across all selected titles, a total of 70 op-ed articles were published which were directly focused on some aspect of the Rwandan genocide or the subsequent refugee exodus. This, in itself, is a rather small figure when one considers that the op-ed section is generally reserved for commenting on the more topical issues at any given time. It also represents only 18.2 per cent of the total of 384 such pieces which were dedicated to discussing Bosnia. Certainly, such a discrepancy between the coverage of these two regions is further evidence to support the notion that the racial identity of victims is a key determinant of media coverage. Further, that the Rwandan genocide could be regarded as sufficiently important to warrant the publication of an opinion piece on only 70 occasions further highlights how *naturalised* the notion of violence in Africa had become within Western discourse by 1994. Described in terms of news values, the most relevant concept is again that of cultural proximity, as the greater focus on Bosnia (despite the conflict recording around one-eighth of the total deaths suffered by Rwanda) helps to illustrate. Despite claiming the lives of some 800,000 people in a little over three months – a fact which, by any definition, would be expected to satisfy the criteria for a newsworthy story – the Rwandan genocide failed to command consistent media interest *except* on those occasions where Rwanda was seen to be affecting, or being affected by, outside actors.

The publications which afforded Rwanda the most op-ed space were the *Guardian* and the *Los Angeles Times,* which devoted 14 and 12 pieces respectively. The *Washington Post* and the *Independent* each featured eleven op-ed articles, whilst the *Chicago Tribune* and the *New York Times* both included seven comment pieces. The titles which printed the fewest op-ed articles concerning Rwanda were *The Times* and the *Daily Telegraph* – with the former printing five articles and the latter publishing only three over the period studied. On a month-to-month comparison, July again proved to be the most productive in relation to the publication of such articles, seeing 24 comment pieces published in total. May was the next most prolific month with 17 op-ed articles published within the eight chosen titles, whilst eight were produced in April and 13 in June. This pattern of coverage conforms to the overall trends observed with the other variables analysed (news, editorials etc.), in that comment was seen to rise between April and May, regress again in June, and then noticeably spike upwards in July.

In addition, there were the 63 letters which were published between 7 April – 29 July 1994, of which the *Guardian* printed the greatest number with 18. The *Daily Telegraph,* on the other hand, only printed two relevant letters during the duration of the crisis.[36] Again, when measured against the number of letters published which referenced the crisis in the Balkans, a dramatic contrast is revealed. With the violence in the Balkans prompting the publication of 457 letters, this equates to the Rwandan genocide provoking a total number of letters which was only 13.8 per cent of the Bosnian total. Race and realpolitik are evidently the most crucial determinants of media coverage – infinitely more so than the objective scale of such violence.

Taken together, these statistical observations provide clear evidence that the apocalyptic violence in Rwanda was simply not considered to be a major story and, when compared with the comparatively generous coverage afforded to the crisis in Bosnia, further demonstrates the marked difference in Anglo–American press coverage of mass violence in different parts of the globe. Evidently, factors such as proximity, strategic interest and race are all more influential in provoking Western press interest than body counts are – even when reaching levels indicative of perhaps the worst genocide of the late twentieth century.

Themes within Coverage

Whilst the statistical evidence provided clearly demonstrates an overall lack of interest in the Rwandan crisis, to gain a more nuanced understanding of these dynamics it is revealing to investigate the manner in which various aspects of the crisis were framed. The framing of the genocide within these reports was of crucial importance, as this inevitably had an impact on how the conflict was understood by the vast readership of these newspapers. As has been commented upon in the years since, the Rwandan genocide was misinterpreted from the very beginning, and this filtered into how it was reported on in the press. Although it was, in reality, a meticulously planned exercise, the violence was more often than not characterised as anarchic, and resulting from 'ancient tribal hatreds.' This level of ignorance, misrepresentation and racism fed into established stereotypes about African society which still exist today. Indeed, Aidan Hartley's recollection of an editor dismissing the unfolding carnage in Africa as 'your classic Bongo story' is unlikely to have been an isolated incident.[37] This can be partially explained, however, when one considers the pressures put on the limited number of journalists in Rwanda during this period. The number of reporters in the country never rose above 15 during the entire duration of the genocide, on account of both the developments in South Africa (where some 2,500 reporters were placed in May 1994) and the fact that the country was, obviously, a very dangerous place to be a journalist. As a result, a number of media correspondents resorted to recycling the same mistaken narratives, and often borrowed phrases and entire articles from other reporters – with this 'cross-fertilisation' of course leading to the same misconceptions being regularly reiterated throughout the conflict.

The importance of such frames (e.g. *tribalism, anarchy*) being invoked so frequently in the early weeks of the conflict is also crucial. Accepting Robert Entman's observation that 'Challenging first impressions is difficult, particularly when they are supported by emotional language and visual images of threat,' it is likely that references to tribalism, savagery and the like in the early reporting subsequently characterised the conflict in such terms for a proportion of the Anglo–American newspaper audience.[38] Writing in May 1994, Richard Dowden stated that: 'Perhaps one day someone will try to explain why it happened, how human beings could do these things. At the moment the scenes and images must simply be recorded.'[39] Dowden, one of the few editors to apparently attempt to draw attention to the carnage as it was taking place, was correct in what he was recommending. The problem was, however, that the scenes and images from the genocide were recorded in a manner which was often misleading, uninformed or otherwise distorted.

Tribalism and Anarchy

Despite the fact that the Rwandan genocide was the result of several interconnected factors – including economic volatility, colonial history, and the cynical manipulation of a population who were among the poorest in the world – throughout its duration the most commonly cited 'explanation' for the violence was that it was simply the result of a deeply held 'tribal' animosity between the Hutu and Tutsi. Echoing the 'ancient ethnic hatreds' frame which was prominent in the media coverage of Bosnia, and overlooking (or perhaps not taking the time to investigate) the fact that the two groups are not even 'tribes' in the generally accepted sense of the term, Rwanda's violence was framed in this manner from the very beginning. Many commentators alluded to this dynamic, positioning the mass violence within 'a competition for land unlike anywhere else in Africa,' whilst others described the violence as being simply 'one more round of the tribal bloodletting that has plagued this part of Africa for centuries.'[40] Some contributions even rejected the colonial influence on the region entirely, with one letter to the *Chicago Tribune* asserting that the violence was 'a legacy of African tribalism, not colonialism.'[41]

Such allusions to a violent tribal history, though misguided, were (again) perhaps due to most Western journalists having little, if any, knowledge of the political dynamics of the region; and thus this simplistic explanation for the violence was therefore the easiest means to (wrongly) contextualise the violence in the early days of the crisis. What is telling about framing the conflict in terms of *tribalism*, however, is the persistence in which this characterisation was invoked. Even into July, when the genocide was all but over and there had been ample time to ascertain the true dynamics of the conflict, the press continued to characterise the violence as tribal in origin. Several months into the conflict, a *Washington Post* article in late July 1994 continued to describe how 'Even before Rwanda gained independence from Belgium in 1962, the country was plagued by tribal warfare', a means of framing the carnage as simply the latest bout in a cycle of violence which was practically endemic between Hutu and Tutsi.[42] However, perhaps the most illustrative example of this trend – in explaining the conflict in terms of tribalism and savagery – came from Bernard Levin of *The Times*. Whilst the tone of the piece was intended to illustrate the larger point that violence between various rival groups was occurring across the world, the somewhat satirical language invoked is nonetheless telling in the context presented here:

> [Burundi] was in the late 1970s, but savages have long memories, and just as no one can truly understand the murderous crossfire in Yugoslavia, so no one can understand the reasons that lead Hutus and Tutsis, Tutsis and Hutus, to pile up bodies until the pile blacks out the sun […] There are those who would ask, disdainfully, what else can you expect from a pack of illiterate niggers – or rather, a vast pack of illiterate niggers – who have only just come down from the trees, but that is why I began with Yugoslavia. There are no niggers in Yugoslavia, and I am told there is almost 100 per cent literacy across the entire range of warring factions there, yet the slaughter continues, so it can't be that.[43]

In many ways, though the term was largely obsolete in relation to the Hutu and Tutsi, the 'tribal' label proved difficult to dislodge once it had become established. As will be discussed shortly, this was no doubt related to the fact that defining the participants in such terms fit within an ingrained

Western discourse regarding Africa and its inhabitants; a discourse which also (mistakenly) saw the violence as being rooted in a centuries-old feud between the inhabitants of the region.

In addition to the tribal narrative, and in many ways strengthening its appeal, was the persistent argument that violence between Hutu and Tutsi dated back hundreds of years. This assertion (which again mirrored similar language used in relation to Bosnia) had little basis in reality. In the first weeks of coverage in April and early May 1994, the genocide was often framed as having its roots in the 'fifteenth century', whilst other reporting would be less specific in establishing a timeline; such as when Jonathan Howard of the *Daily Telegraph* claimed that 'The present carnage has its roots in the centuries of tension between the two communities.'[44] By establishing a narrative suggesting that the violence engulfing Rwanda conformed to a pattern which pre-dated even the colonial period by several hundred years, the modern conflict was therefore characterised as simply being symptomatic of Rwanda's historical dynamics. This imbued the carnage with a sense of inevitability which not only misrepresented the real history of Rwanda (where mass violence had been seldom witnessed, particularly in the period before European colonisation), but also contributed to a lack of calls for outside intervention. If the violence was perceived as being merely the *latest* example of such destruction, then active involvement – with the aim of stopping the killing – was implied as being something of a wasted effort. Indeed, some contributors went as far as describing the reasons for the conflict as being a mystery even to those engaged in it, with the words of Bernard Levin once again illustrating this trend:

> More to the point, mass hatred such as we are seeing in this carnage, in its Yugoslav and Rwanda forms, is literally meaningless, and if someone tested hate-fuelled individuals for their hate, few, perhaps none, could answer the question. How many of the tribal murderers – Yugoslav and Rwandan – have any notion of what their hatred stems from? We know that the slaughter is not for food or money or even power. There is a residue of tribal oppression which can fill up a reservoir of hate, but such feelings are invariably matched, hate for hate, and no one could say who started it.[45]

Reporting Genocide

Though largely mistaken, describing Rwanda's carnage in 1994 in such terms – of tribalism and ancient hatreds – largely mirrored those persistent reports which had explained the crisis in the Balkans in much the same manner. As opposed to contextualising the brutality within a wider framework of global politics and sociodemographic factors, the perpetrators (and often the victims) in both cases were instead categorised as essentially brainless – acting out violent impulses which, in contrast with the *civilised* Western world, were inherent in both the region and the people themselves. Of course, given that both the perpetrators and victims in the Rwandan instance were largely rural, poor and, most importantly, black, such stereotyped and simplistic descriptions of the violence fit easily into an existing Western schema.

Another way in which Rwanda's genocide was largely misrepresented from the very beginning was the manner in which the violence itself was described in terms of anarchy and chaos, an observation which is also likely to have its roots in an established Western narrative of sub-Saharan Africa as being savage and out of control. Particularly in the early days and weeks of the conflict – by which time Rwanda was already being referred to as 'a savage killing field, a place where human life is cheap and vengeance the prevailing emotion' – the genocidal process, which was in reality a meticulously planned operation, was instead framed as being something of a free-for-all.[46]

Tellingly, and perhaps indicative of the fact that many reporters recycled the language and framing of other journalists, the term 'orgy' is cited with notable regularity. A *Chicago Tribune* article described the 'long-troubled country' descending into an 'orgy of bloodletting', whilst a later editorial in the same title spoke of a 'rampage' taking place amidst 'an orgy of killing whose enormity is mind-boggling.'[47] The *New York Times*, speculating on the assassination of Habyarimana, asserted that 'the presumptive blame for the orgy of slaughter falls on Tutsi warriors seeking to impose their past dominance,' with a *Guardian* headline from the same period declaring: 'Army on orgy of killing in Rwanda.'[48] Framing the unfolding violence in such a manner gave the impression that there was little organisation among the killers in Rwanda, thus contributing to the mistaken belief – which persisted throughout the months to come – that the violence was

150

instead akin to an entire country collectively going insane. In the period immediately following Habyarimana's assassination, however, when Kigali temporarily became the most violent city on the planet, even the UN were both shocked and confused by the level of violence being witnessed. One official observer, Moctor Gueye, was quoted as saying, 'So far as we can see, it seems like there are a lot of guns in a lot of hands, and we don't really know who is giving orders to shoot at whom and for what reason.'[49] Evidently then, the grotesque atrocities engulfing the country, especially in the early days of the violence, were difficult to properly identify or distinguish with any certainty. However, that the violence continued to be described in terms of 'anarchy' for several months is likely because the idea conformed to existing Western notions concerning Africa and its people.

Indeed, a number of commentators from the time explicitly linked the destruction in Rwanda to wider issues concerning Africa, many of which were rather cynical in their descriptions of the continent and its prospects, with Richard Dowden noting in the *Independent* that Rwanda 'seemed to confirm the worst fears of the most cynical Afro-pessimists.'[50] This assertion, that the conflict was symptomatic of a violent trend within African society, was also echoed by other journalists at the time. Martin Woollacott, for one, highlighted how industrialised countries 'after a burst of optimism about Africa's prospects' were coming once again 'to the conlusion that many African countries are hopeless cases.'[51] An editorial in *The Times* also echoed such a belief, describing Africa as 'a rudderless continent, starved of democracy and stultified by war and misrule,' whilst Barbara Amiel – wife of Conrad Black, owner of Telegraph Newspapers – lamented that 'Ever since I can remember, Africa has been the stuff of penny dreadfuls. Ibos and Watusis, the Shona versus the Matabele, cannibalism, mad dictators such as Idi Amin, mass starvation, and corruption and scientific social-ism.'[52] Essentially, Africa was projected as somewhere in which *these things* happened; a violent, backward region of the globe far below the level of perceived civility and progress of the Western world. This generalised dis-course on Africa, which essentially viewed all black African countries as being politically synonymous, was racialised in the coverage of Rwanda to an extent not replicated in media discussion of the Balkans. Whilst Bosnia was seen as symptomatic of ethnic tensions and ancient hatreds that purportedly afflicted the Balkans region, the violence in Rwanda was linked to various other instances of atrocity and upheaval across the entirety of the African continent. Events on the continent (from Idi Amin; to Somalia; to Biafra; to Rwanda…) were thus contextualised within a wider racialised historical narrative, that saw black Africa as savage, tribal and violent.

It should be stated, however, that this framing of the Rwandan genocide – as tribal, anarchic and ultimately representative of Africa as a whole – was indeed challenged on occasion. While never concentrated or persistent enough to subvert – or even influence – the dominant narratives surrounding the conflict (and ideas of Africa more generally), it nonetheless remains the case that there were a minority of voices within the Anglo–American press which sought to question the assumptions permeating the reporting of the violence. The main aspect of the conflict which was challenged within the more nuanced coverage of the genocide was the assertion that the antagonists were 'tribes', a position which was critiqued by a few notable experts. In a letter to *The Times*, for example, Director of Christian Aid, Michael H. Taylor, though being somewhat generous in describing the title's coverage as 'laudibly extensive', argued that 'it would be an over-simplification to suggest that divisions are based solely on tribal hatred.'[53] Continuing this, Donatella Lorch quoted Alison Des Forges' correction that the violence was 'not a tribal conflict, but a ruthless cynical plot.'[54] Indeed, some contributors even tried to properly articulate the reasons as to *why* the two groups could not be accurately referred to as tribes. One notable example came from Richard Dowden, who stated:

> Nor can the mass exterminations in Rwanda and Burundi simply be dismissed as another ghastly example of African tribalism. These two former kingdoms are unique, and the Hutu and Tutsi people cannot be defined as tribes. They speak the same language, share the same culture, live on the same hills and in recent years began to intermarry.[55]

This attempt to explain the illegitimacy of the 'tribal' narrative was later echoed by Alex de Waal – co-director of African Rights – who was quoted in an unattributed article in the *Guardian* as saying: 'It is difficult to define a tribe, but tribal peoples do have a distinct language, a distinct territory and a distinct culture. This is not the case with these groups.'[56] By the time of the refugee crisis, amid recurring allusions to the genocide as having its roots in a centuries-old feud between Hutu and Tutsi, Kenan Malik of the *Independent* would state, succinctly, that the divisions were 'neither ancient nor natural.'[57]

Attempts, such as those listed, to counteract the prevailing narrative framing of the Rwandan crisis were, however, a distinct minority. Being remarkably few in number, they were never going to be enough to act as a balance against the dominant frames through which the conflict was generally discussed. Further to this, such was the prevalence of the previously discussed framing of Rwanda (in that it was generally presented as a clash between two tribes who had had been at war for centuries) in the early reporting of the genocide, that attempts to counteract this narrative were largely an impossible task. Describing Africa in terms which repeated notions of savagery, chaos and lack of progress fitted easily into the existing discourse concerning the continent, and so most of the oft-repeated (though largely mistaken) means of characterising Rwanda throughout the summer of 1994 were, to many in the Anglo–American world, in line with what they already *knew*. This was perhaps best expressed at the time by Matthew Parris of *The Times*, who argued:

> Nothing better illustrates the undeclared racism of the English intelligentsia than our silence over the latest atrocities in east central Africa. We have plenty of news but no comment. This is not because the English have no opinions but because they have the same opinion. They think these people are savages and there's nothing to be done about it. To save a fuss, they think that's better left unsaid.[58]

Prospects of Intervention

As had been the case within reporting on Bosnia and the related atrocities there, the carnage in Rwanda also saw the prospect of intervention being discussed; albeit briefly and generally accompanied by some form of disclaimer. And, again like the coverage of the Balkans, the subject of intervention – in terms of how it should proceed and, more importantly, who should be responsible for such an undertaking – was a topic which divided opinion.

Given that it was assumed that the responsibility for any interventionist measures to stop the violence would lie with the United States, it is unsurprising that most of the directly anti-interventionist commentary found within this study appeared in American newspapers. Indeed, many such articles actually attempted to explain their anti-interventionist position as being acceptable and rational, if not entirely keeping with self-professed notions of morality. Stephen Kinzer of the *New York Times* alluded to as much when he noted how 'In this conflict between humanitarian impulses and cold calculation of national interest, realpolitik is winning', and it is certainly true that American interests were often explicitly invoked to substantiate this position in a number of related articles.[59] One such piece argued that, 'In a world of parish-pump genocides, morality cannot, by itself, provide a key to intervention', going on to justify this stance by stating that 'Only when morality intersects with economic and strategic interests does a policy begin to emerge.'[60] Others also echoed this position, with one editorial stating coldly that 'realism is not the same as heartlessness… America has no vital interest in Rwanda', whilst another lead article simply asserted that it made 'good sense for the United States to refrain from sending troops to curtail the horrors of genocide and war in Rwanda.'[61] The common thread running through each of the examples cited is the manner in which non-intervention in Rwanda was portrayed, to varying degrees, as either a matter for someone else, or simply not important in relation to what were perceived as America's (vaguely defined) national interests. Whilst some commentators had campaigned vocally and insistently for some form of action in response to atrocities in Bosnia – not least to save the faltering credibility of the UN and the wider notion of the 'international community' – the Rwanda crisis had a much more difficult job in finding support for intervention. Indeed, the contrast in the response to Bosnia and Rwanda was regularly cited, with the following extract from a piece by Henry S. Bienen largely representative of a wider trend which attempted to explain why intervention in the Balkans was generally seen as more desirable, and achievable, than such an action in Rwanda:

The life of a Rwandan is as precious as the life of a Bosnian. The maiming of Angolans and Sudanese is no more tolerable than the maiming of Muslim Bosnians in Gorazde. We should value human lives equally but this does not compel the United States to intervene with military force in every place where individuals and groups are persecuted [...] to argue, as some do, that, unless we intervene for peace everywhere we cannot act in Bosnia is the height of folly and itself is a morally specious argument.[62]

If the costs of intervention, both financially and politically, were viewed as too steep, the actual physical risks of intervening in Rwanda were also cited during this period. A related argument, which was regularly invoked in order to dissuade calls for intervention, was the explicit referencing of 'Somalia' – used to illustrate the potential for a well-intentioned humanitarian mission to go horrifically wrong. With the Rwandan genocide being one of the first African news stories to feature (temporarily) within mainstream Western media since the US-led debacle in Mogadishu in October 1993, it was perhaps inevitable that this high-profile failure – which saw 18 US Rangers killed – would impact on the prospects of intervention in Rwanda. Even though the situations in Somalia and Rwanda were radically different, the fact that both were perceived as generic war-torn African countries was enough for comparisons between the two – especially in a negative context designed to dissuade action in the latter – to hold sufficient weight to be influential in the framing of potential foreign-policy objectives. A *New York Times* editorial stated as much, asserting that 'the disasters of Somalia showed all too graphically the problems of responding to horrific television images with ad hoc forces under multinational command' – in doing so also implying that the blame for Mogadishu lay with the UN.[63] Another comment piece, this time in the *Los Angeles Times*, situated US policy in the context of a dynamic post-Cold War environment whilst also citing the lessons which were supposedly learned by the ill-fated action of the previous year:

Until a few years ago, US interest in Africa was largely confined to supporting friendly – and frequently repressive – regimes as bulwarks against Soviet adventurism. As the Cold War ended, the United States took even a lesser a role in African affairs.

Somalia was a radical departure, and if the debacle there accomplished nothing else, it helped to crystallize the concept that US policy in Africa would no longer be interventionist.[64]

An editorial in the *Chicago Tribune* that suggested African led-intervention also followed such a line, opening with the argument that 'Only the most callous person [...] can see pictures of slain Rwandans [...] and not be moved to wonder, "Can't something be done?"', before warning against US involvement or even 'one step toward what could be a Somalia-like experience.'[65] Evidently, in much the same manner that Bosnia was consistently viewed as having the potential to be another Vietnam, Rwanda was often framed as a Mogadishu-waiting-to-happen. Indeed, as Richard Dowden commented at the time, 'Rwandans are dying because the US messed up in Somalia.'[66] Given the vast geographic and cultural distance between Rwanda and Somalia, the fact that the two states could be so easily compared within the Anglo–American media is again indicative of a racial factor in the framing of African events.

In contrast to the crisis in the Balkans, which at least prompted some limited enthusiasm for Western-led intervention, Rwanda rarely generated consistent calls for outside action to contain the violence. The closest equivalent to such a stance came in the form of a handful of contributors advocating some type of African-led mission, though most of these completely overlooked the logistical and material hindrances to such a policy. The *Chicago Tribune* forwarded a similar proposal, arguing that the US was correct in seeking to 'support and encourage an African initiative', a position seconded a day later by a *Los Angeles Times* editorial which asserted: 'Intervention is in order – but Africans must take the lead.'[67] Indeed, barely a week into the crisis, as Western nationals were fleeing the country, commentator George Ayittey was already attempting to pass the burden of responsibility onto African nations, arguing that:

In Burundi and Rwanda, the UN Security Council should pass its peacekeeping mandate on to the OAU. The solution to the cycle of war lies in Africa itself and the ultimate responsibility of saving Africa lies with its leaders. If they are not willing to save their continent, there is little the world community can do.[68]

Another notable example of this trend came from analyst Charles Krauthammer, who offered a possible solution to the crisis by advocating something resembling a South African protectorate over Rwanda. Though highly unlikely to have ever been feasible, not least because of the enormous political change which had taken place in South Africa only weeks before, this instance was also somewhat unique, in that it was one of the only comment pieces written during the genocide which actually advocated, however tentatively, direct intervention by the United States:

> But tinged as it is with the memory of imperialism, trusteeship by the Great Powers would not have a chance of worldwide support. Trusteeship by a country like South Africa would. And there is precedent [...] Why not grant the majority black government of South Africa trusteeship over some of the wreckages of the post-colonial era? [...] But what if South Africa declines to lead in Rwanda? Then America should step in as the last resort. Somalia again? Yes, but this time we do it right: in and out in 90 days. No nation-building fantasies, just rescue and protection. Create the havens, then turn them over to the multi-national African force. Genocide demands no less.[69]

This comment piece was virtually alone in demanding some form of intervention from a Western power (at least in the period before France took unilateral action – which will be discussed in a later section), an illustration of just how disinterested the overall media response to Rwanda generally was. Indeed those sections of the Anglo–American press which weren't directly anti-intervention were not necessarily pro-intervention either, but instead more concerned with explaining how such undertakings were no longer a necessity in the post-Cold War political landscape. Essentially, the rules and demands of peace-keeping and intervention had changed with the fall of Soviet communism, in that American interests were no longer intrinsically tied to combating, in the words of Stephen Chapman, the 'mortal threat' faced in previous decades.[70] This reasoning was also discussed at the height of the refugee crisis in late July, in a *Washington Post* lead article which criticised the slow response to the humanitarian situation by highlighting that, in the past, 'anti-communism reinforced humanitarianism.'[71]

In a similar vein, and again mirroring a debate which had been high-lighted in relation to the conflict in the Balkans, was discussion of the potential damage to the UN which could result from a misguided intervention in Rwanda's catastrophe. As in the Bosnian case, institutional prestige and viability were seen to easily supersede the plight of the actual victims in this instance, even as the genocide reached its murderous peak in late April and early May. Though articles criticising the UN appeared throughout the duration of the violence in Rwanda – both for abandoning the country early on *and* for being perceived to be pressuring the US to do more – other written contributions saw the Rwandan conflict as either an opportunity for good publicity or, in some instances, a further potential disaster. Handled well, argued Peter Pringle of the *Independent*, Rwanda 'could greatly ease the UN's terrible public relations problems', whilst an editorial in the *New York Times*, anxious over the potential for any such intervention to go wrong, quoted Madeleine Albright's warning that such a failure would 'only further undermine UN credibility and support'.[72] In both these instances, as was often the case in discussions of the legitimacy or feasibility of UN action in relation to both Bosnia and Rwanda, the people actually suffering the privations and brutality of war and genocide were generally an afterthought, at best. This subjugation of the physical wellbeing of actual human beings to the potential damage to supranational institutions is itself a further indication of where the true priorities of the press (itself an institution) indeed lay – a point illustrated by the following extract from a *Chicago Tribune* editorial from late April 1994: 'The saddest part of the Rwandan tragedy is the thousands of lives lost. *Almost as sad* is the sobering lesson about what the UN, for which hopes were so high after the Cold War, can and cannot do' [Emphasis added].[73]

Evidently then, the Rwandan genocide struggled, throughout its murderous duration, to provoke calls from the Anglo–American press for their governments to do more to halt the violence. However, when combined with an analysis of the manner in which the *scale* of the violence was consistently marginalised within the Anglo–American press, such indifference should not be regarded as particularly surprising.

Lack of Focus on the Genocide

In addition to the statistical observations cited earlier in the chapter, which demonstrated how the Rwandan genocide was rarely considered a main story for any length of time, the lack of focus devoted to the sheer scale of the violence can also be highlighted as evidence to illustrate the fact that the crisis was frequently marginalised throughout its duration.

For example, the overall scale of the carnage – in terms of numbers killed – was not given front page prominence until 22 April, when the *Washington Post* published an article headlined: 'Rwanda Death Toll said to Top 100,000'.[74] This is interesting in itself, as despite the fact that estimates had been cited in news articles from the beginning of the conflict, it was not until a total of 100,000 was reached that it was seen to be important enough to warrant inclusion in the front page headline of an American newspaper. This observation can arguably be cited as further evidence of the importance of race in relation to determining media interest during instances of mass violence, given that the deaths of hundreds of thousands of black African victims seemed to illicit such little concern from the Anglo–American media. Further, despite having a difficult time even *making* the front page, the Rwandan genocide was to find it even more challenging to stay there. Though the fact that the death the death toll obviously continued to spiral as the summer of 1994 progressed, on many occasions the front page coverage went in the opposite direction. Revealingly, at a conference of newspaper editors and media moguls at the time, coincidentally dealing with how to cover genocide in the press, Ted Koppel said to an audience of journalists: 'I'll bet you a quarter none of you have Rwanda on page 1 next week.'[75] Although this was something of an overstatement, he was certainly accurate in describing the general practice of many of the sources in this study. A partial explanation for this – as some analysts have noted in the years since – was that the realisation that the violence was *genocidal* in nature came very slowly.[76] With the press 'stunned in incomprehension,' the magnitude of the carnage has been said to have escaped the majority of onlookers for the better part of April, and there is probably at least some degree of truth to this. Indeed, even Romeo Dallaire, the UN force commander in Rwanda at the time of the violence, claims that he initially found it difficult to fully accept what was developing in front of him.[77]

On the face of it, these seem like perfectly reasonable arguments – that is until one analyses the print coverage of the Rwandan crisis and realises that the facts were there for all to see. The sheer numbers coming out of Rwanda, not forgetting the gruesome nature of most of the killing, were a clear indicator of what was taking place, and yet the press rarely made a determined effort to highlight what was unfolding.[78] Though the term 'genocide' was rarely used explicitly in the first weeks of the conflict, the argument that the scale of the violence was not quickly appreciated does not stand up to close scrutiny.[79] For example, less than a week into the slaughter, a *Washington Post* article cited the estimate that perhaps 100,000 people had already been killed. Revealingly, despite citing this figure only five days into the conflict – meaning that an average of 20,000 people had been murdered *every day* since the plane crash – this estimate was hidden away within the body of an article which itself was relegated to page 13.[80] The figure of 100,000 dead was widely circulated in the weeks that followed, though it seldom got the attention which it surely should have commanded. Even as hardened aid workers were describing a death toll so high that it was 'meaningless,' the scale of the violence continued to struggle for prominent placing within the print media.[81] Certainly, the estimate of 100,000 was quoted in a variety of articles, but it was often in an easily missed section of the newspaper.[82] In one notable instance on 24 April the number was relegated to inclusion in a box-sized article, on page 13, of no more than 150 words. And by 28 April, *The Times* had confined this figure to a 34-word piece hidden away on page 15.[83] This trend was also seen in those articles which were slightly more ambiguous about the exact nature of the violence. One article, written barely three weeks into the carnage, and despite describing 'bodies littering the streets,' could only muster a paltry 23 words for the entire piece.[84]

On the rare occasions where the extent of the violence *was* a focal point within the media, there was normally some way in which it continued to be marginalised. For example, the figure of 100,000 dead occasionally featured in the headlines during this period, but rarely on the front page. Coincidentally, three separate newspapers featured this horrific figure in the headline of an article on the same date – 21 April. Not one of them, however, featured it on page one.[85] In fact, in one of the newspapers selected, this shocking death toll was still of secondary importance on the individual page on which it featured – with the news that tennis star Boris Becker was being blackmailed taking prime position.[86] This subjugation of the violence to celebrity culture was a common feature throughout the conflict, though. For example, on 10 April, the headline '"8,000 butchered" in Rwanda capital' did actually make it onto the front page, though it was relegated to a corner mention as the fact that comedian Freddie Starr's horse had won the Grand National was considered to be of greater importance.[87]

Though it is true that the generally political nature of genocide can make it a difficult crime to positively identify, figures in excess of 100,000 gave a blindingly clear indication of a ferocious instance of mass violence, and would generally be expected to gain concentrated coverage by way of satisfying the 'news value' conditions of conflict and intensity.[88] Certainly, the examples provided contradict the false proclamations that Britain and the US learned of the genocide much later than is commonly thought.[89] On the contrary, the extent of the violence was readily apparent – the problem, evidently, was that such figures no longer had any meaningful impact (especially when the victims were black Africans). Even though the first few weeks of the genocide witnessed the most concentrated and organised violence of the entire campaign, a range of other domestic and international events continued to dominate the media glare. Meanwhile, the death of 100,000 civilians was often relegated to easily missed articles buried deep within the various newspapers.[90]

As the mass violence in Rwanda continued into May 1994, further increases in the estimated death toll also failed to prompt any significant change in the overall coverage. By mid-May, the figure of 200,000 dead was being frequently cited and yet this still failed to push the genocide further up the news agenda. Despite indicating the deaths of a quarter-of-a-million people in the space of just six or seven weeks, most reporting on the genocide continued to be confined to the inside pages of Western newspapers. One notable example appeared in the *New York Times* on 11

May, in which an article citing between 100,000 and 200,000 deaths was relegated to page nine, which itself was dominated by an advertisement for cheap flights to Europe.[91] In another instance, a small headline stating, 'Rwandan Death Toll May Exceed 200,000' only managed inclusion above the briefest of articles within the 'Around the World' section.[92] Indeed, on a number of occasions, the citing of such figures actually appears to be little more than an 'add-on' at the end of an article. In several reports on the violence in Rwanda, the total of 200,000 killed is only mentioned within the last paragraph of the piece – often appearing in the very last sentence.[93] A further notable example appeared in the following editorial from the *Orlando Sentinel* – which was reproduced in the *Chicago Tribune* in late May 1994. In tentatively arguing that the UN should have responded to the violence with greater urgency, what is most revealing within this article is found in the following extract:

> Yes, the battles were raging more than a month ago. The death toll, however, stood at about 20,000. No one could have anticipated today's obscene statistics – an estimated 200,000 dead, 500,000 wounded and 2 million refugees.[94]

The fact that this article stated, in plain English, that the death toll of 20,000 was not particularly noteworthy, gives a clear indication of the fact that the tolerance for mass violence had extended considerably by the 1990s. As Susan Moeller has noted, 'indifference in the face of horror has a long history,' but to so easily dismiss the loss of 20,000 people is as concrete an example as one could hope to find.[95] As also stated by Moeller, body counts alone do not determine the extent of coverage, but when a death toll numbering in the hundreds of thousands begins to emerge one would assume that news editors and the like would feel compelled to highlight such developments.[96] The reality as the genocide progressed, however, was quite to the contrary. As some journalists have noted since, a number of editors – even only a few weeks into the slaughter – actually wished to scale back the (already limited) coverage of Rwanda.[97]

Expectedly, then, this trend continued even as the death toll grew past half a million. Since earlier estimates of 100,000 to 200,000 had been downplayed within the media, it should perhaps be little surprise that the figure of 500,000 – despite vividly illustrating the worst instance of mass violence of the post-Cold War world – also failed to provoke an increase in the attention paid to Rwanda. On barely a handful of occasions did this incredible figure appear in a main headline, and it rarely featured prominently within the main news section.[98] Even when it was cited for the very first time in most newspapers, it was given very little coverage. For example, when the 500,000 estimate was first mentioned in the *Guardian*, it was featured in the 'World news in brief' section. Similarly, the first mention of this number within the *Daily Telegraph* only managed to warrant inclusion on page 15.[99] One exceptional case deserves a mention though, in that the 500,000 figure prompted one of the few journalistic 'number-comparisons' ever used to highlight the scale of the slaughter. An article by Patrick Bishop of the *Daily Telegraph* invoked a comparison to the Armenian genocide of 1915 and went on to describe how the total of half a million equated to one in every 15 Rwandans being killed since 7 April.[100] Whilst it is of course true that recent decades have witnessed a noticeable decline in overall print-media coverage of foreign developments (meaning that fewer events will be reported on), established news values would lead one to assume that concentrated coverage *would* be extended to the extermination of more than half a million people – even accepting the previously mentioned general lack of coverage devoted to Africa.[101] Former *Boston Globe* correspondent Tom Palmer once argued that, 'People being killed is definitely a good, objective story', adding 'And innocent people being killed is better.'[102] This reasoning certainly sounds like it would be adhered to but, as press coverage of Rwanda demonstrates, this is by no means the rule. By the middle of June and into July, the estimated numbers of Rwanda's dead began to figure even less than in the previous months. Despite the fact that the death toll continued to rise, in addition to being confirmed by a greater number of reliable sources, by July the focus of the media gradually moved away from the genocide and onto the developing refugee crisis.

As the evidence of organised genocide, and not merely 'senseless' mass violence, became undeniable, the events in Rwanda continued to be firmly stuck deep within the inside pages of the various titles analysed. One particular report described a massacre at a convent in which it was noted that some 20,000 people had been killed in one operation – certainly a monstrous atrocity by any standards – and yet this only warranted a place on page 14 of the *Daily Telegraph*.[103] The fact that the estimated death toll, by early June, was occasionally being cited as up to one million also did little to reverse the trend of media disinterest in the genocide.[104] This figure was quoted in several articles, but never found its way into anything which resembled a prominent report. That such catastrophic numbers of innocents killed could be so easily dismissed – one such article which cited one million dead was reduced to a tiny corner-mention on page 14 – is indicative that genocide, in itself, was not considered a particularly important story by this point. An old newsroom truism has it that one dead fireman in Brooklyn is worth '500 Africans,' but as these examples show, the media trade-off is actually far greater – with the deaths of several hundred thousand Africans often failing to command any sizable presence in the Anglo–American print media.[105] Certainly, from this evidence at least, Stalin's reported assertion that one million deaths are simply a statistic holds true. What is perhaps most disheaterning though is that, come 1994, the threshold at which human lives (particularly those in Africa) became a mere abstract number was actually several hundred thousand short of Stalin's original estimate.[106]

It should be noted, for purposes of clarity, that a handful of articles did at least attempt to draw attention to the magnitude of the violence in Rwanda as it was unfolding. One example came from Mark Huband, who forcefully described Rwanda as 'the greatest genocide since Germany in the 1930s and Cambodia in the 1970s.' Highlighting that Rwanda had been an obscure country to Westerners prior to the genocide, he also went on to highlight the fact that the presence of the media had ensured that any claims of 'ignorance' over what was occurring in Rwanda were blatant falsities.[107] Another commentator also likened the atrocities to what had taken place in Nazi-occupied Europe, adding though that what he had witnessed in Rwanda 'was different than anything [he had] seen before'; whilst Richard Dowden continued allusions to the Nazi era by describing the violence as 'an African Final Solution.'[108] It should be noted here, however, that such explicit references were remarkably few in number in the reporting of Rwanda, and in no way comparable to the prevalence of 'Holocaust framing' recorded in the media coverage of Bosnia.

A small number of journalists also tried to contrast the suffering in Rwanda with that in Bosnia, such as Charles Krauthammer, who argued that: 'For all the hyperbolic use of such terms as genocide and holocaust to describe Bosnia, the worst violence on earth today is occurring in Rwanda.'[109] This is notable in that such comparisons were rarely made within the 'News' sections of the various titles. Another article from the same author virtually dismissed Bosnia altogether, describing Rwanda as 'the one unequivocal case of genocide occurring in the world today.'[110] Unfortunately though, such lamentations on the crisis in Rwanda were extremely rare, and so these strongly worded articles generally failed to make much of an overall impact on how the genocide was being treated in the press.

Theories relating to the concept of psychophysical numbing may argue that it is a natural human response to fail to comprehend death in such vast numbers, and there is more than a grain of truth to this.[111] The human capacity for compassion cannot be multiplied indefinitely and so perhaps it is inevitable that, at least on a psychological level, the numbers involved in the likes of Rwanda can become somewhat abstract. However, just because the ability to properly absorb such death tolls is beyond human comprehension, this does not mean that these same figures should be of only secondary importance within the media. Indeed, many commentators would testify to the very opposite of this, arguing that the severity of a news event is often a clear indicator of its potential for extensive reporting within the media. As an event unfolds, it is often the case that media coverage will intensify in line with the suffering of those involved.[112] This can relate to 'minor' catastrophes, such as floods or hurricanes, but is supposed to be most prominent when related to mass violence and war. Indeed, as the old newsroom saying states, 'if it bleeds, it leads.' As the coverage of the Rwandan genocide testifies, however, there are major exceptions to this.[113]

Rwanda can rightfully be described as being 'among history's truly horrible moments', and yet it seldom gained concentrated coverage within the Anglo–American print media.[114] Even as the death toll escalated to almost unbelievable levels the genocide continued to be relegated to marginalised articles and side-mentions at best, often struggling against celebrity news and advertising space. Further to this, in those articles which *did* appear in the press concerning Rwanda, the genocide itself was rarely the main focus of the narrative. Death tolls numbering in the hundreds of thousands were often tacked on at the end of a piece, and it was only when the genocide was seen to affect, or be affected by, foreign nationals (as will be discussed shortly) that it commanded greater attention from the media. What this all demonstrates, therefore, is that genocide, as a news story, can rarely break through on its own merits. During the Rwandan genocide, this process perhaps reached its zenith in modern times. As hundreds of thousands of innocent people were murdered in what would be the fastest genocide in history, the press coverage of the carnage actually receded as the violence intensified. Certainly, as Herman Cohen wrote at the time, 'Another Holocaust may have slipped by, hardly noticed.'[115]

Rare Instances of Press Focus

Given the combination of quantitative and qualitative observations discussed thus far, it is fair to argue that the Rwandan genocide did not generally command the focused attention of the Anglo–American elite press. Even when the extent of the violence was beyond any reasonable doubt, the media coverage was generally fleeting, insubstantial and a misrepresentation of the underlying dynamics of the conflict. On a handful of occasions, however, the crisis in Rwanda did indeed generate a degree of concentrated – though short-lived – coverage from the newspapers which informed this study. In chronological order, these exceptions were: the period surrounding the initial massacres, during which time white nationals were evacuated from the country; the French intervention which took place in June; and the refugee crisis which followed the RPF victory in mid-July. As will be highlighted in the following section, in each of these instances the clear focal point of the reporting was the actions of outsiders or – in the case of the refugees – the fact that the crisis in Rwanda was seen to be spreading beyond its own immediate borders, with the genocide itself remaining of secondary importance.

Western Evacuation

The main reason that the days following Habyarimana's plane crash saw the conflict being covered comparatively fully in the press had little to do with the suffering of Rwandans. On the contrary, a large part of the press attention devoted to Rwanda during this period was instead concerned with the handful of white foreigners who were living there at the time. Even though the violence reached horrific proportions almost immediately – with one reporter describing a 'blood soaked Rwanda' – the initial coverage focused predominantly on the evacuation of foreign nationals, whilst the violence was generally relegated to lesser prominence.[116] Granted, it could be argued that this focus at least led to Rwanda gaining some manner of concentrated coverage and front page exposure for a few days, but it is still surprising that the violence itself could be automatically constructed as being of secondary importance within the context of the story. Fergal Keane would later note that focus on the actions of white nationals was essentially standard practice within Western coverage of African conflicts, but also added the disclaimer that the total number of dead – if not the politics and social dimensions behind the violence – would normally be highlighted prominently as well.[117] In the Rwandan case, this was rarely true. Although estimates of the numbers of dead were included within the body of several articles, these figures were seldom highlighted as the most relevant part of the report. Perhaps this was inevitable though, since journalism is generally driven by public interest and, in the developed world, the immediate interest was on securing the safe passage of (mostly white) foreign nationals. Comment to this effect, with several journalists (mostly from British titles) highlighting this process, was explicitly cited during this period. Martin Woollacott described Rwanda as getting 'the standard emergency treatment', which he defined as 'send in the paratroopers, get the whites home, and let the fires burn themselves out.'[118] An editorial in the *Independent* also commented on this aspect in Rwanda, arguing that the violence there would 'reinforce a widespread view that Africa is a lost continent, so barbarous, so deeply sunk in tribal conflict and so remote from our concerns that nothing can be done to help it', going on to state that the dominant view was that 'Rescuing the lives of white nationals is about the only reason for becoming involved.'[119] Perhaps the most cynical lament on the unfolding crisis, however, came from Matthew Parris of *The Times*, who stated:

> There is no hope for Africa, no hope at all. And in the end we are going to airlift our own people, mostly white people, and leave the Africans to their fate. Why don't we just cut the crap, and say so now?[120]

The mass evacuation of foreign nationals also had a secondary implication for the coverage of Rwanda, in that a number of journalists and reporters followed civilian evacuees out on the final transports. This meant that first-hand coverage from inside Rwanda dropped dramatically and, as a result, the majority of the reporting in the weeks immediately following the end of the evacuation process came from journalists based outside of the country. Alan J. Kuperman would later exaggerate this point by stating that European newspaper coverage stopped cold on 18 April, further emphasising this point by describing how the *Guardian* featured nothing on Rwanda for seven days.[121] After analysis of these same sources, it can be concluded that Kuperman is largely correct in his statements. Coverage did indeed stop cold on 18 April for four out of the eight selected publications in this study (including three of the British titles) – that is, featuring no news on Rwanda whatsoever on 19 April – though his description of the *Guardian's* week-long lack of coverage is mistaken. The *Guardian* did fail to feature Rwanda on three separate occasions during April, including the 19th, but this falls short of the reported seven-day blackout.[122] What is certainly apparent though is that there was a noticeable difference between the first 12 days of reporting (7–18 April), when the evacuation of foreigners was taking place; and the last 12 days in April (19–30 April), after which this same process had been completed. Across the eight selected titles, a total of 157 articles were produced concerning Rwanda in the first 12 days following Habyarimana's assassination. In the 12 days up to 30 April, however, only 92 articles were published. This is a clear indication that the removal of foreigners was viewed as a much more important event than the genocide itself – a fact compounded by the realisation that the 'evacuation period' saw only one two occurrences when a title did not feature Rwanda at all, whereas the 'post-evacuation period' saw 16 such occasions – an average of two for every newspaper.

What makes these statistics all the more revelatory is that the period following the evacuation of Western nationals ushered in the most intensive period of killing of the entire genocide. While 4,000 white nationals were escaping the country, some 20,000 Rwandans were killed, and yet the press actually scaled back their coverage during this time. Indeed, one letter published on 14 April correctly surmised that the 'press attention on Rwanda [was] sure to drop to near zero following the evacuation of Europeans,' showing that this phenomenon was even identified, to a degree, during the crisis itself.[123]

French Intervention

As Livingstone has noted, the news media is fickle, 'shifting from one crisis to the next.'[124] Between the evacuation of foreign nationals in early April and the onset of the refugee crisis in late July, the genocide rarely led the news – with the occasional exception. One of these came in mid- to late May, as the fact that several thousand bodies had washed down the Kagera River into Uganda – 'creating a new form of ecological disaster' – caused Rwanda to receive a brief resurgence of interest within the press.[125] This increased reporting barely lasted a few days though. An article, written by Donatella Lorch, about the flood of bodies into Uganda is notable in that the author claimed that the magnitude of the slaughter was 'shocking the world.'[126] Whilst this may have been true for a brief period, to argue that the world was truly shocked by these events – at least judging by the press coverage it received – was a gross miscalculation on her part. The ten thousand bodies which had flowed out of Rwanda were, apparently, not sufficient to hold the attention of the press, which by early June was devoting increasingly less coverage to the violence in general.

A development which did briefly fall within the glare of the media spotlight, however, was the intervention of the French – known as *Operation Turquoise* – which took place in mid- to late June 1994. Although by this point in the conflict the majority of the victims were already dead, the French involvement in Rwanda (given that the crisis now directly involved

what is considered an *elite nation*) reignited a degree of interest from certain areas of the press. Being first discussed seriously around the middle
of the month, by 21 June the French intervention was well underway;
and between then and the end of the month, the media focus on Rwanda
increased considerably. For example, the first occasion in which the
Independent devoted an entire page to covering Rwanda came on 21 June,
a development which was highly dependent on French intervention.[127] To
further illustrate the increase in coverage prompted by the French intervention, consider the following statistics: Between 1 June and 15 June,
before the intervention took place, 115 articles were produced concerning Rwanda. Between the 16–30 of June, on the other hand, during which
period the French were heavily involved in Rwanda, the number of articles
devoted to the crisis rose to 155. This increase in coverage was especially
apparent among British sources, which devoted only 46 articles to Rwanda
in the first half of June and 81 in the second. As there were few other notable developments during this time, then it is safe to assume that it was the
'French angle' which prompted this increase. In relation to judging press
priorities, however, it should be remembered that a change in the death toll
from 10,000 to 100,000, or even 500,000, never provoked the same increase
in press coverage as that which accompanied a handful of French troops
entering the country.

Upon closer analysis, it is apparent the French intervention greatly
divided opinion among contemporary analysts – a development which,
in itself, contributed to a brief increase in coverage concerning Rwanda
(even though, as noted, this largely focused on the actions of the French, as
opposed to the violence which the intervention was purportedly intended
to stop). Whilst calls for intervention (in the period before the unilateral French action) had until this point been largely dismissive of such a
venture, the French operation nonetheless gathered a fair degree of support once it had started. An editorial in the *Chicago Tribune*, for example,
lauded the effort, hailing it as 'viscerally satisfying in the way that bold,
assertive action often is. The more so in this case, since no other power
has offered a better plan – or *any* plan – for responding in a hurry to such
an awful situation'.[128] That 'Only France was willing and able to act' was
also praised by the *New York Times*, with the same lead article further

stating that such 'decisiveness' contrasted with 'the inability of Washington and the United Nations to speed promised armored personnel carriers to Africa.'[129] Certainly, positive comment about the French action was most vocal among American media outlets, with such support perhaps being a subtle means of ensuring that calls for American intervention would recede. The following extract from Scott Kraft, of the *Los Angeles Times*, provides an illustrative example of the manner in which this intervention, when supported, was framed in positive terms:

> The experts doubted it would work. They suspected the French would take sides. And they spoke darkly of 'another Somalia,' from where US troops had been forced by American public opinion to beat an ignominious retreat. But three weeks ago, as the United States and every other nation did little more than wring their hands about the ethnic bloodletting in Rwanda, France airlifted 2,500 of its young sons and daughters in uniform into the heart of the Central African conflict.[130]

This positive framing of the French intervention was also seen in some of the headlines from the period – such as 'French troops warmly welcomed in Rwanda'; 'French aim in Rwanda "is to save lives"'; and 'Rwandans put their faith in God and their trust in paratroopers' – all of which demonstrably portrayed the action in a favourable light.[131] To many, apparently, France's intervention was indeed 'justified', but there was also, of course, a great deal of comment which was critical of the French undertaking.[132]

The French intervention quickly prompted suspicion and disapproval, with notable regularity, from some commentators in British publications. For example, citing France's previous involvement with the Habyarimana regime, Victoria Brittain of the *Guardian* argued that there was 'no country less able to contribute to peace in Rwanda than France', emphasising this point by stating that the French intervention marked 'the lowest point of the catastrophic current record of UN peacekeeping operations in Africa.'[133] A negative opinion of the operation linked to a wider criticism of the actions of the UN also appeared in a later editorial, once again in the *Guardian*, where France's decision was regarded as giving peacekeeping 'a bad name.'[134] French intervention, at least in those reports which were explicitly against such an undertaking, was in turn often framed as being little more than a display of military strength by the French, with the aim of reaffirming the country's status as a world power. Certainly, there may be more than an element of truth to this, and commentary pieces from the time were quick to explicitly highlight this factor. Richard Dowden, himself a reserved advocate – at times – for some form of intervention, criticised France's decision nonetheless, stating: '[Mitterand] needed a grand gesture to show his friends in Africa that France could still act an imperial part. Mr Mitterand chose Rwanda.'[135] This position was echoed by Mark Huband, who argued:

> France's determination to be seen to be doing something is as
> much a recognition of the ineptitude and hostility of the outside
> world to Rwanda as it is an attempt by the Balladur government
> to keep up its credentials as a world power.[136]

Those commentators who criticised France's intervention in Rwanda were also quick to highlight the former's long and complex history of colonial interference in African affairs, a complicating factor which was highlighted with notable regularity in anti-interventionist corners of the press (especially those in the UK – itself, of course, a former colonial power). A letter published in the *Guardian* drew attention to this, arguing that, 'Since the 19th century France [had] a history of attempting to assert its grandeur and maintain its position as a major power in the world through involvement, particularly of a military nature, in Africa.'[137] This citing of France's colonial past was also invoked in an *Independent* editorial column, which described France's 'long post-colonial history of military intervention on behalf of deeply unpopular and discredited African leaders.' This was said to represent a 'source of shame to many in France,' and the current intervention was argued as being part of an 'essentially anti-democratic tradition.'[138] This same editorial also speculated on another factor which was seen to be influencing the French decision to intervene in Rwanda – an apparent desire to stop the spread of the English language in Africa. Emphasising this point, the lead article in question argued that 'however strong France's fears may be of the onward march of the English language, preserving the boundaries of Francophonia is no ground for military action.'[139] This linguistic aspect was also commented upon in a letter to the *New York Times* in which the author, highlighting the fact that France was in fact sheltering many of those who were directly responsible for the massacres in Rwanda, cynically stated: 'What, after all, is a little genocide compared with the spectre of such cultural loss?'[140]

The above aspects considered, the French intervention can therefore be seen to have both prompted a brief increase in the overall coverage of Rwanda whilst also provoking a wider discussion (both positive and negative) regarding the legitimacy of such a venture. What is most telling, however – and conforming to the wider pattern discussed in this section of how press coverage of Rwanda only rose at certain times – is that the genocide itself was once again rarely an issue on its own merits. The most obvious example of this persistent trend, however, came after the massacres had all but ended, with the refugee crisis which escalated in late July of 1994.

Refugee Crisis

Though media attention had been slowly moving away from the genocide since sometime in May, the full weight of media scrutiny finally descended on Rwanda only in mid-July – when the rebels declared victory and thus prompted a mass refugee movement of Hutus into surrounding countries. Hundreds of thousands, if not millions, of people fled in what was to be one of the swiftest mass population movements of modern times. Indeed, as one headline described, it was 'The exodus of a nation.'[141] When this small period, from 15 July – 29 July, is analysed it becomes immediately clear just how prominently the crisis featured in the Western press for a short time. In the eight newspapers selected, 270 articles were published between these two dates. This is quite remarkable in that this equals the total number of articles published for the *entire* month of June, and surpasses the total of 249 recorded for 7–30 April. Indeed, some 21.9 per cent of all articles dedicated to Rwanda were produced in this 15-day period, in a study which focused on a time period of just over 16 weeks. The most prolific titles in terms of reporting during this period were the *New York Times* and the *Daily Telegraph*, which published 50 and 38 articles, respectively, from 15–29 July 1994. The newspapers producing the fewest number of articles in this short period were the *Los Angeles Times* (23) and the *Independent* (24); though, as an indication of how much the refugee crisis outmatched the genocide for coverage, it is notable that this 15-day total for the *Independent* was only marginally fewer than the 29 articles it published during almost the full month of April.

Further analysis also presents other examples illustrating how the refugee crisis was apparently far more newsworthy than the genocide itself. For one, in the four days between 22–25 July, the *Daily Telegraph* published 18 separate articles on the unfolding crisis. Considering that this number represents almost two-thirds of this newspaper's entire total for the month of April – when the worst massacres were unfolding – this should provide ample illustration of how the refugees provoked a level of interest which the violence rarely achieved. Another example can be found in *The Times*, which featured four articles concerning Rwanda in each edition on 23, 24 and 27 July 1994. This is of relevance when it is also noted that, before 23 July, *The Times* never featured more than three articles on any one date. Similarly, for six days between 22–27 July, the *New York Times* featured *at least* four articles each day. On 23 July, this newspaper even printed six full articles in one edition – a feat which, by coincidence, was matched by the *Daily Telegraph* on the very same day. Richard Dowden once remarked that he found it difficult to find the appropriate words to describe what was occurring during the genocide, but as the above statistics imply, there were certainly few difficulties for the press, as a whole, in finding the right words to describe the plight of the refugees.[142] Also, for almost the first time in the entire conflict, some newspapers devoted two front page headlines to the unfolding refugee problem within a single edition – a level of publicity which had only been seen during prior coverage of the genocide on one occasion. Specifically, from 16–29 July 1994 there were 12 occasions where a given newspaper devoted *two* front page articles to the crisis in Rwanda – a level of publicity only ever recorded in the 13 April edition of the *Independent*. Statistically then, it is apparent that the refugee crisis which followed the RPF victory in mid July 1994 received proportionally greater newspaper coverage than the genocide itself.

Also revealing were the various journalistic techniques used to illustrate the suffering of the refugees, with the crisis often framed as being of importance to the international community in a manner which the genocide rarely was. One example, a 20 July front page article concerning the refugee movement, featured a table highlighting the 'top four refugee crises since 1945', illustrating that Rwanda was by far the swiftest – creating some 730,000 refugees per month.[143] It is interesting, though, that few similar comparisons were made in the previous months to draw attention to the fact that the genocide itself was easily the fastest on record. Another commonly used method of drawing attention to the developing crisis in Goma and elsewhere was highlighting the rate at which the refugees were dying – which one report put at 1,800 per day. Again, similar numerical comparisons were rarely utilised during the genocide.[144] A further example of a similar approach, by Anna Quidlen, explicitly referenced this technique in order to publicise the scale of the refugee crisis, saying: 'there are now more Rwandan refugees than there are people living in Detroit. This statistical comparison is an old journalistic trick to make the unimaginable comprehensible, to make the other side of the world seem like the town next door.'[145] An editorial in *The Times* highlighted how a refugee population of 600,000 was akin to every person in Washington amassing on the same spot, though the same report failed to highlight that the genocide had claimed the lives of a greater number of people.[146] Such journalistic techniques are generally utilised only in reference to those issues which the press *want* to draw attention to – that is, the refugee crisis was framed in this accessible manner because the Anglo–American media wished to highlight the suffering in Goma, in marked contrast with the lack of such coverage in the months when the mass killing was at its peak. Indeed, to use Herman & Chomsky's conceptualisation, the refugee crisis helped to finally transform Rwandans into 'worthy victims' in the eyes of the press.[147] Of course, this is not to say that the suffering of the refugees did not warrant such emotive coverage. Around 50,000 people did eventually die of disease, exposure or malnutrition, but the fact that the genocide had claimed *at least* ten times as many victims was evidently lost sight of. As Prunier states, suffering 'cannot be measured by numbers alone,' but if the refugees could inspire 270 articles within only 15 days then one would assume that the genocide should have warranted *at least* a comparable level of coverage.[148]

Beyond the aforementioned rise in terms of the sheer quantity of journalistic attention devoted to Rwanda during this time, also of note is the fact that, with the developing refugee crisis, the Anglo–American press discovered a hitherto unheard-of level of unanimity in terms of supporting some form of involvement in the region. Although France had been praised (by some) for its intervention in June, the genocide was rarely constructed as being of concern to other Western countries. The refugee crisis, on the other hand, soon became *the* global issue within the Anglo–American media, prompting a flurry of calls for more to be done to aid the refugees. In stark contrast to the lack of suggestions regarding intervention in the killing spree of the preceding months, calls on the US and UK to help were immediate and strongly worded, with several articles invoking the idea that basic morality dictated a proper response. One such editorial, in the *Chicago Tribune*, whilst noting that the US had 'no long-term role to play in Rwanda', alluded to this sentiment by asserting that 'human decency alone makes helping in the short-term imperative.'[149] Lead articles were also quick to highlight the responsibility of the wealthy nations of the world, in particular, to respond to the humanitarian catastrophe. One editorial argued that their 'prosperity and heritage require[d] the United States to respond humanely, and immediately,' whilst another called on 'all countries with available resources and skills [to] match America in speed and determination.'[150] The fact that the United States should be seen to take the lead in any large-scale response was also commented upon, and rarely challenged in the manner which possible intervention in the preceding genocide had been. As an editorial in the *Observer* put it: 'President Clinton's decision to launch a round-the-clock relief airlift should be the signal for other countries to act with more positive energy than they have shown so far over a catastrophe that has been staring the world in the face for weeks.' This echoed the previously quoted *Chicago Tribune* editorial from two days prior which argued that the refugees 'must be given the benefit of the fastest, most ambitious and effective humanitarian relief operation the United States and other countries can put together and carry out. The US, with the lion's share of resources at its disposal, has to take the lead in a herculean effort.'[151]

Evidently then, the refugee crisis generated a degree of sympathy and concern which was beyond anything which had been seen during the genocide itself, and for a brief period Rwanda (and the surrounding region) found itself holding the attention of the Anglo–American media. Gone were the anxious references to Somalia, and the cholera-stricken refugees were now constructed as human beings who merited assistance from all who could provide it. This was a notable detachment from the dismissive framing of the genocide in terms of tribalism and anarchy, which in turn had implied that little could (or should) be done in response. Even the prior concerns over potential negative effects resulting from intervention in the crisis were temporarily brushed aside, as in the following extract from the *Guardian*: 'Save the sick; feed the starving: get those who can travel home in safety. And only then, surely, worry about what comes next.'[152] This newly found insistence that the crisis in Rwanda demanded a response, regardless of the risks, was further highlighted by Robert B. Oakley, who said of the refugees: 'the threat they pose to international civilian and military humanitarian workers cannot be ignored. Nor can the possibility of casualties. If casualties among humanitarian workers should occur, the American public need to realise the cause is worth the price.'[153] Such emotive framing of this crisis is further evidence of the fact that the refugee crisis was constructed as being a more newsworthy event than the genocide which preceded it. Indeed, whilst Romeo Dallaire's later argument that the *génocidaires* in the camps received ten times the publicity of the genocide itself is an exaggeration, it remains evident that the press devoted far more attention to the refugees than to an organised campaign of extermination which claimed the lives of around 350 people *every hour*.[154]

Conclusion

As Kenneth Harrow remarked, 'genocide has become banal, much more banal than Hannah Arendt thought possible.' The observations presented here certainly bear this out.[155] The British and American news media had sufficient resources to cover the unfolding catastrophe and yet, on most occasions, concentrated coverage was not forthcoming. As the analysis of these newspapers demonstrates, the Rwandan genocide rarely progressed to the level of being a major story. Apart from a few specific occasions where some form of foreign involvement provoked an increased level of interest in the conflict, the media coverage of the Rwandan crisis exhibited few indicators that the slaughter was considered to be of global importance. Front page publicity was often sparse, while the news coverage devoted to Rwanda generally included the genocide only as a secondary issue to some other development. Editorials and op-ed pieces rarely called for a meaningful Western response and some went as far as openly discouraging any sort of effort to aid the victims. Even as the death toll passed some 500,000 within only six weeks, the Anglo–American print media continued to devote only partial attention to Rwanda.

Although it is true that the organised nature of the violence was not completely understood until some weeks into the slaughter, the *magnitude* of the human cost of the massacres was widely known and this alone would have been expected to elicit a sizable press response. Instead, in several instances, coverage of Rwanda actually decreased as the conflict wore on – a development which goes against most accepted ideas about how violence commands the attention of the media. Almost exactly one year before the genocide in Rwanda began, an article appeared in the *New York Times*, asking the question: 'Does the World Still Recognise a Holocaust?' The answer, it may be argued, is a resounding 'yes' – but the Western world may only immediately recognise genocide if it resembles *the* Holocaust. What was surely a more pertinent question, however, was 'Does the world still *care* about a Holocaust?'[156] As the media coverage of Rwanda indicates, this is a far more difficult question to answer in the affirmative. By any measure, the Rwandan genocide should have surely been given greater attention by the Anglo–American print media. Genocidal violence, almost by definition, is exceptional in nature and the Rwandan crisis was a prime example of this phenomenon. Indeed, it proved to be the fastest mass extermination of modern times, claiming somewhere in the region of 800,000 people in little over three months; and yet the press response to this violence from British and American outlets was generally indifferent, at best.

Romeo Dallaire once said that 'To properly mourn the dead [...] we need accountability, not blame.'[157] What is also required is a realisation that the United Kingdom and the United States may no longer find such crimes to be particularly shocking (especially when taking place in black Africa). A key conclusion resulting from the findings of this study therefore is that, for all the rhetoric to the contrary, genocide is simply not as important an issue within the Western world as most people would like to believe. As discussed in this chapter and the one which preceded it, the extent of news media coverage of genocide (regardless of its hugely destructive impact) is as dependent on established news values – and as susceptible to forms of framing – as virtually any other event.

Lamenting the overall lack of response to the Rwandan genocide, an American correspondent admitted bleakly at the time that 'the realisation that a holocaust, a genocide, is in progress in our own times and with our full knowledge diminishes us all,' and that the former excuse of 'not knowing' simply didn't apply.[158] That the genocide could be allowed to happen in the first place indeed diminished us all, but the fact that it continued to unfold with such little scrutiny from the Anglo–American media is a far more revealing development. Whilst other factors were, of course, important in explaining this lack of attention – not least that the genocide took place in a resource-poor, landlocked, obscure African country – it is still notable that such apocalyptic violence was unable to command the concentrated attention of the Anglo–American media for any length of time.

5

From Disbelief to Disinterest

The old newsroom expression may indeed affirm that 'if it bleeds, it leads' but, as the examples in this book demonstrate, this was not necessarily the case by the early 1990s.[1] Whilst coverage by the Anglo–American news media was forthcoming in the cases of Bosnia and Rwanda, the reporting of these instances of mass violence was regularly subject to forms of marginalisation through news frames of varying influence. Taking place half-a-century after the end of World War II – the first time in which the Western world had been properly exposed to such atrocities through the media – the reporting of Rwanda and Bosnia suggests that mass violence, in itself, is not a priority for the Western press. Instead, coverage was characterised at various times by: a lack of understanding of the dynamics of each conflict; a racist discourse which had its roots in established Western notions regarding the peoples of Africa and the Balkans; a general trend towards marginalising coverage of the violence itself in favour of reporting other developments, notably those involving Western actions or interests; and, ultimately, an indifference to the suffering which can be demonstrated by a number of quantitative and qualitative observations. Before offering theoretical comments on these trends though, it is important to first reiterate some of the key findings from this research.

Reporting Genocide

Following a 114-day analysis of newspaper coverage of both the Bosnian and Rwandan genocides, it is evident that the oft-repeated sentiment that these events were *ignored* by the Anglo–American press is an exaggeration. Though there *were* several instances in which the Rwandan genocide did not feature whatsoever in an edition of one of the Anglo–American titles chosen, this event nonetheless provoked a total of 1,222 articles in the period from 7 April to 29 July 1994. When combined with editorials, comment articles and letters, 'total reporting' of the Rwandan genocide equates to some 1,409 separate inclusions over the dates selected – an indication that this event did receive at least some limited attention from Western journalists, though it should also be remembered that many of these pieces were small in size and often relegated to poor placing within the publications in which they appeared. With regards to the Bosnian example, a total of 3,028 articles were published across the its comparable 114-day study, a number which rises to 4,048 when all other types of reporting are included. This contrast in overall press engagement, in that coverage of Bosnia outmatched Rwanda by a ratio of 2.87:1, is again further evidence that race and proximity are crucial determinants of Western press focus.

These quantitative observations do not, however, provide an entirely accurate reflection of the level of attention given to these two instances of genocide by the Anglo–American press. Upon closer analysis, a trend emerges in which the violence itself was only the main focus of the reporting in certain instances, being repeatedly superseded by other considerations. In the case of Bosnia, coverage of the actual violence unfolding generally held the focus of the Anglo–American press for only a few days at most before being replaced by reporting and discussion of diplomatic considerations or possible military engagement. This was seen to be particularly prevalent when outside involvement in the Balkans – such as potential responses from NATO or Russia – became a possibility, with the suffering of the victims themselves generally relegated to secondary importance. This was especially notable in the aftermath of the two Sarajevo artillery attacks discussed in Chapter 3 (in February 1994 and August 1995), and this trend was even replicated in the days and weeks following the now-infamous Srebrenica massacre, where diplomatic concerns were seen to quickly trump coverage of the horrific violence which provoked them.

A similar trend presents itself when Anglo–American reporting of the Rwandan genocide is analysed in depth. Though the violence in the central African state received something approaching consistent (though sparse) coverage throughout its duration, notable increases in press interest only appeared during those periods where the conflict was affecting, or being affected by, outside actors. The most notable examples of this dynamic came during the following periods: the evacuation of foreign nationals out of the country in early April; the French-led intervention in June; and the refugee crisis which peaked in late July. What these trends indicate then is that the violence which actually contributed to these events becoming recognised as 'genocide' was itself generally of secondary importance in determining levels of coverage.

Further to these observations was the fact that, in both case studies, the victims of the violence were often either caricatured according to some pre-existing stereotype or, in some cases, actually implicated in their own suffering. Though the genocidal violence in both Bosnia and Rwanda took place within a larger conflict – thus at times making the distinction between various forms of violence more difficult – in both cases it was abundantly clear that the majority of victims were civilians, most of whom were obviously not connected to the politics behind the violence afflicting them. Nonetheless, these conflicts, both of which had myriad complex reasons for their descent into mass violence, were often explained by way of some existing Western discourse regarding the regions in which they were taking place. In the reporting of the Bosnian conflict, a number of journalists constructed the various factions in the region as being as destructive as each other, despite the fact that Serb forces and their affiliates were responsible for the vast majority of war crimes in the region. Whilst this would sometimes take the form of calls for a greater degree of balance in Anglo–American reporting (due to a perceived pro-Muslim bias in some quarters), others would be more assertive in their claims, stating that it was actually the Serbs who were the main victims of mass violence. The most common 'explanation' for the conflict, however, was that it was somehow endemic to the region, with some commentators arguing that the violence which erupted in the early 1990s was simply the reawakening of ancient hatreds that had plagued the Balkans for centuries. Indeed, the notion that the inhabitants of Bosnia and the surrounding region were somehow destined to be in eternal conflict with one another was, in part, due to existing ideas of the Balkans themselves, a point which was emphasised by Mark Mazower when he stated that historically the term *the Balkans* was 'loaded with negative connotations – of violence, savagery, primitivism.'[2] This narrative, in explaining away such violence as being innate to the people of a region, was also seen in the reporting of the Rwandan genocide. Indeed, in many ways the reductionism of the press in explaining the violence in terms of 'ancient hatreds' and 'tribal savagery' was more pronounced and persistent in the 1994 genocide than was ever the case in Anglo–American reporting of the crisis in the Balkans. From the very first days of the carnage, the violence in Rwanda was framed as simply being the latest outbreak of anarchic tribal violence to afflict the African continent – a characterisation which undoubtedly seemed reasonable to a Western audience which was by the early 1990s all-too-accustomed to media depictions of destruction and upheaval in Africa. With Rwanda being largely unknown to those in West – journalists included – prior to 1994, it is perhaps unsurprising that the coverage of this catastrophe largely conformed to the same racialised discourse which had accompanied various other horrors affecting Africa, a continent which the media generally framed 'only with civil war, famine and AIDS' in mind.[3]

In both Bosnia and Rwanda, though probably more so in the latter, in a number of instances these beliefs were recycled by the press as a result of ignorance about the location in which the violence was unfolding. With little or no prior experience of the regions, journalists often relied on out-of-date, mistaken or decontextualised information. As a result, these 'myths' surrounding both the Balkans and Africa continued to appear, with varying degrees of persistence, throughout the duration of both conflicts. Of course, this reliance on caricaturing the victims was not simply a result of poor research or lack of knowledge. It is also likely that framing the causes of these events through reference to established racialised stereotypes was in some instances used as a deliberate means of dissuading potential outside intervention – with the notion that these 'savage' regions were afflicted by 'ancient' hatreds (thus rendering any involvement redundant in the long term) being the most persistently cited. Indeed, as Power notes, 'no genocide since the Holocaust has been completely black and white, and policymakers have been able to accentuate the grayness and moral ambiguity of each crisis.'[4] It should be noted, however, that in both cases there were, of course, occasional contributors to the Anglo–American press who attempted to question the dominant narratives being presented, but they were generally in the minority and therefore such framing proved difficult to challenge in any meaningful way.

Another observation which emerges clearly from this research is the fact that, in relation to Anglo–American reporting of genocidal events, overall body-counts do not determine the extent of coverage. Though smaller changes in numbers of casualties – such as a particularly serious shelling in Sarajevo – might be seen to rekindle limited interest from the press, there was little by way of increased media engagement when the death tolls became so large as to be abstract. The most obvious illustration for this comes from a direct comparison of press interest in Rwanda and Bosnia. The Rwandan genocide saw the deaths of some 800,000 people in just over three months, whilst the conflict in the Balkans witnessed around 100,000 killed in four years – meaning that the average monthly death toll in Rwanda was some 128 times that which was recorded in Bosnia. Nonetheless, Bosnia completely eclipsed Rwanda in terms of Anglo–American press coverage across any number of measures. Combined with other statistical and thematic observations presented here, this media trade-off is further evidence that, in terms of the Anglo–American news agenda, black lives do not matter. For each and every variable selected within this research, Bosnia received considerably more coverage than Rwanda over their respective 114-day samples. In addition to the aforementioned discrepancy between the number of news articles dedicated to each crisis (1,222 for Rwanda and 3,028 for Bosnia), there were also massive differences in terms of opinion content related to the respective conflicts. In terms of editorial coverage, those with a focus on Bosnia numbered 183 (77.2 per cent) over the 114-day analysis, a total which was more than three times the 54 (22.8 per cent) which were printed about Rwanda. An even greater difference in coverage was recorded in relation to comment pieces, with 383 (84.5 percent) concerning Bosnia being published to Rwanda's total of 70 (15.5 per cent). The greatest quantitative difference recorded, however, was in relation to the number of letters published over the respective periods analysed. Whilst 63 letters were published between 7 April and 29 July 1994 that directly concerned the conflict in Rwanda, this was dwarfed by the 454 letters printed in relation to Bosnia – a comparison which equates to a ratio of almost 7.5-to-1 in favour of the latter example. Listed together, these dramatic differences in coverage surely provide further evidence of the importance of race, at least in determining which victims of mass violence will hold the focus of the Western media.

These dynamics should not come as a huge surprise, given the well-established principle that the Anglo–American press tend to devote far more column inches to developments in regions which are constructed as 'culturally proximate' than they do for crises affecting the developing world. As Wolfgang Sofsky has put it, indignation has local limits of attention, and this was clearly illustrated by the notable differences in the press coverage of Bosnia and Rwanda; the former generated far more media attention than the latter – despite the fact that, in terms of sheer scale and ferocity, the Rwandan genocide was far more destructive.[5] A key reason for this, of course, was that the crisis in the Balkans was taking place mere hours from the heart of Europe and, as such, had the potential to pull the likes of NATO (and potentially Russia) into a wider conflict. Rwanda, on the other hand, was a landlocked African state which was of little interest to any Western power except France, and so as long as the genocide remained contained within its own borders it continued to suffer from a lack of media focus. Given the findings of this research then, Jacques Derrida's assertion that we 'do not count the dead in the same way from one corner of the globe to the other' appears accurate, and is entirely in keeping with dominant conceptions of news framing and news values presented in this research.[6]

This pattern was not, however, only recorded during a comparison between the examples of Bosnia and Rwanda. Upon closer analysis of the sources selected, it was discovered that this same trend – of death tolls providing little by way of indication towards levels of Anglo–American press interest in a given event – was also apparent *within* each conflict as well. In Rwanda, the refugee crisis which peaked in late July 1994 was seen to receive far more press attention, proportionally, than the genocide which had preceded it – despite the fact that the organised violence which had ravaged the country had claimed *at least* ten times as many victims as had disease and starvation in the camps of Goma. Coverage of the Bosnian genocide also followed this trend, with coverage from August 1992 (when the concentration camps were uncovered) seeing notably more articles produced within a 28-day period than was the case for the now-infamous massacre at the fallen safe haven of Srebrenica in July 1995. The predominance of reporting on Sarajevo – to the detriment of coverage of the wider and far more deadly campaign of ethnic cleansing affecting the more remote parts of the region – is another illustration of this Anglo–American trend in which magnitude of violence proved to have little bearing in relation to overall press interest.

All of this leads one to the conclusion that, by the early 1990s, genocide *in itself* was not considered to be as important an issue as years of prior Western rhetoric would suggest. Certainly, to quote Ian Kershaw, 'the liberal assumption that people will instinctively defend other human beings against mass slaughter seems at least questionable.'[7] As the analysis of Rwanda and Bosnia demonstrates, the victims of mass violence are generally of little importance to the Anglo–American press, particularly so when these victims are black. Though when describing the press response to both Bosnia and Rwanda it would be inaccurate to speak of these events being 'ignored', it remains the case that an in-depth study of a wide range of newspaper sources from the time indicates an overall lack of Western concern for such crimes. In particular, that the actual violence taking place in these case studies could be so often superseded or minimised by a range of secondary concerns indicates that the Anglo–American press, by the 1990s, did not consider crimes of a genocidal nature to be particularly newsworthy.

Violence in the Media

A phenomenon which helps to explain the reaction of the Anglo–American press to the violence in both Bosnia and Rwanda is a fundamental dynamic of the mass media age in which we live; a progressive process of desensitisation towards both violence, and human suffering in general. Reports and images that would have shocked the world in 1945 had, by the early 1990s, become simply another item amongst many in the Western news agenda.

Pass any newsstand in the country, or tune in to any news bulletin, and one is bound to be confronted with reports of some violent act occurring somewhere in the world. We take in this 'desensitizing horror' everyday, to the point where 'the excruciations of war have [...] devolved into a nightly banality,' and this has contributed to a situation whereby even the most extreme outbreaks of violence now fail to provoke any notable reaction.[8] Certainly, Elliot Cohen is correct when he states that 'the exhibition of sadism and slaughter does not automatically cause revulsion and rejection. On the contrary, it may make the forbidden and horrible seem familiar and customary.'[9]

For example, the evening news generally highlights *at least* three or four instances of human suffering every night – such as famine, civil war, terrorism and so on – which would mean that a regular news consumer could be exposed to more than 1,000 such stories every year. Combined with the increased realism within fictional depictions of war and violence – such as in film and television – it could certainly be argued that the Western world is now bombarded by images of violence, poverty and suffering.[10] This is a development which began in the 1960s, when the media began to be less conservative in what they presented to their audience. Films became more 'realistic' – meaning more graphic – and reporting of world events became less restricted. Perhaps the American coverage of the conflict in Vietnam is the most illustrative example of this, where the civilian population of the US was presented with stories and images which were more vivid than anything previously depicted.[11]

This barrage of atrocity, which has been fed to the West in past decades largely through the media, has also ensured that there is virtually *nothing* which is beyond human comprehension. An illustration of this change in the relative 'shock value' of mass violence can be seen in a comparison of the coverage of the liberation of the camps in 1945 and the reporting of the case studies from the 1990s. Whilst reporters in April and May 1945 were often at pains to emphasise that what they were reporting was indeed real – this being, predominantly, due to the fact that such crimes were at this point beyond the expectations of many – by the 1990s this had ceased to be necessary, since the knowledge of such atrocities was by then an established part of Western discourse. Essentially, mass violence no longer grips the imagination of the press in the way it once did, with the coverage of Bosnia and Rwanda providing sufficient evidence to support this observation.

Of course, this is in contrast to the manner in which genocide is depicted in a number of contemporary scholarly and non-scholarly accounts. That such killing defies the imagination, is beyond understanding, or that its 'sheer wrongness – remains uncircumscribable,' is a staple of Holocaust and genocide studies.[12] Indeed, one could make the argument that genocide, by its very nature, invokes hyperbole. However, it is conceivable that the very opposite is true. In the Anglo–American world, the problem is not that these crimes are *unimaginable* but rather that they are *all too imaginable*. After several decades of knowledge of the gas chambers, mass slaughter, nuclear annihilation and international terrorism – all of which have also been presented for the purposes of entertainment – the argument that humans cannot comprehend such atrocity simply does not stand up to scrutiny. In Bosnia, only particular instances of violence provoked attention from the press, and in Rwanda not even death tolls estimated to be in the hundreds of thousands could stir the media from its collective apathy. In a sense then, the Anglo–American world has indeed become 'emotionally anaesthetized' as a result of a greater familiarisation with such atrocious acts.[13]

It is sometimes argued that such horror 'seems to overload our powers of imagination and evaluation alike,' meaning that people do not react to these crimes because they cannot fully comprehend their magnitude.[14] On the contrary, however, most people (who generally only engage with such things through the media) see these atrocities and remain indifferent for the simple reason that they understand and *accept* that these things can happen. Essentially; violence can be envisioned all too vividly, to the point where its spectacle no longer has any shock value for the majority of those who witness it. Media reports of cruelty and barbarity are, apparently, something to which the Anglo–American public has become accustomed. This, it must be argued, is strongly influenced by depictions of such violence in the media. Without any prior knowledge of these atrocities, it is unlikely that people would be so callous when presented with them. This position, of course, can be substantiated by reference to the shocked response to similar crimes in 1945, from a generation which was still unaccustomed to being exposed to mass violence in such vivid terms.

It is not the case, of course, that there was a single date in the post-1945 era in which the Western world suddenly decided that genocide was simply not worthy of its proper attention. Rather, representations of this violence within the media became gradually more 'acceptable' – and this is something which is continuing even now. One could call this the 'gradualism of indifference' – a process which could be thought of as resulting from one of humanity's greatest assets: the ability to adapt. The reason that mankind has not been rendered extinct by any number of social and environmental threats is that virtually anything can become tolerable. Certainly, as Sofsky remarks, 'mankind has the disturbing ability to adapt to almost anything.'[15] So, whilst the Holocaust may well be 'an event that has ruptured our sense of what human nature is,' society has adapted in a way so as to not allow subsequent cases of genocide to be as psychologically impacting.[16] In *Anna Karenina*, Tolstoy states that 'there are no conditions of life which a man cannot get accustomed, especially if he sees them accepted by everyone around him' – and it is perfectly reasonable that this same process had occurred in relation to responding to genocide and mass violence by the 1990s. Whilst such atrocities may have been traumatic and shocking in 1945, by the 1990s they had become an accepted aspect of the human condition.[17] As a letter published only days before the 6 February 1994 mortar attack on the Markale marketplace asked, 'Have we really become desensitized to the murder and suffering of others?' The findings of this research certainly seem to provide evidence that this may be the case. Accepting this position, the final section of this conclusion will discuss one of the key catalysts of this trend – the growing centrality of the Holocaust within Western consciousness.[18]

The Holocaust in the Anglo–American World

As detailed in Chapter 2, by the early 1990s the Holocaust was a well-established phenomenon within Western culture. Particularly in the United States, the Holocaust – through a series of mass-culture representations – came to be one of the most recognised events of the twentieth century. Indeed, in a somewhat ironic twist of timing, the zenith of this process came in the midst of the crises in Bosnia and Rwanda, with the opening of the United States Holocaust Memorial Museum coinciding with the 1993 release of *Schindler's List*. With this in mind, Doneson's assertion that 'the Holocaust no longer stands outside of society, it has become an integral part of society' is a position which is hard to argue against.[19] In relation to one of the key findings of the empirical chapters of this book – that the Anglo–American press response to Bosnia and Rwanda was somewhat at odds with a by-then established Western commitment to the protection of human rights – the centrality of the Holocaust within Western culture has had an impact for myriad reasons. The first of these is that whilst the Holocaust undoubtedly had a massive influence in first making 'human rights' a matter for global concern (at least rhetorically), in doing so this ensured that the notion of *genocide* would forever be intrinsically linked to the form which it took under the Third Reich.

A critique which has therefore resulted from this – as has been argued several times – is that the Holocaust has now become the standard bearer for what genocide is. Certainly, as Susan Moeller states, 'the Holocaust is to a massacre as the assassination of Lincoln or JFK is to a murder.'[20] The major issue with this development is that, as the term 'genocide' is essentially synonymous with the Holocaust in most people's minds, this means that it is easy to dismiss anything which does not meet with the Holocaust standard. This is crucial when one considers that historical comparisons are an established means of making sense of a news story and, as a result, several subsequent instances of genocide have been automatically explained through reference to the Holocaust – for example, 'we haven't seen anything like this since the Nazis.'[21] Therefore, those instances which mirror the Holocaust, at least on an aesthetic level, are seen to gain some level of legitimacy and thus further coverage. Factors such as scale or organisation are little by way of a determinant, however, as evidenced by the relatively weak media response to the Rwandan genocide.

It may be therefore argued that the notably extensive press response to Bosnia in 1992 was primarily due to the cultural relevance of concentration camp iconography in Western society. In essence, representations of the Holocaust may have inadvertently made the Anglo–American world sensitive to only one certain form of genocide, to the detriment of those which do not fit into this 'Holocaust frame'. This particular 'frame' is that of trains, gas chambers and, most importantly, concentration camps. Described by Sofsky as 'the central institution of violence in modern persecution', the concentration camp has a distinct place in the history of twentieth-century atrocities; becoming something of a by-word for organised persecution and regularly used as an attention-grabbing slur by a variety of politically active groups.[22] The crucial dynamic of this, however, is that genocide has rarely, if ever, taken this form *since* the era of the Third Reich. Nonetheless, this particular method of persecution has become the defining example of what constitutes genocide – and one which the slaughter of Rwanda, for example, despite its rigorous organisation, thus failed to conform to on an aesthethic level.

This concept is also important in explaining the general press reaction to 1990s mass violence, as it is the Holocaust through which most lay people identify with what genocide is: evidence for which is seen in the comparatively large press response to the camp revelations of August 1992. Despite the fact that the likes of Omarska, whilst being undeniably brutal, were actually responsible for proportionally fewer deaths than the wider, slow-burning campaign of ethnic cleansing, it was the 'hook' of the concentration camps which dominated Anglo–American reporting of Bosnia. Patrick Cockburn of the *Independent* stated as much when, following the first revelations of the camps in eastern Bosnia, he asserted that: 'The symbol of real horror in the West is not feckless butchery by militia bands, but the systematic and organised liquidation of a population in death camps run like factories.'[23] In fact, in relation to total coverage of both Rwanda and Bosnia, this period from 1–28 August 1992 was seen to be by far the most publicised, particularly within British publications.

In considering how central the Holocaust is to modern media representations of genocide, it is important to recognise that it was the Holocaust that originally led to the construction of genocide as the ultimate crime. Yet in becoming the *ultimate example* of this same crime, this event has taken precedence over all other such incidents within media representations of genocidal violence. As a result of people in the West becoming more familiar with this specific example of genocide, they have inadvertently become indifferent to mass killing – with the exception of those few atrocities which could be framed as being similar to the Holocaust.

A related trend which can also result from 'Holocaust' and 'genocide' being regarded as synonymous is that this dynamic can inadvertently produce unhelpful comparisons. By throwing terms like 'Holocaust' at every case of genocide, one encourages the audience to relate the current crisis to a better-known historical example. However, linking something which is clearly not comparable in method or magnitude to the Holocaust, even if it is indeed genocidal in its implications, allows the audience to dismiss the comparison as illegitimate and, in doing so, weakens the impact of the contemporary example. In fact, William Shawcross made a similar point a decade before Bosnia and Rwanda, arguing that 'only when something can be compared, perhaps rightly, perhaps wrongly, but always plausibly, with the Holocaust will it assume truly disastrous proportions in our perceptions.'[24]

In terms of sheer scale, the Holocaust has assumed the mantle of the greatest crime in history – 'the emblematic horror against which all other horrors are measured.' Through popular representations – such as *Holocaust* or *Schindler's List* – and other forms of publicity, the Holocaust had by the 1990s emerged as 'the archetype and yardstick of evil.'[25] Raul Hilberg noted in the aftermath of the Holocaust that 'against this single occurrence, one would assess all other deeds' and there is evidence that this has been the case on several occasions.[26] This is a crucial consideration, as comparison to the Holocaust can render almost any tragedy as second-rate and it is certainly conceivable that this was the case during later instances of genocide. One of the best explanations of this process comes from Peter Novick, and deserves to be quoted in full:

> Apart from the Holocaust's alleged uniqueness, its extremity, which made it so potent a rhetorical weapon, also meant that compared to the Holocaust, anything else looked not so bad. The comparison, by raising the threshold of outrage, could easily desensitize. Certainly desensitization hadn't been the intention of those who have talked about the lessons of the Holocaust – quite the reverse. But there is a curious anomaly in how Americans have responded to mass death abroad. And that anomaly makes one wonder whether desensitization may, in fact, have been an unintended consequence of our making the Holocaust our central symbol of atrocity.[27]

Essentially, the Holocaust becoming so well-recognised in the Western world by the early 1990s had a secondary impact on how the citizens of Britain and America reacted to contemporary examples of mass violence. From the initial outburst of societal shock at the liberation of Nazi camps, through decades of representation and discussion in various forms of media, the Holocaust was by the 1990s intrinsically linked to the Western conceptualisation of genocide. In turn, although they were horrific in their own right, the dominance of the Holocaust in establishing a paradigm for what constituted genocide ensured that only certain aspects of the *violence* in Bosnia and Rwanda were reported in depth. Though the Anglo–American press did not *ignore* these respective crises, it remains the case that the violence itself was often marginalised to make way for other considerations – with the visceral shock and disbelief which accompanied the liberation of Belsen and Buchenwald not replicated in the media response to the mass violence in Bosnia and Rwanda.

Conclusion

As has been argued throughout this book, whilst genocide is regularly described as being the ultimate crime against humanity, it is less apparent that this same crime can, in itself, be expected to automatically provoke media attention simply by virtue of the suffering such violence causes. If this *were* the case, in that reporting of mass violence correlated with the relative severity of the incident, then the Rwandan genocide would be expected to have gained more coverage than the Bosnian conflict as a result of the former's much higher death toll. As was demonstrated in the preceding chapters, however, this was not the case, with certain established news values being seen to exert a far greater influence on levels of coverage than the quantitative scale of the violence. Two of the most important influences in this regard were proximity and race. In essence; (1) the well-established principle that events closer to a given media outlet are more likely to gain coverage than those further away; and (2) that victims of mass violence are less likely to receive extensive coverage if they are non-white. Quantitative analysis of Anglo–American press coverage of Bosnia and Rwanda provides further evidence of these trends; with British coverage of Bosnia seen to outmatch that of the geographically more distant United States, whilst the reporting of (European) Bosnia by both British and American newspapers was seen to dwarf that which was afforded (African) Rwanda. Further to this was the observation that the violence in each country was often of secondary importance within Anglo–American press coverage. These observations, taken together, illustrate how genocidal violence is not, in itself, seen as a priority for Western news media. Instead, instances of such violence are as susceptible to various social, cultural and economic influences as virtually any other type of story.

The manner in which these respective conflicts were framed – both in an overall sense and in relation to specific developments in each case – was also seen to have an impact on the intensity and general focus of coverage. In the Anglo–American coverage of both Bosnia and Rwanda, particularly in the earlier reporting of each conflict, the framing of these events was often influenced by a pre-existing Western discourse about the people of these respective regions. The most dominant frames in this regard tended to be a negative stereotyping of the inhabitants of Rwanda and Bosnia, with both conflicts being explained in terms of 'ancient ethnic hatreds' endemic to each region or the inherently violent tendencies of the people them-selves. The use of such framing thus frequently misrepresented the dynam-ics of these respective conflicts, and in turn helped to dissuade calls for intervention through the insinuation that little could be done in the long term.

Whilst the reporting on Bosnia and Rwanda can largely be explained via reference to dominant news values and the influence of news fram-ing, it is also argued in this book that Anglo–American coverage of these catastrophes can be cited as evidence of an overall lack of concern for genocidal mass violence. Though both Rwanda and Bosnia received some degree of coverage from the Anglo–American print media, a deeper analysis of these same press reports reveals that the violence itself (which, in both cases, constituted genocide) was often superseded by focus on other concerns. The mass violence of the 1990s in Bosnia and Rwanda was by no means ignored, as has been asserted by scholars in the past, but it remains the case that these events were generally afforded concen-trated coverage only in those instances where the violence was seen to be: (1) affecting, or being affected by, foreign nationals or other members of the international community; or (2) bearing a sufficient aesthetic resemblance to the Holocaust. Despite rhetorical assertions to the contrary, genocide may well be the crimes of crimes, but within the context of Anglo–American news coverage, it is certainly not the story of stories.

Speaking to the Stockholm International Forum on Preventing Genocide in January 2004, Kofi Annan lamented that he longed for 'the day when we can say with confidence that, confronted with a new Rwanda or a new Srebrenica, the world would respond effectively.'[28] Given the observations presented here regarding press responses to such violence, it appears that he may be waiting a considerable time. In a century where factors such as global warming, over-population and civil conflict will no doubt prove to be catalysts for further outbreaks of genocidal mass violence, it is likely that such occurrences will be met with the same general indifference as those cases which scarred the final decade of the last century.

Appendix

* Selected totals provided are for the respective 114-day date ranges for the studies of press coverage concerning Bosnia and Rwanda.

** For the *Daily Telegraph*, the *Guardian*, *The Times* and the *Independent*, statistics provided also include those from their Sunday equivalents.

Front Page Coverage	Bosnia	Rwanda
Daily Telegraph	89	10
Guardian	92	15
The Times	96	17
Independent	102	24
Los Angeles Times	209	28
Washington Post	103	40
Chicago Tribune	59	23
New York Times	103	47
Total	**853**	**204**

Editorial Coverage	Bosnia	Rwanda
Daily Telegraph	28	4
Guardian	29	8
The Times	31	7
Independent	17	7
Los Angeles Times	12	7
Washington Post	24	8
Chicago Tribune	21	5
New York Times	21	8
Total	**183**	**54**

Comment Articles	Bosnia	Rwanda
Daily Telegraph	34	3
Guardian	68	14
The Times	61	5
Independent	42	11

Comment Articles	Bosnia	Rwanda
Los Angeles Times	41	12
Washington Post	52	11
Chicago Tribune	29	7
New York Times	56	7
Total	**383**	**70**

News Article Coverage of Bosnia	(*114)	Aug '92	Feb '94	Jul '95	Sep '95
Daily Telegraph	**427**	123	118	100	86
Guardian	**444**	149	96	116	83
The Times	**482**	140	115	124	103
Independent	**466**	126	94	135	111
Los Angeles Times	**246**	62	64	63	57
Washington Post	**344**	89	106	76	73
Chicago Tribune	**238**	68	51	57	62
New York Times	**381**	100	105	93	83
Total	**3028**	**857**	**749**	**764**	**658**

News Article Coverage of Rwanda	(*114)	Apr '94	May '94	Jun '94	Jul '94
Daily Telegraph	**144**	28	35	28	53
Guardian	**161**	32	39	34	56
The Times	**136**	27	41	25	43
Independent	**151**	29	42	40	40
Los Angeles Times	**122**	27	37	24	34
Washington Post	**155**	37	32	34	52
Chicago Tribune	**165**	24	46	42	53
New York Times	**188**	34	42	43	69
Total	**1222**	**238**	**314**	**270**	**400**

Notes

Chapter 1   The Crime of Crimes?

1. William D. Rubinstein, *Genocide: A History* (Harlow: Pearson Education Limited, 2004), p. 1.
2. Berel Lang, *Post-Holocaust: Interpretation, Misinterpretation and the Claims of History* (Bloomington: Indiana University Press, 2005), p. 145.
3. Frank Chalk, 'Genocide in the 20th century: Definitions of genocide and their implications for prediction and prevention', *Holocaust and Genocide Studies* 4/2 (1989), p. 15.
4. Barbie Zelizer, *Remembering to Forget: Holocaust Memory Through the Camera's Eye* (Chicago: University of Chicago Press, 1998), p. 203.
5. Yehudith Auerbach & Yaeli Bloch-Elkon, 'Media framing and foreign policy: The elite press vis-a-vis US policy in Bosnia, 1992–95', *Journal of Peace Research* 42/1 (2005), p. 85; Myers et al., 'The inscription of difference: News coverage of the conflicts in Bosnia and Rwanda', *Political Geography* 15/1 (1996), p. 26; Robert Entman, *Projections of Power: Framing News, Public Opinion, and U.S. Foreign Policy* (Chicago: University of Chicago Press, 2004), p. 77.
6. Karen S. Johnson-Cartee, *News Narratives and News Framing: Constructing Political Reality* (Oxford: Rowman and Littlefield, 2005), p.231.
7. Peter Shiras, 'Big problem, small print: A guide to the complexity of humanitarian emergencies and the media', in R.I. Rotberg & T.G. Weiss (eds), *From Massacres to Genocide: The Media, Public Policy and Humanitarian Crisis* (Washington, DC: The Brookings Institution, 1996), p. 97; Brian McNair, *Journalism and Democracy: An Evaluation of the Political Public Sphere* (London: Routledge, 2000), p. 16.
8. For example, see: Alan J. Kuperman, *The Limits of Humanitarian Intervention: Genocide in Rwanda* (Washington, DC: Brookings, 2001); Myers et al., 'The inscription of difference'; Auerbach & Bloch-Elkon, 'Media framing'.
9. Samantha Power, *'A Problem From Hell': America and the Age of Genocide* (London: Flamingo, 2003), p. xvi.

Chapter 2   Bringing Darkness to Light

1. See: Daniel Dayan & Elihu Katz, *Media Events: The Live Broadcasting of History* (London: Harvard University Press, 1992).

2. Samantha Power, *'A Problem From Hell': America and the Age of Genocide* (London: Flamingo, 2003), p. 47.
3. Cited in: Antony Kushner, 'Ambivalence or Antisemitism?: Christian attitudes and responses in Britain to the crisis of European Jewry during the second world war', *Holocaust and Genocide Studies* 5/2 (1990), p. 177.
4. Robert H. Abzug, *Inside the Vicious Heart: Americans and the Liberation of Nazi Concentration Camps* (New York: Oxford University Press, 1987), p. 44.
5. Laurel Leff, *Buried by The Times: The Holocaust and America's Most Important Newspaper* (New York: Cambridge University Press, 2005), p. 296.
6. Cited in: Ben Shephard, *After Daybreak: The Liberation of Belsen, 1945* (London: Pimlico, 2006), p. 91.
7. Norman G. Finkelstein, *The Holocaust Industry: Reflections on the Exploitation of Jewish Suffering*, 2nd edition (London: Verso, 2003), p. 125.
8. Express Staff Reporter, 'M.P.s brought evidence – Frau Koch's lampshade', *Daily Express*, 28 April 1945, p. 3.
9. Harold Marcuse, *Legacies of Dachau: The Uses and Abuses of a Concentration Camp, 1933–2001* (Cambridge: Cambridge University Press, 2001), p. 49.
10. Barbie Zelizer, *Remembering to Forget: Holocaust Memory Through the Camera's Eye* (Chicago: The University of Chicago Press, 1998), p. 63; David Hackett (translation), *The Buchenwald Report* (Colorado: Westview Press, 1995), pp. 317–34.
11. Tim Cole, *Selling the Holocaust: From Auschwitz to Schindler: How History is Bought, Packaged and Sold* (New York: Routledge, 2000), p. 125.
12. Martin Gilbert, *The Holocaust: The Jewish Tragedy* (London: Fontana Press, 1987), p. 805.
13. Reilly, *Belsen: The Liberation*, p. 11.
14. Ibid., p. 22; Paul Kemp, 'The British army and the liberation of Bergen-Belsen, April 1945', in Jo Reilly et al. (eds), *Belsen in History and Memory* (London: Frank Cass, 1997), p. 137.
15. BBC Radio 4, 'The archive hour: Images of Belsen', recorded 14 May 2000 – Imperial War Museum sound files.
16. Kemp, 'The British army', p. 140; Shephard, *After Daybreak*, p. 4.
17. Abzug, *Inside the Vicious Heart*, p. 80.
18. J.L.Garvin, 'How Nazi Germany has been barbarised: Scientific satanism and world's revolt', *Daily Telegraph*, 26 April 1945.
19. Jean-Claude Favez, *The Red Cross and the Holocaust*, edited and translated by John and Beryl Fletcher (Cambridge: Cambridge University Press, 1999), p. 251; Marcuse, *Legacies*, p. 48; Hitchcock, *Liberation*, p. 294; Shephard, *After Daybreak*, p. 15.
20. Reilly, *Belsen: The Liberation*, p. 17.

21. Richard Breitman, *Official Secrets: What the Nazis Planned; What the British and Americans Knew* (London: Penguin Books), p. 161.

22. Cited in: Bernd Wegner, 'The ideology of self-destruction: Hitler and the choreography of defeat', *German Historical Institute*, London Bulletin 26/2 (2004), p. 28; The self-destructive nature of Nazism is also discussed in: Laurence Rees, *The Nazis: A Warning from History* (London: BBC Books, 2005), p. 357.

23. Wolfgang Sofsky, *Violence: Terrorism, Genocide, War*, translated by Anthea Bell (London: Granta Books, 2003), p. 232; See also: Reilly, *Belsen: The Liberation*, p. 76.

24. Combined American Press Dispatch, 'Congressmen plan to see more camps', *New York Times*, 27 April 1945, p. 1; Zelizer, *Remembering to Forget*, p. 64.

25. Lawrence Baron, 'The Holocaust and American public memory, 1945–1960', *Holocaust and Genocide Studies*, 17/1 (2003), p. 64.

26. Tony Kushner, *The Holocaust and the Liberal Imagination: A Social and Cultural History* (Oxford: Blackwell, 1994), p. 206.

27. Leff, *Buried by The Times*, p. 301.

28. Edgar Ainsworth, 'Victim and prisoner', *Picture Post* 27, 22 September 1945, p. 13.

29. Reilly, *Belsen: The Liberation*, p. 56.

30. Don Whitehead, 'Legislators See horrors in Nazi camp', *Washington Post*, 23 April 1945, p. 1; 'British M.P.s at Buchenwald watch a scene too terrible to print', *Daily Express*, 24 April 1945, p. 4.

31. Special Correspondent, 'Woman M.P.'s 3 hours of tears', *Daily Mirror*, 23 April 1945, p. 4; Cable, 'Buchenwald tour shocking to M.P.'s', *New York Times*, 23 April 1945, p. 6; U.P., 'Editors inspect Buchenwald', *New York Times*, 26 April 1945.

32. Combined American Press Dispatch, 'Congressmen plan to see more camps', *New York Times*, 27 April 1945.

33. Christopher Buckley, 'German's reaction to camp horrors', *The Scotsman*, 26 April 1945, p. 5.

34. U.P., 'Buchenwald "factory" for extermination', *Washington Post*, 29 April 1945, p. 8.

35. Zelizer, *Remembering to Forget*, p. 85; The breakdown of language in representations of the Holocaust is not restricted to journalism – see: John Filstiner, *Paul Celan: Poet, Survivor, Jew* (New Haven: Yale University Press, 2001); Aspects of this concept, especially the 'Humane Literacy' research of George Steiner, are also discussed in: Robert Black, 'Looking back at Mr. spectator, given Srebrenica: A tail-piece', *Media History* 14/3 (2008), p. 373.

36. This was commented upon in the following: Lord Addison, M.P., 'Europe's problem: What M.P.s say of the Nazi horror camps', *Picture Post* 27/6, 27 May 1945, p. 25.

37. Zelizer, *Remembering to Forget*, p. 8.
38. Reilly, *Belsen: The Liberation*, p. 61.
39. 'Horror camp pictures', *Daily Express*, 30 April 1945, p. 3.
40. Richard Dimbleby at Belsen, 15 April 1945 – Imperial War Museum sound files (17714); David Cesarani, 'Great Britain', in David S. Wyman (ed.), *The World Reacts to the Holocaust* (Baltimore: The John Hopkins, 1996), p. 610.
41. B.B.B., 'Didn't everyone know?', *Daily Mirror*, 17 April 1945, p. 2; see also: Reilly, *Belsen: The Liberation*, pp. 56–7.
42. Letter from Howard Smith, 'Film as evidence', *History Workshop* 3 (1977), pp. 195–7.
43. *Daily Mirror* Reporter, '"Show horror films to Huns here" demand', *Daily Mirror*, 30 April 1945, p. 5.
44. Raw footage from a variety of camps can be accessed at the Imperial War Museum, London. The following are some of the more graphic examples: IWM Film No: A70 304/03 P 3 A 35; IWM Film A 70 304/04-06 P 3 A35; IWM Film MGH 3349 P 2 A 35.
45. Toby Haggith, 'Filming the liberation of Bergen-Belsen', in Toby Haggith and Joanna Newman (eds), *Holocaust and the Moving Image: Representations in Film and Television since 1933* (London: Wallflower Press, 2005), pp. 33; Reilly, *Belsen: The Liberation*, p. 28.
46. 'Film arrangements for next week', *The Scotsman*, 28 April 1945, p. 4.
47. Judith E. Doneson, 'The use of film in teaching about the Holocaust', in: Gideon Shimoni (ed.), *The Holocaust in University Teaching* (Oxford: Pergamon Press, 1991), p. 19; On Hitchcock film, see: http://www.telegraph.co.uk/news/uknews/11368569/Alfred-Hitchcock-holocaust-film-to-go-on-general-release-70-years-after-suppression.html (accessed 27 January 2015).
48. 'To let you see', *Daily Mirror*, 28 April 1945, p. 4; 'Belsen burial', *Daily Mirror*, 21 April 1945, p. 2.
49. 'The news-reels: Belsen and Buchenwald', *The Times*, 1 May 1945, p. 8; see also: Lead Article, 'Buchenwald report', *The Scotsman*, 28 April 1945, p. 4.
50. Cited in: Nicholas Pronay, Imperial War Museum sound files (19573); Reilly, *Belsen: The Liberation*, p. 61.
51. B.B.B., 'In the sand', *The Times*, 30 May 1945, p. 2; Associated Press, 'Soldiers insist civilians view atrocity film', *Washington Post*, 21 April 1945, p. 2.
52. Reilly, *Belsen: The Liberation*, p. 61.
53. Hitchcock, *Liberation: The Bitter Road*, pp. 299–303.
54. Don Whitehead, 'Legislators see horrors in Nazi camp', *Washington Post*, 23 April 1945, p. 1; William Frye, 'Eyes of breathing cadavers reflect grotesque flicker of hope in Nazi-made hell', *Washington Post*, 21 April 1945, p. 1; see also: Gene Currivan, 'German civilians view Nazi horrors', *New York Times*, 18 April 1945, p. 8.

55. Leff, *Buried by The Times*, p. 308.
56. Power, *'A Problem From Hell'*, p. 42.
57. Lead Article, 'Barbarism vs. civilization', *New York Times*, 25 April 1945, p. 22.
58. For example, see: 'The shackled monster of Belsen', *Daily Express*, 21 April 1945, p. 1; 'Mad doctor of Belsen', *Daily Mirror*, 28 April 1945, p. 4.
59. Reilly, *Belsen: The Liberation*, pp. 50–60; Antoine Capet, 'The liberation of the Bergen-Belsen camp as seen by some British official war artists in 1945', in Suzanne Bardgett & David Cesarani (eds), *Belsen 1945: New Historical Perspectives* (London: Vallentine Mitchell, 2006), p. 174; Kushner, *The Holocaust and the Liberal Imagination*, p. 211.
60. UNIDENTIFIED (Male), Mass Observation Diary Entry, 19 April 1945.
61. Leo Kuper, *Genocide: Its Political Use in the Twentieth Century* (London: Yale University Press, 1981), p. 48.
62. Letter from Mrs Rose Spencer, 'All these horrors must be known', *Daily Mirror*, 23 April 1945, p. 2.
63. Lead Article, 'The victims', *The Times*, 20 April 1945, p. 5; Other sources have noted the great psychological impact felt on both sides of the Atlantic – see: Reilly, *Belsen: The Liberation*, p. 55; Kushner, *The Holocaust and the Liberal Imagination*, p. 212; Cited in: Haggith, 'Filming the liberation', p. 33.
64. From Robert Burns, 'Man Was Made to Mourn', in: *The Complete Poems and Songs of Robert Burns* (New Lanark: Geddes & Grosset, 2002), p. 43.
65. Shephard, *After Daybreak*, p. 4.
66. Albert S. Lindemann, *Anti-Semitism Before the Holocaust* (Essex: Pearson Education Limited, 2000), p. 57.
67. Niall Ferguson, *War of the World: History's Age of Hatred* (London: Penguin, 2006), p. 235.
68. Letter from Margery Annan Bryce, 'German atrocities', *The Times*, 27 April 1945, p. 5.
69. Lord Denham was quoted as saying that 'every single German was responsible for conditions in these camps' – a view which was expressed by others in government. For example, see: 'Parliament: The German defeat', *The Times*, 2 May 1945, p. 8.
70. Letter from W.B. Moonte, 'Nazi crimes', *The Scotsman*, 26 April 1945, p. 4; The assertion that English-speaking peoples could not be guilty of similar crimes was also expressed by others: Sir Henry Morris-Jones, M.P., 'Europe's problem: What M.P.s say of the Nazi horror camps', *Picture Post* 27/6, 12 May 1945, p. 25; 'German atrocities', Mass Observation (2248), 5 May 1945, p. 9.
71. The idea that the German people had received the government they deserved was also voiced. See: Letter from Comiston, 'German crimes', *The Scotsman*, 26 April 1945, p. 4.

72. Rex Bloomstein, 'Human rights: does anyone care?', in Haggith & Newman, *Holocaust and the moving image*, p. 261; David Cesarani, *Eichmann: His Life and Crimes* (London: Vintage, 2005), p. 17.

73. B.B.B., 'Monuments of shame', *Daily Mirror*, 20 April 1945, p. 2.

74. Cited in: Lead Article, 'German horrors', *Washington Post*, 23 April 1945.

75. Letter from T.H. Minshall, 'Germany and the camps', *The Times*, 24 April 1945, p. 5.

76. Michael Burleigh, *The Third Reich: A New History* (London: Pan MacMillan, 2001), p. 784.

77. Susan Sontag, *Regarding the Pain of Others* (London: Penguin Books, 2003), p. 99; Kushner, *The Holocaust and the Liberal Imagination*, p. 209.

78. Eugen Kogon & R.A. Gutman, 'Hitler's concentration camps: An examination of conscience', *The Review of Politics* 9/1 (January 1947), p. 38.

79. Charles E. Egan, 'All Reich to see camp atrocities', *New York Times*, 24 April 1945, p. 6; Lead Article, 'German crimes', *The Scotsman*, 19 April 1945, p. 4.

80. 'Belsen burial', *Daily Mirror*, 21 April 1945, p. 2; Rev. Fr. Edmund Swift, S.J. (R.C. Chaplain to 81 British General Hospital), *Indelible Memories of Belsen*, p. 28.

81. Reilly, *Belsen: The Liberation*, p. 69.

82. *Daily Mirror* Reporter, 'Show horror films to Huns here demand', *Daily Mirror*, 30 April 1945, p. 5; Gruson, 'British anger deep', p. 3.

83. U.P. 'War crimes group to inspect camps', *New York Times*, 25 April 1945, p. 6.

84. Julius Ochs Adler, 'Buchenwald worse than battlefield', *New York Times*, 28 April 1945, p. 6; A selection of such statements are also provided in: Reilly, *Belsen: The Liberation*, p. 68–9.

85. Correspondent, 'Congressman and Nazi command', *The Times*, 24 May 1945, p. 3.

86. George Gallup, 'U.S. public favours punishing minor Nazis for war crimes', *Washington Post*, 27 April 1945, p. 12.

87. It may also be argued that the subsequent hardening of postwar Anglo–American policy, at least in regards to the weakening of Germany by various means, was not, of course, a knee-jerk reaction to the horrific revelations from the camps. Given that Germany was now viewed as being responsible for two devastating conflicts in Europe, the atrocities discovered in 1945 may have simply provided a stronger argument for those who, for months beforehand, had been advocating such punitive policies against Germany. See: John L. Chase, 'The development of the Morgenthau plan through the Quebec conference', *The Journal of Politics* 16/2 (1954), pp. 325–59.

88. By Wireless to *New York Times*, 'British confirm worst details', *New York Times*, 28 April 1945, p. 6; Words of the Archbishop of Canterbury, Dr Fischer, cited in: 'Parliament: The German defeat', *The Times*, 2 May 1945, p. 8.

89. Eve Garrard & Geoffrey Scarre, 'Introduction', in Eve Garrard & Geoffrey Scarre (eds), *Moral philosophy and the Holocaust* (Aldershot: Ashgate Publishing Limited, 2003), p. x.

90. Abzug, *Inside the Vicious Heart*, p. 128; Laurence Rees, *Auschwitz: The Nazis and the Final Solution* (London: BBC Books, 2005), p. 338; Laurence Wilkinson, 'British cowed prison guards with a glance', *Daily Express*, 4 May 1945, p. 3.

91. Abzug, *Inside the Vicious Heart*, p. 30.

92. Associated Press Wire Photo, 'Long rows of German victims at Belsen await burial', *Washington Post*, 29 April 1945, p. 8; Sydney Gruson, 'British anger deep at atrocity proof', *New York Times*, 20 April 1945, p. 3; Bertrand Russell, 'Whose guilt? The problem of cruelty', *Picture Post* 27/10, 16 May 1945, p. 12.

93. Kushner, *The Holocaust and the Liberal Imagination*, p. 211.

94. 'M.P.s Saw horrors', *The Scotsman*, 23 April 1945, p. 5.

95. William Frye, 'Eyes of breathing cadavers', p. 1; See also: James Wellard, 'Horror camp slaves terrify Germans', *Daily Express*, 24 April 1945, p. 1.

96. 'British troops, sick with fury, drive SS to bury victims', *Daily Mirror*, 21 April 1945, p. 1.

97. Cited in: Shephard, *After Daybreak*, p. 43; Letter home from Kathleen J. Elvidge, printed in: 'Serving at Belsen: South Kirkby woman in horror camp', *Daily Express*, 9 June 1945; See also: Anthony Mann, 'R.A.M.C. brigadier on Belsen scenes: Worse than anything seen in war', *The Scotsman*, 19 September 1945, p. 5.

98. Leff, *Buried by The Times*, p. 315; Zelizer, *Remembering to Forget*, p. 82.

99. Zelizer, *Remembering to Forget*, p. 82–3.

100. Paul Bartrop, 'The relationship between war and genocide in the twentieth century: a consideration', *Journal of Genocide Research* 4/4 (2002), p. 523.

101. Power, *'A Problem From Hell'*, p. 9; P. Lochner, *What About Germany?* (New York: Dodd, Mead & Co, 1942), p. 2; Peter Balakian, *The Burning Tigris: A History of the Armenian Genocide* (London: Pimlico, 2005), p. xiii.

102. One notable publication which did detail the atrocities from the Armenian case was the Bryce-Toynbee report (1916), though it should be noted that the authors characterised much of the Armenian suffering as part of a process of 'deportation.' See: James Bryce & Arnold J. Toynbee (eds), *The Treatment of Armenians in the Ottoman Empire, 1915–1916: Documents Presented to Viscount Grey of Falloden* (London: Gomidas Institute, 2005), pp. 626–35.

103. Breitman, *Official Secrets*, p. 104.

104. Abzug, *Inside the Vicious Heart*, p. 4; For a contemporary description, see: Letter from K. Alexander, 'Germany and the camps', *The Times*, 26 April 1945,

p. 5; Laurence Rees, *Auschwitz: The Nazis and the Final Solution* (London: BBC Books, 2005), p. 30.

105. Leff, *Buried by The Times*, p. 309.

106. Cited in: Rubinstein, *Genocide*, p. 155.

107. Lead Article, 'The victims', *The Times*, 20 April 1945, p. 5.

108. Samantha Power, 'Raising the cost of genocide', in Nicolaus Mills & Kira Brunner (eds), *The New Killing Fields: Massacre and the Politics of Intervention* (New York: Basic Books, 2003), p. 253.

109. Mark Mazower, *Dark Continent: Europe's Twentieth Century* (London: Penguin Books, 1999), p. 170.

110. Zelizer, *Remembering to Forget*, p. 30.

111. A.J.P. Taylor, cited in: David S. Wyman, *The Abandonment of the Jews: America and the Holocaust, 1941–1945* (New York: Pantheon Books, 1984), p. 27; This is not to say, however, that other German atrocities were not committed. Horne & Kramer's study reveals details of a number of such atrocities, whilst proposing that the 'Allied propaganda' argument – which ultimately minimised the degree of Anglo–American awareness of the afore-mentioned German war crimes – became firmly entrenched in the interwar years. See: John H. Horne & Alan Kramer, *German Atrocities 1914: A History of Denial* (London: Yale University Press, 2002), pp. 366–418.

112. Breitman, *Official Secrets*, p. 104; see also: Reilly, *Belsen*, p. 63; Leff, *Buried by The Times*, p. 6.

113. Leslie Mitchell, cited in: Toby Haggith, 'British relief teams in Belsen concentration camp: Emergency relief and the perception of survivors', in Bardgett & Cesarani, *Belsen 1945*, p. 110.

114. Zelizer, *Remembering to Forget*, p. 143.

115. 'The news-reels: Belsen and Buchenwald', *The Times*, 1 May 1945, p. 8; see also: Letter from A. Guy Bettany, 'The parliamentary delegation', *The Times*, 21 April 1945, p. 5; Cable, "Buchenwald tour shocking to M.P.s', *New York Times*, 23 April 1945, p. 6.

116. Martin Gilbert, *The Holocaust: The Jewish Tragedy* (London: Fontana Press, 1987), p. 826.

117. It should be noted, however, that World War II was of course rendered for cinematic representation after the war; though the majority of the most popular releases had more of a triumphalist tone, rather than any serious reckoning with German war crimes. For example, see: *The Colditz Story* (1955; Guy Hamilton); *Ice Cold in Alex* (1958; J. Lee Thompson); *The Dambusters* (1955; Michael Anderson).

118. Deborah E. Lipstadt, 'America and the memory of the Holocaust, 1950–1956', *Modern Judaism* 16/3 (1996), p. 197. Quote is from: Marouf Hasian Jr, 'Anne Frank, Bergen-Belsen, and the polysemic nature of Holocaust memories',

Rhetoric & Public Affairs 4/3 (2001), p. 358; see also: Lawrence James, *Warrior Race: A History of the British at War* (London: Abacus, 2002), p. 700; Alan Mintz, *Popular Culture and the Shaping of Holocaust Memory in America* (Seattle: University of Washington Press, 2001), p. 6.

119. Ilan Avisar, *Screening the Holocaust: Cinema's images of the unimaginable* (Indianapolis: Indiana University Press, 1988), p. 105; Lipstadt, 'America and the memory', p. 198.

120. Lawrence Baron, 'The Holocaust and American public memory, 1945–1960', *Holocaust and Genocide Studies* 17/1 (2003), p. 63.

121. Peter Novick, *The Holocaust in American Life* (New York: Mariner Books, 2000), p. 110.

122. Daniel Levy & Natan Sznaider, *The Holocaust and Memory in the Global Age* (Philadelphia: Temple University Press, 2006), pp. 87–94.

123. Wulf Kansteiner, 'Testing the limits of trauma: the long-term psychological effects of the Holocaust on individuals and collectives', *History of the Human Sciences* 17/2–3 (2004), p. 99; Novick, *The Holocaust in American Life*, p. 83.

124. Joanne Reilly, *Belsen: The Liberation of a Concentration Camp* (London: Routledge, 1998), p. 77.

125. Raphael Lemkin, *Axis Rule in Occupied Europe: Laws of Occupation, Analysis of Government, Proposals for Peace* (Washington, DC: Carnegie Endowment for International Peace, 1944).

126. Linda Melvern, 'Rwanda and Darfur: The media and the security council', *International Relations* 20/1 (2006), p. 93. See also: Levy & Sznaider, *The Holocaust and Memory*, p. 193.

127. For example: 'Soviets opposition to human rights charter – genocide outlawed', *The Scotsman*, 10 December 1948, p. 5.

128. Jeffrey Shandler, 'Aliens in the wasteland: American encounters with the Holocaust on 1960s television', in Hilene Flanzbaum, *The Americanization of the Holocaust* (London: The John Hopkins University Press, 1999), p. 34. See also: David Cesarani, *Eichmann: His Life and Crimes* (London: Vintage, 2005), p. 335; Lipstadt, 'America and the memory', p. 196.

129. These titles, and others, are discussed in the following: Baron, 'The Holocaust and American', p. 69; Tony Kushner, *The Holocaust and the Liberal Imagination: A Social and Cultural History* (Oxford: Blackwell, 1994), p. 242.

130. Lipstadt, 'America and the Memory', p. 204.

131. Levy & Sznaider, *The Holocaust and Memory*, p. 59.

132. Kushner, *The Holocaust and the Liberal*, p. 5; Judith E. Doneson, 'The American history of Anne Frank's diary', *Holocaust and Genocide Studies* 2/1 (1987), p. 150; Mintz, *Popular Culture*, p. 17; Baron, 'The Holocaust and American public', p. 77.

133. Quoted in: Hasian Jr, 'Anne Frank, Bergen-Belsen', p. 349.
134. Yehuda Bauer, cited in: Tim Cole, *Selling the Holocaust: From Auschwitz to Schindler, How History is Bought, Packaged and Sold* (New York: Routledge, 2000), p. 46.
135. Judith E. Doneson, *The Holocaust in American Film* (New York: Syracuse University Press, 2002), p. 68; Cole, *Selling the Holocaust*, p. 30; Alvin H. Rosenfeld, 'Popularization and memory: The case of Anne Frank', in Peter Hayes (ed.), *Lessons and Legacies: The Meaning of the Holocaust in a Changing World* (Illinois: Northwestern Press, 1991), p. 254; Novick, *The Holocaust in American Life*, p. 117.
136. Cole, *Selling the Holocaust*, p. 29; Novick, *The Holocaust in American Life*, p. 117; Doneson, 'The American history', p. 154; http://www.imdb.com/title/tt0052738/awards – accessed 19 March, 2012.
137. Rosenfeld, 'Popularization and Memory', p. 248.
138. Lipstadt, *Denying the Holocaust: The Growing Assault on Truth and Memory* (London: Penguin, 1993), p. 230; Lawrence Baron, 'Not in Kansas anymore: Holocaust films for children', *The Lion and the Unicorn* 27 (2003), p. 395; Cole, *Selling the Holocaust*, p. 38.
139. Cole, *Selling the Holocaust*, p. 23; Rosenfeld, 'Popularization and memory', p. 244.
140. Rosenfeld, 'Popularization and memory', p. 245.
141. Cesarani, *Eichmann*, p. 242; Cole, *Selling the Holocaust*, p. 47.
142. Novick, *The Holocaust in American Life*, p. 129; Norman G. Finkelstein, *The Holocaust Industry: Reflections on the Exploitation of Jewish Suffering*, 2nd edition (London: Verso, 2003), p. 19.
143. Cesarani, *Eichmann*, p. 3; Doneson, *The Holocaust in American Film*, p. 157.
144. Niall Ferguson, *The War of the World: History's Age of Hatred* (London: Penguin Books, 2006), p. 225; Robert Braun, 'The Holocaust and problems of historical representations', *History and Theory* 33/2 (1994), p. 183.
145. Trudy Gold, 'An overview of Hollywood cinema's treatment of the Holocaust', in Toby Haggith & Joanna Neman (eds), *Holocaust and the moving Image: Representations in film and television since 1933* (London: Wallflower Press, 2005), p. 194.
146. Cole, *Selling the Holocaust*, p. 60; Mintz, *Popular Culture*, p. 11.
147. Michael R. Marrus, *The Holocaust in History* (Toronto: Key Porter Books, 2000), p. 5; Kushner, *The Holocaust and the Liberal*, p. 13; Mintz, *Popular Culture*, p. 11.
148. Cole, *Selling the Holocaust*, p. 67; Cesarani, *Eichmann*, pp. 254–5.
149. Shandler, 'Aliens in the wasteland', p. 34; Cesarani, *Eichmann*, p. 254.
150. Lipstadt, 'America and the memory', p. 205; Kushner, *The Holocaust and the Liberal*, p. 248.

151. Cesarani, *Eichmann*, p. 268.
152. Cole, *Selling the Holocaust*, p. 68; Cesarani, *Eichmann*, p. 72.
153. Levy & Sznaider, *The Holocaust and Memory*, p. 42; Berel Lang, *Post-Holocaust: Misinterpretation and the Claims of History* (Bloomington: Indiana University Press, 2005), p. 48; Cesarani, *Eichmann*, p. 325; Philip Zimbardo, *The Lucifer Effect: How Good People Turn Evil* (London: Rider, 2007), p. 288.
154. Cole, *Selling the Holocaust*, p. 64.
155. Kushner, *The Holocaust and the Liberal*, p. 3.
156. Samantha Power, 'To suffer by comparison?', *Daedalus* 128/2 (1999), p. 40; Lang, *Post-Holocaust*, p. 101; Samantha Power, 'A Problem From Hell': *America and the Age of Genocide* (London: Flamingo, 2003), p. 73; Cesarani, *Eichmann*, p. 336; Levy & Sznaider, *The Holocaust and Memory*, p. 109.
157. Mintz, *Popular Culture*, p. 12.
158. Power, 'A Problem From Hell', p. 73.
159. Levy & Sznaider, *The Holocaust and Memory*, p. 116; Henry Greenspan, 'Imagining survivors: Testimony and the rise of Holocaust consciousness', in Helene Flanzbaum (ed.), *The Americanization of the Holocaust* (London: The John Hopkins University Press, 1999), p. 57.
160. Geoffrey Hartman, *The Longest Shadow: In the Aftermath of the Holocaust* (London: Palgrave, 2002), p. 20; Wulf Kansteiner, 'Testing the limits of trauma', p. 100; Raul Hilberg, 'Opening remarks: The discovery of the Holocaust', in Peter Hayes (ed.), *Lessons and Legacies: The Meaning of the Holocaust in a Changing World* (Illinois: Northwestern Press, 1991), p. 18; indeed, *Holocaust* was an example of a new form of 'popular history', the type of which had become increasingly common in the late 1960s and 1970s. Added to this was the fact that historical documentaries tended to have a rather narrow set of themes – most of which were related to the Nazis and World War II – meaning that the 'groundwork' for *Holocaust* had already been established. See: Kevin Williams, 'Flattened visions from timeless machines: History in the mass media', *Media History* 13/2–3 (2007), pp. 136–43.
161. Doneson, *The Holocaust in American Life*, p. 145; Kushner, *The Holocaust and the Liberal*, p. 258; Mintz, *Popular Culture*, p. 23.
162. Levy & Sznaider, *The Holocaust and Memory*, p. 117; Doneson, *The Holocaust in American Life*, p. 159.
163. Annette Insdorf, *Indelible Shadows: Film and the Holocaust* – 3rd edition (Cambridge: Cambridge University Press, 2003), p. 6; Doneson, *The Holocaust in American Film*, p. 227.
164. Novick, *The Holocaust in American Film*, p. 210; Doneson, *The Holocaust in American Film*, p. 188.

165. Levy & Sznaider, *The Holocaust and Memory*, p. 116; Jeffrey Shandler, 'Schindler's discourse: America discusses the Holocaust and its mediation, from NBC's miniseries to Spielberg's film', in Yosefa Loshitzky, *Spielberg's Holocaust: Critical Perspectives on Schindler's List* (Indianapolis: Indiana University Press, 1997), p. 154; Doneson, *The Holocaust in American Life*, p. 189.

166. Levy & Sznaider, *The Holocaust and Memory*, p. 116; Cole, *Selling the Holocaust*, p. 12; Insdorf, *Indelible Shadows*, p. 5.

167. Shandler, 'Schindler's discourse', p. 154; Insdorf, *Indelible Shadows*, p. 4; Stefan E. Hormuth and Walter G. Stephen, 'Effects of viewing "Holocaust" on Germans and Americans: A just-world analysis', *Journal of Applied Social Psychology* 11/3 (1981), p. 240; Michael R. Marrus, 'The use and misuse of the Holocaust', in Peter Hayes (ed.), *Lessons and Legacies: The Meaning of the Holocaust in a Changing World* (Illinois: Northwestern Press, 1991), p. 108.

168. Quoted in: Doneson, *The Holocaust in American Film*, p. 196.

169. Ibid, p. 177.

170. Shandler, 'Schindler's discourse', p. 158; Elie Wiesel, 'Trivializing the Holocaust', *New York Times*, 16 April, 1978, p. 2:1.

171. Mintz, *Popular Culture*, p. 24.

172. Novick, *The Holocaust in American Life*, p. 209; Shandler, 'Schindler's discourse', p. 155; Lawrence Baron, 'X-Men as J-Men: The Jewish subtext of a comic book movie', *Shofar: An Interdisciplinary Journal of Jewish Studies*, 22/1 (2003), p. 49; Doneson, *The Holocaust in American Film*, p. 144.

173. Frank Manchel, 'A reel witness: Steven Spielberg's representation of the Holocaust in Schindler's List', *The Journal of Modern History* 67/1 (1995), p. 91; Novick, *The Holocaust in American Life*, p. 214; Greenspan, 'Imagining survivors', p. 45. See also: Michael Darlow, 'Baggage and Responsibility: The World at War and the Holocaust', in Toby Haggith & Joanna Newman (eds), *Holocaust and the Moving Image: Representations in Film and Television Since 1933* (London: Wallflower Press, 2005), p. 145.

174. Baron, 'Not in Kansas anymore', p. 395; Quoted in: Power, *A Problem From Hell'*, p. xxi.

175. T. Fabre – quoted in: Doneson, *The Holocaust in American Film*, p. 186.

176. Adam Jones, *Genocide: A Comprehensive Introduction* (London: Routledge, 2006), p. 352.

177. Ward Churchill, *A Little Matter of Genocide: Holocaust and Denial in the Americas 1492 to Present* (San Francisco: City Lights Books, 1997), p. 21; Deborah Lipstadt, *Denying the Holocaust*, p. 94, 143 & 195.

178. Robert Braun, 'The Holocaust and problems', p. 180.

179. Hasian, 'Anne Frank, Bergen Belsen', p. 367; Bernard Weinraub, 'Reagan's German trip: Furor over remembrance', *New York Times*, 18 April, 1985, p. A1; a further controversy, which erupted a year after Bitburg, were the

allegations that Kurt Waldeim – the former UN Secretary-General – had been a Nazi war criminal. Although not experiencing the same impact of Reagan's visit, it nonetheless contributed to keeping the Holocaust in Western focus. See: Novick, *The Holocaust in American Life*, p. 227.

180. Cole, *Selling the Holocaust*, p. 147; Finkelstein, *The Holocaust Industry*, p. 92.

181. Kushner, *The Holocaust and the Liberal*, p. 264; 'Queen opens Holocaust Exhibit' – http://news.bbc.co.uk/1/hi/uk/778774.stm – accessed 1 March 2012.

182. Alison Landsberg, 'America, the Holocaust, and the mass culture of memory: Toward a radical politics of empathy', *New German Critique* 71 (1997), p. 74; Doneson, *The Holocaust in American Film*, p. 191; Quoted in: Cole, *Selling the Holocaust*, p. 149.

183. Cole, *Selling the Holocaust*, p. 1; David Rieff, *Slaughterhouse: Bosnia and the Failure of the West* (New York: Touchstone, 1996), p. 26.

184. Quoted in: Philip Gourevitch, *We Wish to Inform You That Tomorrow We Will Be Killed With Our Families* (London: Picador, 2000), p. 152; Judith Doneson, 'Holocaust revisited: A catalyst for memory or trivialisation?', *Annals of the American Academy of Political and Social Science* 548 (1996), p. 76; Cole, *Selling the Holocaust*, p. 14.

185. Levy & Sznaider, *The Holocaust and Memory*, p. 153; Jeffrey Karl Oschner, 'Understanding the Holocaust through the U.S. Holocaust museum', *Journal of Architectural Education* 48/4 (1995), p. 240.

186. Greenspan, 'Imagining survivors', p. 111; Omer Bartov, 'Chamber of horror: Holocaust museums in Israel and the United States', *Israel Studies* 2/2 (1997), p. 70.

187. Alehandro Baer, 'Consuming history and memory through mass media products', *European Journal of Cultural Studies* 4/4 (2001), p. 497; Cole, *Selling the Holocaust*, p. 147.

188. James Carroll, 'Shoah in the news: Patterns and meanings of news coverage of the Holocaust', Discussion Paper D-27, October 1997, Harvard University.

189. Shandler, 'Schindler's discourse', p. 164; Yosefa Loshitzky, 'Introduction', in Yosefa Loshitzky, *Spielberg's Holocaust: Critical Perspectives on Schindler's List* (Indianapolis: Indiana University Press, 1997), p. 3.

190. Mintz, *Popular Culture*, pp. 91–3; Insdorf, *Indelible Shadows*, pp. 25–32; Another pop-culture artefact, the impact of which was influenced by the resurgent interest in the Holocaust during this period, was Art Spiegelman's graphic-novel, *Maus* – see: Baer, 'Consuming history', p. 494; Landsberg, 'America, the Holocaust', p. 67; Thomas Doherty, 'Art Spiegelman's Maus: Graphic art and the Holocaust', *American Literature* 68/1 (1996), pp. 69–84.

191. Mintz, *Popular Culture*, p. 125.

192. David Margolick, 'Schindler Jews find deliverance again', *New York Times*, 13 February, 1994, p. E1; Fred Bruning, 'The problem with Schindler's List', *Macleans*, 25 April, 1994, p. 9; This 'documentary' style of filming which is utilised throughout *Schindler's List* is explored further in: David James, *Schindler's List: Images of the Steven Spielberg Film* (New York: Newmarket Press, 2004).
193. Frank Manchel, 'A reel witness', p. 89; Cole, *Selling the Holocaust*, p. xvii; David Gritten, 'The eyes have it', *Daily Telegraph*, 8 February 1994, p. 15.
194. Cole, *Selling the Holocaust*, p. 74; Power, 'To suffer by comparison?', p. 41; Trudy Gold, 'An overview of Hollywood cinemas', p. 196; http://www.imdb.com/title/tt0108052 – accessed: 14 May 2013; the higher estimate of box-office sales is taken from: Duncan Wheeler, 'Goddard's list: Why Spielberg and Auschwitz are number one', *Media History* 15/2 (2009), p. 193; Omer Bartov, 'Hollywood tries evil', in Yosefa Loshitzky, *Spielberg's Holocaust: Critical Perspectives on Schindler's List* (Indianapolis: Indiana University Press, 1997), p. 55.
195. Mintz, *Popular Culture*, p. 35; Novick, *The Holocaust in American Life*, p. 207; Jonathan Margolis, 'The horror story that Hollywood is right to tell', *The Times*, 13 February, 1994, Section 4, p. 6; Geoffrey Hartman, *The Longest Shadow*, p. 82.
196. In my experience, Schindler's List has placed as high as #2 on the imdb.com (one of the 10 most visited sites on the internet) 'top 250' list, and has rarely left the Top 10; Levy & Sznaider, *The Holocaust and Memory*, p. 141; Shandler, 'Schindler's discourse', p. 163; Cole, *Selling the Holocaust*, p. 73.
197. Quoted in: Mintz, *Popular Culture*, p. 157; see also: J. Hoberman, 'Schindler's List: Myth, movie and memory', *Village Voice*, 29 March, 1994, p. 24.
198. Cole, *Selling the Holocaust*, p. 73; Mintz, *Popular Culture*, pp. 34–5.
199. Miriam Bratu Hansen, 'Schindler's List is not Shoah: The second commandment, popular modernism, and public memory', *Critical Inquiry* 22/2 (1996), p. 292; see also: Loshitzky, 'Introduction', p. 2.
200. Insdorf, *Indelible Shadows*, p. 258; Doneson, *The Holocaust in American Film*, p. 227; Alan E. Steinweis, 'The Holocaust and American culture: An assessment of recent scholarship', *Holocaust and Genocide Studies* 15/2 (2001), p. 296.
201. Levy & Sznaider, *The Holocaust and Memory*, p. 136; Cole, *Selling the Holocaust*, p. 72; Wheeler, 'Goddard's list', p. 192.
202. Hansen, 'Schindler's list is not Shoah', p. 300; Doneson, 'Holocaust revisited', p. 71; Barbie Zelizer, *Remembering to Forget: Holocaust Memory Through the Camera's Eye* (Chicago: The University of Chicago Press, 1998), p. 12.
203. Doneson, 'Holocaust revisited', p. 70; Loshitzky, 'Introduction', p. 3.
204. Manchel, 'A reel witness', p. 89; Loshitzky, 'Introduction', p. 2; See also: Cole, *Selling the Holocaust*, p. xiii; Baer, 'Consuming history', p. 494.

205. Cole, *Selling the Holocaust*, p. 7; Katherine Bischoping, 'Method and meaning in Holocaust-knowledge surveys', *Holocaust and Genocide Studies* 12/3 (1998), p. 458 (Table 1); Novick, *The Holocaust in American Life*, p. 233; see also: Tom W. Smith, *Holocaust Denial: What the Survey Data Reveal* (New York: American Jewish Committee, 1994).

206. Cole, *Selling the Holocaust*, p. 3; Kushner, *The Holocaust and the Liberal*, p. 260.

207. Hartman, *The Longest Shadow*, p. 49; Novick, *The Holocaust in American Life*, p. 240.

208. Mick Hume, 'Nazifying the Serbs, from Bosnia to Kosovo', in Philip Hammond & Edward S. Herman, *Degraded Capability: The Media and the Kosovo Crisis* (London: Pluto Press, 2000), p. 71; 'Holocaustizing' is borrowed from: Power, 'To suffer by comparison?', p. 44.

Chapter 3   Inconveniently Close

1. Samuel P. Huntington, *The Clash of Civilizations and the Remaking of the World Order* (London: Pan Books, 1996), p. 226.

2. Alan E. Stenweis, 'The Auschwitz analogy: Holocaust memory and American debates over intervention in Bosnia and Kosovo in the 1990s', *Holocaust and Genocide Studies* 19/2 (2005), p. 277; Nicolaus Mills, 'The language of slaughter', in N. Mills & K. Brunner (eds), *The New Killing Fields: Massacre and the Politics of Intervention* (New York: Basic Books, 2003), p. 5.

3. David Rieff, *Slaughterhouse: Bosnia and the Failure of the West* (New York: Touchstone, 1996), p. 20; see: Josip Glaurdic, 'Yugoslavia's Dissolution: Between the Scylla of Facts and the Charybdis of Interpretation', in Florian Bieber, Armina Galijas & Rory Archer (eds), *Debating the End of Yugoslavia* (London: Routledge, 2014), pp. 23–38.

4. Robert J. Donia; *Radovan Karadzic: Architect of the Bosnian Genocide* (Cambridge: Cambridge University Press, 2014), p. 18. This book also provides an overview of the contesting positions regarding classifying the violence in Bosnia as 'genocide'; see: p. 16–19.

5. Barbie Zelizer, *Remembering to Forget: Holocaust Memory Through the Camera's Eye* (Chicago: The University of Chicago Press, 1998), p. 206.

6. Laura Silber & Allan Little, *The Death of Yugoslavia* (London: Penguin, 1996), p. 244.

7. Noel Malcolm, *Bosnia: A Short History* (London: Pan Books, 1996), pp. 226–36.

8. David Rohde, *End Game: The Betrayal and Fall of Srebrenica: Europe's Worst Massacre Since World War II* (Colorado: Westview Press, 1998), p. 349; on

the revised figures, see: http://news.bbc.co.uk/2/hi/europe/6228152.stm accessed 28 March 2017.

9. Norman Cigar, *Genocide in Bosnia: The Policy of 'Ethnic Cleansing'* (Texas: Texas A & M University Press, 1995), p. 9.

10. William D. Rubinstein, *Genocide: A History* (Harlow: Pearson Education Limited, 2004), p. 281.

11. Cited in: Philip Hammond, 'Reporting 'humanitarian warfare: Propaganda, moralism and NATO's Kosovo war', *Journalism Studies* 1/3 (2000), p. 380.

12. Theodore I. Geshkof, *Balkan Union: A Road to Peace in Southeastern Europe* (New York: Columbia University Press, 1940), p. 47.

13. Maria Todorova, *Imagining the Balkans* (Oxford: Oxford University Press, 2009), p. 47.

14. Lene Hansen, *Security as Practice: Discourse Analysis and the Bosnian War* (London: Routledge, 2006), pp. 99–100.

15. Mary Edith Durham, *Twenty Years of Balkan Tangle* (London: George Allen & Unwin, 1920), p. 238; Roger Cohen, 'A Balkan gyre of war, spinning onto film', *New York Times*, 12 March 1995, sec. 2, p. 24.

16. For further discussion of these beliefs, and how they continued into the 1990s, see: Hansen, *Security as Practice*, pp. 85–94.

17. Todorova, *Imagining the Balkans*, p. 188.

18. Ibid, p. 57.

19. Geshkof, *Balkan Union*, p. 4.

20. Todorova, *Imagining the Balkans*, p. 59.

21. Malcolm, *Bosnia*, p. 271.

22. Ibid, p. xix.

23. Hsiang Iris Chang, Seth C. Lewis & Nan Zheng, 'A matter of life and death? Examining how newspapers covered the newspaper "crisis"', *Journalism Studies* 13/3 (2011), p. 310.

24. George F. Kennan, *The Other Balkan Wars. A 1913 Carnegie Endowment Inquiry in Retrospect with a New Introduction and Reflections on the Present by George F. Kennan* (Washington, DC: Carnegie Endowment for International Peace, 1993), p. 1.

25. Ibid, p. 14.

26. The concept of 'mental communities' has been researched since at least the beginning of the twentieth century – see: Wilhelm Max Wundt, *Outlines of Psychology* (Leipzig: Engelman, 1907), pp. 296–8; George Mead, *Mind, Self, and Society: From the Standpoint of a Social Behaviorist* (Chicago: University of Chicago Press, 1934).

27. Hubert J. O'Gorman, 'The discovery of pluralistic ignorance', *Journal of the History of the Behavioral Sciences* 22 (1986), pp. 333–47; see also: Karen S.

Johnson-Cartee, *News Narratives and News Framing: Constructing Political Reality* (Oxford: Rowman & Littlefield, 2005), pp. 34–6.

28. Jack Lule, *Daily News, Eternal Stories: The Mythological Role of Journalism* (New York: Guilford Press, 2001), p. 15.

29. Todorova, *Imagining the Balkans*, p. 7.

30. For example: Garth Myers, Thomas Klak & Timothy Koehl, 'The inscription of difference: News coverage of the conflicts in Rwanda and Bosnia', *Political Geography*, 15/1 (1996), pp. 21–46.

31. Editorial, 'Catch-22 on refugees', *Observer*, 16 August 1992, p. 18.

32. Thomas Cushman and Stjepan G. Mestrovic, 'Introduction', in T. Cushman and S. Mestrovic (eds), *This Time We Knew: Western Responses to Genocide in Bosnia* (New York: New York University Press, 1996), p. 9.

33. Janine Di Giovanni, 'One last hope that sent a cynic back to Sarajevo', *Sunday Times*, 13 February 1994, p. 15.

34. Robert Crampton, 'The lessons of war', *The Times*, 5 February 1994, Magazine, p. 21.

35. John Pomfret, 'Washington TV newsman killed by Sarajevo sniper', *Washington Post*, 14 August 1992, p. A26; For a more detailed survey of the material conditions within Sarajevo, see: Peter Andreas, *Blue Helmets and Black Markets: The Business of Survival in the Siege of Sarajevo* (London: Cornell University Press, 2008).

36. Tim Page, 'Images of war: the human condition exposed', *Independent*, 1 September 1995, section 2, p. 4; Festus Eribo, 'Russian newspaper coverage of Somalia and the Former Yugoslavia', *Issue: A Journal of Opinion*, 22/1 (1992), p. 30; 'TV reporter wounded', *The Times*, 26 August 1992, p. 1.

37. Jacques Semelin, *Purify and Destroy: The Political Uses of Massacre and Genocide* (London: Hurst & Company, 2007).

38. Silber & Little, *The Death of Yugoslavia*, p. 250.

39. Jonathan Miller, 'Death-camp scoop made the world sit up', *Sunday Times*, 9 August 1992, p. 18.

40. Adam Jones, *Genocide: A Comprehensive Introduction* (London: Routledge, 2006), p. 215.

41. Walter Goodman, 'TV Images of Bosnia ignite passions and politics', *New York Times*, 6 August 1992, p. C20; Chicago Tribune Wires, 'UN demands access to camps', *Chicago Tribune*, 5 August 1992, p. 3; Ed Vulliamy, 'Shame of camp Omarska', *Guardian*, 7 August 1992, p. 1.

42. Niranjan S. Karnik, 'Rwanda & the media: Imagery, war & refuge', *Review of African Political Economy* 25/78 (1998), p. 620.

43. Will Bennett & Marcus Tanner, 'The nightmare of Bosnia', *Independent*, 7 August 1992, p. 1.

44. Michael A. Sells, *The Bridge Betrayed: Religion and Genocide in Bosnia* (Los Angeles: University of California Press, 1998), p. 75.
45. Roy Gutman, 'Witnesses call teenager's rape in camp typical', *Guardian*, 10 August 1992, p. 1; Thom Shanker, 'Sex slavery joins list of Balkan "atrocities"', *Chicago Tribune*, 6 August 1992, Section 1, p. 1.
46. Craig R. Whitney, 'Europe's caution on Bosnia provokes growing criticism', *New York Times*, 1 August 1992, p. A5; Editorial, 'Atrocity in Bosnia', *Washington Post*, 3 August 1992, p. A18.
47. Letter from Ruth Cohen & Reuven Silverman, 'Precedents for keeping the peace, pacifying the Balkans and saving the choldren', *Independent*, 11 August 1992, p. 14.
48. Mark Danner, 'America and the Bosnia genocide', *New York Review of Books*, 4 December 1997, p. 5.
49. Patrick Bishop, 'Bullet-pocked wall bears testimony to former death camp', *Daily Telegraph*, 10 August 1992, p. 8; Simon Tisdall, John Hooper and Michael Simmons, 'Bosnia: US and UK at odds', *Guardian*, 8 August 1992, p. 1; Michael Binyon, 'Evidence mounts of executions and beatings in Serb-run camps', *The Times* 7 August 1992, p. 1.
50. Philip Sherwell, 'Serbs impose reign of terror in Bosnia', *Daily Telegraph*, 7 August 1992, p. 8; Editorial, 'A matter of conscience – as well as policy', *Los Angeles Times*, 5 August 1992, p. B6; Bob Greene, 'You have seen their faces', *Chicago Tribune*, 9 August 1992, Section 5, p. 1.
51. Robert Shrimsley, '"He was dying in front of us"', *Daily Telegraph*, 14 August 1992, p. 8; Foreign Staff, 'Nazi camps comparison is rejected', *Guardian*, 12 August 1992, p. 6; 'Term for Serb camps is being disputed', *New York Times*, 16 August 1992, p. A14.
52. Peter Spielmann, 'Atrocities known to UN team in May', *Guardian*, 8 August 1992, p. 9; James Bone, 'UN had execution details weeks ago', *The Times*, 8 August 1992, p. 1; Trevor Rowe, 'U.N. Knew of Serb camps a month ago, Bosnian says', *Washington Post*, 6 August 1992, p. A31.
53. Roy Gutman, *A Witness to Genocide* (Dorset: Element Books, 1993, p. 36.
54. Louise Lief et al., 'Europe's trail of tears', *U.S. News & World Report* 113, 27 July 1992, p. 41.
55. Con Coughlin & Philip Sherwell, 'The week the world woke up', *Sunday Telegraph*, 9 August 1992, p. 17.
56. Geoffrey Hartman, *The Longest Shadow: In the Aftermath of the Holocaust* (London: Palgrave, 2002), p. 40.
57. Anthony Lewis, 'Yesterday's man', *New York Times*, 3 August 1992, p. A19; see also: Editorial, 'Milosevic isn't Hitler, but...', *New York Times*, 4 August 1992, p. A18.
58. Rubinstein, *Genocide*, p. 147.

59. Letter from Mike Bamborn, 'Helping Bosnia', *Chicago Tribune*, 7 August 1992, p. 12.
60. Tony Kuschner, *The Holocaust and the Liberal Imagination: A Social and Cultural History* (Oxford: Blackwell, 1994), p. 271.
61. Peter Novick, *The Holocaust in American Life* (New York: Mariner Books, 2000), p. 251.
62. Editorial, 'UN overstretched', *Sunday Telegraph*, 16 August 1992, p. 18; Letter from Jonathan Sacks, 'Bosnia and conscience of the world', *The Times*, 8 August 1992, p. 11.
63. Editorial, 'Bosnian horrors', *The Times*, 7 August 1992, p. 11.
64. Robert Jay Lifton, 'Can images of Bosnia's victims change the world?', *New York Times*, 23 August 1992, section 2, p. 26.
65. Rieff, *Slaughterhouse*, p. 31; see also: Letter from David Weinberg, 'Situation in Bosnia isn't like Holocaust', *New York Times*, 19 August 1992, p. A20.
66. Coughlin & Sherwell, 'The week the world', p. 17.
67. From the journal of Richard Holbrooke – recounted in: Holbrooke, *To End a War*, p. 36.
68. Editorial, 'Strike Serbia', *Sunday Times*, 9 August 1992, section 2, p. 3; Conor Cruise O'Brien, 'Winning votes in Sarajevo', *The Times*, 11 August 1992, p. 10; Editorial, 'Give Serbs a taste of their own medicine', *Observer*, 9 August 1992, p. 18; Nancy Hill-Holtzman, 'Images of atrocities in Bosnia stir protest', *Los Angeles Times*, 8 August 1992, p. B1.
69. Mick Hume, 'Nazifying the Serbs, from Bosnia to Kosovo', in Philip Hammond & Edward S. Herman (eds), *Degraded Capability: The Media and the Kosovo Crisis* (London: Pluto Press, 2000), p. 72; it should be noted that Hume was later involved in a libel case with ITN, in which he alleged pictures were misleading and that comparisons to the Holocaust were unjustified; see also: Brendan Simms, 'Bosnia: The lessons of history', in Cushman & Mestrovic, *This Time We Knew*, p. 68.
70. [Empahsis added] Alan M. Deshowitz, 'Prosecute the Balkan murderers', *Los Angeles Times*, 7 August 1992, p. B7.
71. Auberon Waugh, 'A rare opportunity', *Daily Telegraph*, 1 August 1992, p. 15; Michael Novak, 'The call to arms is all-American, *Los Angeles Times*, 11 August 1992, p. B7.
72. David Campbell, 'Atrocity, memory, photography: imaging the concentration camps of Bosnia – the case of ITN versus Living Marxism, Part 2', *Journal of Human Rights* 1/2 (2002), pp. 143.
73. Patrick Cockburn, 'Sight that shook the world', *Independent on Sunday*, 9 August 1992, p. 23; Letter from Jeremy Black, 'Intervention is a dangerous habit', *Daily Telegraph*, 20 August 1992, p. 14; Sara Rimer, 'Bosnian wa bewilders a Midwestern town', *New York Times*, 24 July 1995, p. A1.

74. Robert Fox, 'Tribal war poses new threat to Europe', *Daily Telegraph*, 11 August 1992, p. 8; Julie Burchill, 'Jaw-jaw not war-war in the bar', *Sunday Times*, 23 July 1995, section 3, p. 6.

75. Mark Mazower, *The Balkans: From the End of Byzantium to the Present Day* (London: Phoenix Press, 2001), p. 143; Cockburn, 'Sight that shook', p. 23.

76. Editorial, 'Being realistic about Bosnia', *Chicago Tribune*, 2 August 1992, section 4, p. 2; Auberon Waugh, 'Something we can do', *Daily Telegraph*, 19 August 1992, p. 17.

77. Conor Cruise O'Brien, 'Only fools step in', *The Times*, 6 August 1992, p. 10; see also: Rieff, *Slaughterhouse*, p. 42.

78. Letter from Dr Cornella Sorabji, 'Serbia and the lessons of history', *Guardian*, 14 August 1992, p. 17.

79. Daniele Conversi, 'Moral relativism and equidistance in British attitudes to the war in the former Yugoslavia', in Cushman & Mestrovic, *This Time We Knew*, p. 247; see also: Yahya Sadowski, 'Ethnic conflict', *Foreign Policy* 111 (1998), p. 13; Holbrooke, *To End a War*, p. 370; Silber & Little, *The Death of Yugoslavia*, p. 25.

80. Entman, *Projections of Power*, p. 7.

81. Malcolm, *Bosnia*, p. 230.

82. Zlatko Dizdarevic, 'Deaths from natural causes', *New York Times*, 2 February 1994, p. A15.

83. Emma Daly, 'Sarajevans face imprisonment in mental state of siege', *Independent*, 15 September 1995, p. 12.

84. Silber & Little, *The Death of Yugoslavia* (London: Penguin, 1996), p. 220.

85. Holbrooke, *To End a War*, p. 48; Misha Glenny, *The Fall of Yugoslavia* (London: Penguin, 1996), p. 220.

86. Carol J. Williams, 'Sarajevo siege creating city of suicidal children, U.N. Finds', *Los Angeles Times*, 2 February 1994, p. A11; See also: Robert Fox, '16,500 children killed in Bosnia', *Daily Telegraph*, 18 February 1994, p. 2.

87. Joel Brand, 'Nothing but tears in the market of mourning', *The Times*, 7 February 1994, p. 1.

88. Silber & Little, *The Death of Yugoslavia*, pp. 309–10.

89. Victoria MacDonald & Robert Fox, 'Shell kills 58 in Sarajevo market', *Sunday Telegraph*, 6 February 1994, p. 2.

90. Editorial, 'Sarajevo needs relief not revenge', *Observer*, 6 February 1994, p. 22.

91. John Sweeney, 'Carnage in the market place', *Observer*, 6 February 1994, p. 1; see also: John Kifner, 'Toll is worst in 22 months of attacks', *New York Times*, 6 February 1994, p. A1; Danica Kirka, '66 die as shell rips through Bosnia market', *Los Angeles Times*, 6 February 1994, p. 1; Patrick Bishop,

'Massacre increases airstrike demands', *Daily Telegraph*, 7 February 1994, p. 1; John Kifner, 'Sarajevans mourn and rage while life and death go on', *New York Times*, 7 February 1994, p. A8; Glenny, *The Balkans*, p. 647.

92. Some outlets produced lists of previous shellings, in the wake of Markale: Reuter, 'Highest toll for Sarajevo', *Washington Post*, 6 February 1994, p. A26; Editorial, 'Letting the Serbs know we still care', *Guardian*, 7 February 1994, p. 19.

93. Associated Press, '10 killed in Sarajevo's bloodiest day in a month', *Los Angeles Times*, 5 February 1994, p. a13; Reuter, 'Nine killed by mortars in Sarajevo aid queue', *The Times*, 5 February 1994, p. 10; Associated Press, '8 killed in Sarajevo', *Washington Post*, 5 February 1994, p. A18.

94. Editorial, 'Letting the Serbs know we still care', *Guardian*, 7 February 1994, p. 19.

95. Susan Sontag, *Regarding the Pain of Others* (London: Penguin Books, 2003), p. 96.

96. Andrew Mar, 'Gamble that NATO cannot afford to lose', *Independent*, 11 February 1994, p. 19; See also: 'Comment', *Independent*, 7 February 1994, p. 1; Editorial, 'D-Day for Bosnia', *The Times*, 8 February 1994, p. 19.

97. The *Washington Post* (with a total of 106 news articles) and the *New York Times* (with 105) surpassed the totals recorded by the *Guardian* (96) and the *Independent* (94). This is also of note due to the fact these figures represent two of the three occasions, across the entire study of Bosnia, in which an American title produced in excess of 100 articles within a 'one-month' period of analysis.

98. Mark Helnrich & Robert Block, 'Sarajevo atrocity turns into bloodbath', *Independent on Sunday*, 6 February 1994, p. 1; See also: Editorial, 'Let Bosnia's Muslims arm themselves', *Chicago Tribune*, 8 February 1994, section 1, p. 16.

99. Walter Goodman, 'Are the TV images father to U.S. Action in Bosnia?', *New York Times*, 14 February 1994, p. C16; Richard Sobel, 'Trends: United States intervention in Bosnia', *The Public Opinion Quarterly* 62/2 (1998), p. 253.

100. Philip Johnston & George Jones, 'Public backs Bosnia action', *Daily Telegraph*, 12 February 1994, pp. 1–2; Reuters, 'World leaders express shock and outrage at blast', *New York Times*, 6 February 1994, p. A12.

101. Frederick C. Cuny, 'The Serbs have lost', *New York Times*, 25 February 1994, p. A29; Boris Johnson & Maurice Weaver, 'Nato ultimatum to Serbs today on air strikes', *Daily Telegraph*, 9 February 1994, p. 13; Noel Malcolm, *Bosnia*, p. 255.

102. Editorial, 'Can it really be America's position to do nothing?', *Los Angeles Times*, 16 February 1994, p. B6.

103. Editorial, 'Rationale for the alliance', *Daily Telegraph*, 10 February 1994, p. 16; for example: Letter from K. Morst, 'Military action in Sarajevo: false parallels, other cities and deadly claims', *Independent*, 10 February 1994, p. 21; David B. Ottoway, 'Mostar's Muslims "living like rats"', *Washington Post*, 21 February 1994, p. A1.

104. Mike O'Connor, 'Investigation concludes Bosnian government snipers shot at civilians', *New York Times*, 1 August 1995, p. A6.

105. Editorial, 'Diplomacy and death in Bosnia', *Chicago Tribune*, 23 August 1995, section 1, p. 24; Ed Vulliamy, 'Sophisticated Sarajevo tortured and broken', *Guardian*, 10 February 1994, p. 10.

106. Bernard-Henri Levy, 'The spirit of Europe lives or dies in Sarajevo', *Independent*, 31 July 1995, p. 11; Editorial, 'To Sarajevo, on wings of desire', *Chicago Tribune*, 16 September 1995, section 1, p. 16; Editorial, 'Limited options', *Daily Telegraph*, 5 August 1992, p. 14; For other discussions of Sarajevo, see: Semelin, *Purify and Destroy*, p. 152; Ed Vulliamy, 'Bosnia: the crime of appeasement', *International Affairs* 74/1, (2008), p. 82.

107. Johnson-Cartee, *News Narratives*, p. 272.

108. David Hoffman, 'Israel returns favor to a Muslim', *Washington Post*, 12 February 1994, p. A14.

109. Jenny Rees, 'The diary girl of Sarajevo makes her grand entry', *Daily Telegraph*, 22 February 1994, p. 6; Owen Bowcott, 'Europe acclaims child's eye view of life during wartime', *Guardian*, 22 February 1994, p. 12; Suzanne Glass, 'Out of the war, into the hype', *Independent*, 24 February 1994, p. 30; Reuters, 'Sarajevo teen still an optimist', *Chicago Tribune*, 23 February 1994, section 1, p. 4; Gavin Cordon, 'Diarist's memories of peace', *The Times*, 22 February 1994, p. 15.

110. Margot Norman, 'Children of the nightmare', *The Times*, 14 February, 1994, p. 14.

111. Peter Preston, 'A faraway country of which we know a lot', *Guardian*, 25 August 1995, p. 17.

112. This particular event was referenced on a few occasions, due to the destruction of the venue where the British pair claimed Olympic gold – see: Joel Brand, 'Sad city rekindles Olympic memories', *The Times*, 9 February 1994, p. 12.

113. Letter from Victoria Bentata, 'Need for immediate action in Bosnia – and the risks', *Independent*, 9 February 1994, p. 15.

114. Charles Krauthammer, 'The good news and the bad: Heeding history with an unworkable plan in Bosnia', *Chicago Tribune*, 21 February 1994, Section 1, p. 11; Walter Goodman, 'Are the TV images father to U.S. action in Bosnia?', *New York Times*, 14 February 1994, p. C16; see also: Peter Simple, 'Monster', *Sunday Telegraph*, 13 February 1994, p. 26.

115. Margaret Shapiro, 'Yeltsin Scoring Points at Home With Bid to Block NATO Airstrikes', *Washington Post*, 19 February 1994, p. A19; Terry Atlas, 'Bosnia split: Allies agree on outrage – and little else', *Chicago Tribune*, 8 February 1994, section 1, p. 1; Tribune Wires, 'Serb pullout is brokered by Russians', *Chicago Tribune*, 18 February 1994, section 1, p. 1; Alan Philips, 'Yeltsin's Master Stroke', *Sunday Telegraph*, 20 February 1994, p. 23; Tony Barber, 'How the Russians stole a march on the West to give 'peace' to Sarajevo', *Independent*, 19 February 1994, p. 1; Paul Richter, 'U.S. wary of Russia offer to Bosnia', 19 February 1994, p. A1.

116. Cited in: Letter from Sally Howe Lineweaver, 'Keep arms embargo on Balkan powder keg', *New York Times*, 20 February 1994, section 4, p. 12.

117. Editorial, 'Yeltsin makes a move: From Russia with love?', *Los Angeles Times*, 19 February 1994, p. B7.

118. Cigar, *Genocide in Bosnia*, p. 94; Silber & Little, *The Death of Yugoslavia*, pp. 309–10.

119. For example, see: Charles Brenner, 'UN tracks source of fatal shell', *The Times*, 19 February 1994, p. 12; David B. Ottaway, 'U.N. probers fail to find who hit Sarajevo market', *Washington Post*, 17 February 1994, p. A31; some UN officials even made the argument that Sarajevo was not technically under siege, as the shelling had been provoked by Muslim initiatives – see: Brendan Simms, *Unfinest Hour: Britain and the Destruction of Bosnia*, (London: Penguin, 2002), p. 24.

120. Silber & Little, *The Death of Yugoslavia*, p. 310.

121. Letter from Donna Millich, 'Deadly shelling in Sarajevo', *Los Angeles Times*, 11 February 1994, p. B6; See also: Letter from Robert Wokler, 'Call for concerted action on Bosnia', *The Times*, 10 February 1994, p. 17.

122. Letter from Vlade Milanovic, 'When the will for peace is weak', *Guardian*, 10 August 1992, p. 20.

123. Ed Vulliamy, 'Bosnia: The crime of appeasement', p. 83; in regards to the use of relativisation in news discussion of Bosnia and policy; this is developed further in: Gregory Kent, *Framing War and Genocide: British Policy and News Media Reaction to the War in Bosnia* (New York: Hampton Press, 2005).

124. Holbrooke, *To End a War*, footnote, p. 23.

125. Cushman & Mestrovic, 'Introduction', p. 18.

126. Jonathan Eyal, 'Lessons in Balkan reality', *Guardian*, 13 August 1992, p. 17.

127. Letter from Peter Smithers [UK delegate, UN General Assembly], 'Out of our depth in the Balkans?', *The Times*, 2 September 1995, p. 17.

128. Eve-Ann Prentice, 'Balkan path to hell is paved with good intentions', *The Times*, 20 July 1995, p. 15.

129. Quoted in: Anna Husarka, 'Tough on crime, murky on genocide', *Los Angeles Times*, 16 February 1994, p. B7.

130. Quoted in: Cigar, *Genocide in Bosnia*, p. 121; A similar analogy was voiced by EEC negotiator Lord Carrington, who stated that: 'Everybody is to blame for what is happening in Bosnia and Hercegovina' – Cited in: Malcolm, *Bosnia*, p. 242.

131. Mebura Topolovac, 'Allegations of Muslim "self-slaughter" in Bosnia', *Independent*, 24 August 1992, p. 18.

132. Michael A. Sells, *The Bridge Betrayed: Religion and Genocide in Bosnia*, (Los Angeles: University of California Press, 1998), p. 86; see also: Cushman & Mestrovic, *This Time We Knew*, p. 17.

133. This was commented upon at the time in the following: Ambrose Evans-Pritchard, 'Washing our hands at the death of a nation', *Sunday Telegraph*, 2 August 1992, p. 20.

134. Ed Vulliamy, 'Bosnia: The crime of appeasement', p. 84.

135. Cited in: Zelizer, *Remembering to Forget*, p. 218.

136. Joel Shapiro & Gordon R. Thompson, 'Myths stand in the way of peace', *Los Angeles Times*, 6 September 1995, p. B9.

137. Letter from George Ivan-Smith, 'Any number of past wrongs don't make right in the Balkans', *Guardian*, 24 August 1995, p. 18.

138. Julie Burchill, 'Jaw-jaw not war-war in the bar', *The Times*, 23 July 1995, Section 3, p. 6.

139. Malcolm, *Bosnia*, p. 221.

140. Semelin, *Purify and Destroy*, p. 132.

141. For example, see: Ian Traynor, '16 years on, the butcher of Bosnia is behind bars', *Guardian*, 27 May 2011, p. 1; David Charter, 'Butcher of Bosnia faces justice at last', *The Times*, 27 May 2011, p. 1; Peter Popham, 'The terrifying face of Serbian brutality', *Independent*, 27 May 2011, p. 5.

142. Chris Watt, 'Psychopath who ordered massacre of 8000 people', *The Herald*, 27 May 2011, p. 2.

143. Simms, *Unfinest Hour*, p. 316.

144. Honig & Both, *Srebrenica*, p. 58 & 177.

145. Ibid, p. 66.

146. Cited in: Patricia Wilson, 'Srebrenica's fall is turning point for UN', *Daily Telegraph*, 12 July 1995, p. 2.

147. Rohde, *End Game*, p. 349.

148. Calculating the exact number of victims of the massacre at Bleiburg, in addition to those who perished as a result of death marches and mass detention, is difficult to estimate; but estimates generally range from 10,000 to 50,000. See: Mark Biondich, *The Balkans: Revolution, War, and Political Violence Since 1878* (Oxford: Oxford University Press, 2011) p. 81; Jozo Tomasevich, *War and Revolution in Yugoslavia, 1941–1945: Occupation and Collaboration* (San Francisco: Stanford University Press, 2001), p. 763; Counting the total

victims of 'Tito's mass shootings, forced death marches and concentration camps in the period 1945–46', Noel Malcolm puts the number at 'up to 250,000.' See: Malcolm, *Bosnia*, p. 193.

149. Rohde, *End Game*, p. 131; Marcus Tanner, 'The damage inflicted by a savage general is more than his trial can repair', *Independent*, 27 May 2011, p. 2.

150. Chris Watt, 'Psychopath who ordered massacre of 8000 people', *The Herald*, 27 May 2011, p. 2.

151. Christopher Brooker, 'Our humbug made the killing fields of Bosnia', *Sunday Telegraph*, 16 July 1995, p. 27; for early coverage, see also: Robert Block, 'Bosnians tell of atrocities', *Independent*, 14 July 1995, p. 1; Associated Press, 'Srebrenica falls to Bosnian Serbs', *Chicago Tribune*, 11 July 1995, Evening Update, p. 1.

152. Lara J. Nettelfield & Sarah E. Wagner, *Srebrenica in the Aftermath of Genocide* (New York: Cambridge University Press, 2014), pp. 258–9.

153. Christopher Bellamy, 'Refugee women "see menfolk shot"', *Independent on Sunday*, 16 July 1995, p. 17; Robert Block, '"Mass slaughter in a Bosnian field knee-deep in blood"', *Independent*, 21 July 1995, p. 1; Robert Block, 'At the mercy of Mladic', *Independent on Sunday*, 23 July 1995, p. 18.

154. Anthony Lewis, 'What Should We Do?', *New York Times*, 21 July 1995, p. A25; See also: Ian Traynor & Agencies, 'Dutch troops tell of atrocities', *Guardian*, 24 July 1995, p. 9; Honig & Both, *Srebrenica*, p. 40.

155. Ian Traynor, 'Serbs bus refugees to front line', *Guardian*, 13 July 1995, p. 1; Reuters, Stacy Sullivan, Eve-Ann Prentice & Philip Webster, 'Rampant Serbs expel the women', *The Times*, 13 July 1995, p. 1; See also: Reuters, 'Serb "ethnic cleansing" of captives charged', *Chicago Tribune*, 13 July 1995, Evening Update, p. 1.

156. Before Srebrenica, the slaughter 'was not an end in itself' – Semelin, *Purify and Destroy*, p. 230; some human rights groups compounded this, believing that the captive men would be 'kept as bargaining chips for future prisoner exchanges, which [had] gone on through the war' – Patrick Bishop, 'Silence in the city "cleansed of all its men"', *Daily Telegraph*, 15 July 1995, p. 11.

157. Editorial, 'Bosnia's human emergency', *New York Times*, 14 July 1995, p. 24; see also: Jonathan Eyal, 'Seizure of "safe area" drags the West in deeper', *The Times*, 12 July 1995, p. 9.

158. Anthony Lloyd, 'Srebrenica's exiles tell grimly familiar stories of murder', *The Times*, 15 July 1995, p. 1; Stacy Sullivan, 'Fears growing for Srebrenica's men', *The Times*, 14 July 1995, p. 1; Christopher Bellamy, 'Survivors tell of Serb killing fields', *Independent*, 19 July 1995, p. 8.

159. Anthony Lloyd, 'Srebrenica's exiles tell grimly familiar stories of murder', *The Times*, 15 July 1995, p. 1; Tribunes Wires, 'Serbs' killing spree reported by

refugees', *Chicago Tribune*, 14 July 1995, section 1, p. 11; See also: Marcus Warren, Toby Helm & Tim Butcher, 'Generals meet to stave off Bosnia blood-bath', *Sunday Telegraph*, 16 July 1995, p. 1; Robert Block, 'Bodies pile up in horror of Srebrenica', *Independent*, 17 July, 1995, p. 1.

160. Robert Block, '"Mass slaughter in a Bosnian field knee-deep in blood"', *Independent*, 21 July 1995, p. 1.

161. Tim Butcher, 'Serb atrocities in Srebrenica are unproved', *Daily Telegraph*, 24 July 1995, p. 10; see also: Stephen Kinzer, 'Muslims Tell of Atrocities in Bosnian Town', *New York Times*, 14 July 1995, p. A1; Patrick Bishop, 'Silence in city "cleansed" of all its men', *Daily Telegraph*, 15 July 1995, p. 11; Stephen Kinzer, 'Bosnian Refugess' Accounts Appear to Verify Atrocities', *New York Times*, 17 July 1995, p. A1.

162. [Emphasis added] Boris Johnson, 'Punish the war criminals – but don't wait 50 years', *Daily Telegraph*, 17 July 1995, p. 18; see also: Robert Block, 'At the mercy of Mladic', *Independent on Sunday*, 23 July 1995, p. 18.

163. Tim Butcher & Patrick Bishop, 'Serbs "take all boys over six years old"', *Daily Telegraph*, 14 July 1995, p. 12.

164. Tim Butcher, 'Serb atrocities in Srebrenica are unproved', *Daily Telegraph*, 24 July 1995, p. 10.

165. Jon Swain & Edin Hamzic, 'We were all screaming and trying to pull back our boys', *The Times*, 15 July 1995, p. 8; See also: John Pomfret, 'Witnesses allege abuses by Serbs', *Washington Post*, 16 July 1995, p. A1.

166. Tim Butcher, 'Refugees' despair in the sweltering fields', *Daily Telegraph*, 15 July 1995, p. 2; See also: Jon Swain, 'Bosnia endures more atrocities', *Sunday Times*, 23 July 1995, p. 13.

167. Holbrooke, *To End a War*, p. 69.

168. Robert Block, 'At the mercy of Mladic', *Independent on Sunday*, 23 July 1995; Reuter, 'Call for war crimes tribunal inquiry into "atrocities"' *Guardian*, 22 July 1995, p. 15.

169. Raymond Bonner, 'U.N. Official Accuses Serbs of "Barbarous" Acts', *New York Times*, 25 July 1995, p. A6; see also: Stacy Sullivan & Eve-Ann Prentice, 'Beleaguered Zepa ready to fight to the finish', *The Times*, 22 July 1995, p. 11.

170. Peter Scnheider, 'False tears over Bosnia', *New York Times*, 30 July 1995, p. A15.

171. In a Dutch context, failure to act over Srebrenica has been often regarded as a source of shame. In regards to debates over damage done to Western/national prestige, this is discussed further in this context in the following: Gloria Wekker, *White Innocence: Paradoxes of Colonialism and Race* (London: Duke University Press, 2016), pp. 4–5.

172. Silber & Little, *The Death of Yugoslavia*, p. 345.

173. Tracy Wilkinson, 'Serbs round up, expel Muslims in "safe area"', *Los Angeles Times*, 13 July 1995, p. A1; Letter from Jack Stewart-Clark & other representatives of the European Parliament, 'Bosnia: no room for appeasement by Britain or the UN', *The Times*, 17 July 1995, p. 19.

174. Rohde, *End Game*, p. 73.

175. Conor Cruise O'Brien, 'The West rattles a toy sabre', *Independent*, 18 February 1994, p. 18.

176. Picture Caption, 'A toast to UN's humiliation: drinks with the butcher of Bosnia', *Sunday Times*, 16 July 1996, p. 1; Ian Traynor, 'Rampant Serbs push UN aside', *Guardian*, 12 July 1995, p. 1.

177. Michael Evans, 'Capture of Srebrenica strikes mortal blow to UN credibility', *The Times*, 12 July 1995, p. 9; Andrew Marr, 'Do we want a Europe ruled by blood?', *Independent*, 13 July 1995, p. 17.

178. Eric Schmitt, 'U.S. and NATO face unhappy choices for U.N. force in the Balkans', *New York Times*, 12 July 1995, p. A6; See also: Michael Dobbs, 'Serbs may have dealt death blow to U.N. peacekeeping', *Washington Post*, 12 July 1995, p. A15.

179. Patrick Bishop, What's best for them?', *Daily Telegraph*, 13 July 1995, p. 17.

180. Holbrooke, *To End a War*, p. 361; The threat to the Western alliance is also discussed in the following: Michael Barnett, 'The politics of indifference at the United Nations and genocide in Rwanda and Bosnia', in Cushman & Mestrovic, *This Time We Knew*, pp. 128–62.

181. Charles A. Kupchan, 'What does the West stand for if it does nothing?', *Los Angeles Times*, 23 July 1995, p. M1.

182. Simms, *Unfinest Hour*, p. 317.

183. Christopher Brooker, 'Our humbug made the killing fields of Bosnia', *Sunday Telegraph*, 16 July 1995, p. 27.

184. For example, see: Christopher Layne, 'Is America marching to folly once again?', *Los Angeles Times*, 9 August 1992, p. M2; Letter from Michael Colvin, 'Need to help Balkan refugees and make sanctions work', *The Times*, 21 August 1992, p. 11.

185. Will Hutton, 'Why Britain must fight in Bosnia', *Guardian*, 30 August 1995, p. 17; Andrew Neil, 'Appeasement is the only war crime that matters', *Sunday Times*, 16 July 1995, Section 3, p. 7.

186. Cited in: Anthony Lewis, 'Weakness as Policy', *New York Times*, 14 July 1995, p. A25.

187. David Fairhall, 'Fears of Bosnian quagmire haunt the Cabinet', *Guardian*, 19 August 1992, p. 6; see also: Harvey Morris, 'The UN chief gives warning of a Vietnam in Yugoslavia', *Independent*, 3 August 1992, p. 1; John Keegan, 'It'll make good TV but...', *Daily Telegraph*, 8 February 1994, p. 17.

188. Novick, *The Holocaust in American Life*, p. 253; For further discussion of the 'quagmire frame' – in particular its development in U.S. circles in the wake of Vietnam – see: Entman, *Projections of Power*, p. 77; Edward S. Herman & Noam Chomsky, *Manufacturing Consent: The Political Economy of News Media* (London: Vintage, 1994), p. 173.

189. Alan Tonelson, 'The wrong war at the worst time', *Los Angeles Times*, 13 July 1995, p. B9.

190. Editorial, 'Ending our shameful silence', *Guardian*, 10 February 1994, p. 22.

191. Walter Russell Mead, 'Peacemakers no match for ancient Bosnian hatred', *Los Angeles Times*, 16 August 1992, p. M2; Edward Heath, 'Air strikes would mean war', *The Times*, 8 February 1994, p. 18; Fareed Zakaria, 'Stay out of Bosnia', *New York Times*, 8 August 1992, p. A21. See also: Walter Russell Mead, 'The Bosnia trap', *Los Angeles Times*, 13 February 1994, p. M6; Letter from Michael Harbottle, 'Precedents for keeping the peace, pacifying the Balkans and saving the children', *Independent*, 11 August 1992, p. 14.

192. Paul Johnson, 'U.S. would have to go it alone', *Los Angeles Times*, 10 August 1992, p. B5.

193. Norman Stone, 'Shooting down the myth of Serbia's mighty guerrillas', *Sunday Times*, 16 August 1992, Section 2, p. 3; Letter from Timothy L. Francis, 'U.N. calls for Serb camp inspections', *Washington Post*, 14 August 1992, p. A 22.

194. Letter from F. Craig, 'Don't let our men die in Bosnia', *Sunday Telegraph*, 23 July 1995, p. 24.

195. Vincent Price & David Tewksbury, 'News values and public opinion: A theoretical account of priming and framing', in George A. Barnett & Franklin J. Boster (eds), *Progress in Communication Sciences: Advances in Persuasion – Vol.13*, (Greenwich, Connecticut: Ablex, 1997), p. 182.

196. Kirk Hallahan, 'Seven models of framing: Implications for public relations', *Journal of Public Relations Research* 11 (1999), p. 214; see also: Daniel Kahneman & Amos Tversky, 'Prospect theory: An analysis of decision under risk', *Econometrica* 47 (1979), pp. 263–91; Entman, *Projections of Power*, p. 97.

197. Peter Beaumont, 'Attack Serbs now, say British public', *Observer*, 23 July 1995, p. 1; Editorial, 'Senate sends a message on Bosnia', *Chicago Tribune*, 26 July 1995, Section 1, p. 18; see also: Editorial, 'Stand up to Serb bully', *Observer*, 16 July 1995, p. 24.

198. Letter from P.J.W. Raine, 'Mortal danger in the heart of Europe', *Independent*, 20 July 1995, p. 14.

199. Letter from Philip L. Comella, 'Hall of shame', *Chicago Tribune*, 22 July 1995, Section 1, p. 16.

200. Mills, 'The language of slaughter', p. 14; On the second point, whilst this is perhaps obvious in relation to the U.S., which had seen the USHMM open in 1993, the Holocaust was also experiencing a 'popular revival' in the UK, with every school in the country receiving a copy of Schindler's List in 1995 – see: Ian Wall, 'The Holocaust, film and education', in Toby Haggith & Joanna Newman (eds), *Holocaust and the Moving Image: Representations in Film and Television Since 1933* (London: Wallflower Press, 2005), p. 205.

201. Letter from John Strawson, 'Sharing the shame and the blame for Bosnia', *Guardian*, 14 July 1995, p. 18. See also: Alex Duval Smith, 'Chirac rhetoric on "new Holocaust" plays to neo-Gaullist patriots', *Guardian*, 17 July 1995, p. 8; Letter from James Sherr, 'Slow Genocide', *The Times*, 24 July 1995, p. 17.

202. Robin Harris, 'War crimes: look who's guilty now', *Sunday Telegraph*, 16 July 1995, p. 27.

203. Letter from Francis Brown, 'Chirac: the lone crusader', *Daily Telegraph*, 17 July 1995, p. 18; Letter from Francis Brown, 'Bosnian refugees: sickening indifference of Western politicians', *Independent*, 17 July 1995, p. 14; Holly Burkhalter, 'What we can do to stop this genocide', *Washington Post*, 20 July 1995, p. A27.

204. Charles Gati, 'Tell it to Srebrenica', *Washington Post*, 13 July 1995, p. A25. See also: Letter from The Board of Deputies of British Jews, 'Britain should back French call to reinforce safe havens', *Independent*, 21 July 1995, p. 14.

205. Andrew Marr, 'Do we want a Europe ruled by blood?', *Independent*, 13 July 1995, p. 17.

206. Editorial, 'Drawing a line in Bosnia', *Independent*, 21 July 1995, p. 14; Peregrine Worsthorne, 'When it is right to be moral', *Sunday Telegraph*, 23 August 1992, p. 16.

207. Roger Cohen, 'Honor, too, is put to fight in Bosnia', *New York Times*, 16 July 1995, Section 4, p. 1.

208. Editorial, 'Genocide and the UN', *Washington Post*, 9 November 1946, p. 8.

209. Worsthone, 'When it is right to be moral', p. 16.

210. Silber & Little, *The Death of Yugoslavia*, p. 351.

211. Carolyn Hughes, 'UN details mass executions of Muslims by Serbs', *Daily Telegraph*, 24 August 1995, p. 17; John Sweeney, 'UN cover-up of Srebrenica massacre', *Observer*, 10 September 1995, p. 19.

212. William Pfaff, 'Serbs caused own violent retribution', *Chicago Tribune*, 5 September 1995, p. 15; see also: Tracy Wilkinson, 'Sarajevo shelled; At least 35 die', *Los Angeles Times*, 29 August 1995, p. A1; Emma Daly & Mary Dejevsky, 'Serbs blamed for Sarajevo carnage', *Independent*, 29 August 1995, p. 1.

213. Early estimates put the death toll between 33 and 37. See: Stacy Sullivan, 'Shell in Sarajevo market kills 33', *The Times*, 29 August 1995, p. 1; David Rohde, *End Game*, p. 338.

214. Roger Cohen, 'Shelling kills dozens in Sarajevo; U.S. urges Nato to strike Serbs', *New York Times*, 29 August 1995, p. A1; Editorial, 'The terrible case for restraint', *Independent*, 30 August 1995, p. 14; see also: Kurt Schork, 'People were just ripped apart', *Independent*, 29 August 1995, p. 6.

215. Associated Press, 'Six killed in shelling of Sarajevo', *Washington Post*, 23 August 1995, p. A27; Tribune Wires, 'UN returns fire on Serbs after shells blast Sarajevo', *Chicago Tribune*, 23 August 1995, p. 6; Reuters, '6 killed, 38 wounded in Sarajevo', *Los Angeles Times*, 23 August 1995, p. A4.

216. Malcolm, *Bosnia*, p. 261; New York Times Service, 'Sarajevans feel betrayed by the West', *Chicago Tribune*, 30 July 1995, p. 11.

217. Hartman, *The Longest Shadow*, p. 100; Semelin, *Purify and Destroy*, p. 153.

218. For example: Tim Butcher, 'Nato hits back with a vengeance', *Daily Telegraph*, 31 August 1995, p. 1; Christopher Bellamy, 'Nato hails success of massive air attacks', *Independent*, 1 September 1995, p. 11; Mark Farland, 'Bombs leave Slobo sitting pretty', *Observer*, 3 September 1995, p. 17; Ed Vulliamy & Reuter, 'Serbs deft new Nato air strikes', *Guardian*, 6 September 1995, p. 1.

219. Robert Fox, 'America for Bosnia peace deal this month', *Daily Telegraph*, 6 September 1995, p. 12; Associated Press, 'NATO's bombers hit Serb targets', *Chicago Tribune*, 30 August 1995, Evening Update, Section 1, p. 1; The fact that U.S. press coverage often 'waxed and waned depending on the likelihood of American military involvement' has been noted in the following: Cigar, *Genocide in Bosnia*, p. 142.

220. Lawrence Freedman, 'Time to inject lessons of Balkan realism into UN operational manuals', *The Times*, 31 August 1995, p. 2; see also: Holbrooke, *To End a War*, p. 362.

221. Editorial, 'Peace is calling to Bosnia', *Chicago Tribune*, 8 September 1995, p. 22; Letter from Donald Pellico, 'U.S. and Bosnia', *Chicago Tribune*, 29 August 1995, p. 10; Letter from Roderick Bridge, 'The day they dropped the bombs', *Guardian*, 1 September 1995, p. 14; see also: Letter from Stuart Wood, 'Have we forgotten Srebrenica already?', *Independent*, 30 August 1995, p. 14.

222. Letter from Tony Benn MP, Tam Dalyell, M.P. et al. 'The day they dropped the bombs', *Guardian*, 1 September 1995, p. 14; see also: Jonathan Steele, 'Americans eager to bomb and talk', *Guardian*, 7 September 1995, p. 1.

223. Julian Brazier, 'Russia's attitude to Balkan conflict', *The Times*, 12 September 1995, p. 17; Letter from John Hermann, 'West's role in Bosnia', *Los Angeles Times*, 21 July 1995, p. B8.

224. Letter from Mike Prijic Knezevic, 'What makes a Serb a Villain and a Croat a hero?', *New York Times*, 16 September 1995, p. A18.

225. 'Russia accuses NATO of genocide', *Chicago Tribune*, 12 September 1995, Evening Update, p. 1; 'Genocide claim by Russia, *The Times*, 13 September 1995, p. 1.

226. Letter from George Tintor, 'The tables turned in Bosnia', *Independent on Sunday*, 17 September 1995, p. 22; Letter from Geoffrey Darnton, 'The day they dropped the bombs', *Guardian*, 1 September 1995, p. 14.

Chapter 4   A Faraway People

1. Steven K. Baum, *The Psychology of Genocide: Perpetrators, Bystanders, and Rescuers* (New York: Cambridge University Press, 2008), p. 9, Michael Dorland, 'PG – Parental Guidance or Portrayal of Genocide: the Comparative Depiction of Mass Murder in Contemporary Cinema', in Allan Thompson (ed.), *The Media and the Rwanda Genocide* (London: Pluto Press, 2007), p. 429.

2. Bill Berkeley, 'Road to a Genocide', in Mills & Brunner (eds), *The New Killing Fields: Massacre and the Politics of Intervention* (New York: Basic Books, 2003), p. 105; Fergal Keane, *Season of Blood: A Rwandan Journey* – 2nd edition, (London: Penguin Books, 1996), p. 29.

3. The UK Committee for UNICEF, Annual Review, 1994/5, p. 5; Nigel Eltringham, *Accounting for Horror: Post- Genocide Debates in Rwanda* (London: Pluto Press, 2004), p. 63, Guy Arnold, *Africa: A Modern History* (London: Atlantic Books, 2005), pp. 851–2.

4. Samantha Power, *'A Problem From Hell': America and the Age of Genocide* (London: Flamingo, 2003), p. 512.

5. S'Fiso Ngesi & Charles Villa-Vicencio, 'Rwanda: Balancing the Weight of History', in Erik Doxtader & Charles Villa-Vecencio (eds), *Through Fire and Water: The Roots of Division and the Potential for Reconciliation in Africa*, (South Africa: David Philip Publishers, 2003), p. 1; John Reader, *Africa: A Biography of the Continent* (London: Penguin Books, 1998), p. 670.

6. Romeo Dallaire, *Shake Hands With The Devil: The Failure of Humanity in Rwanda* (London: Arrow Books, 2003), p. 314; Christian Jennings, *Across the Red River: Rwanda, Burundi and the Heart of Darkness* (London: Victor Gollancz, 2000), p. 91; Eltringham, *Accounting for Horror*, p. 62; Scott Straus, 'How many perpetrators were there in the Rwandan genocide? An estimate', *Journal of Genocide Research* 6/1 (2004), p. 93.

7. Regarding the description of chaos within early discourse on Rwanda, see: Alison Des Forges, *Leave None to Tell the Story: Genocide in Rwanda* (New York: Human Rights Watch, 1999), p. 151 (see also: p. 474).

8. Michael Barnett, *Eyewitness to a Genocide: The United Nations and Rwanda* (New York: Cornell University Press, 2002), p. 1.
9. Martin Gilbert, *First World War* (London: Weidenfeld & Nicolson, 1994), pp. 540–1.
10. Christopher J. Fettweis, 'War as catalyst: moving World War II to the centre of Holocaust scholarship', *Journal of Genocide Research* 5/2 (2003), p. 235.
11. Member of Rwandan Parliament, Kigali 1998 – cited in: Eltringham, *Post-Genocide Debates*, p. 53; Phillip Gourevitch, *We Wish to Inform You That Tomorrow We Will Be Killed With Our Families* (London: Picador, 2000), p. 115.
12. Linda Melvern, *Conspiracy to Murder: The Rwandan Genocide* (London: Verso, 2006), p. 254; Straus, 'How many perpetrators', p. 88.
13. Thomas Hodgkin, *Nationalism in Colonial Africa* (New York: New York University Press, 1957) pp. 174–5.
14. Heather Jean Brookes, '"Suit, Tie and a Touch of Juju" – The Ideological Construction of Africa: A Critical Discourse Analysis of News on Africa in the British Press', *Discourse Society* 6/4 (1995), p. 484; see also: Ammina Kothari, 'The Framing of the Darfur Conflict in the *New York Times*: 2003–2006', *Journalism Studies* 11/2 (2010), p. 209.
15. William A. Gamson, 'News as Framing', *American Behavioral Scientist* 33 (1989), p. 161; Karen S. Johnson-Cartee, *News Narratives and News Framing: Constructing Political Reality* (Oxford: Rowman & Littlefield, 2005), p. 186; For further discussion of the prominence of 'tribalism' in British framing of African conflicts, see: Brookes, 'Suit, Tie', p. 473.
16. Brookes, 'Suit, Tie', p. 488; see also: Brian V. Street, *The Savage in Literature: Representations of 'Primitive' Society in English Fiction, 1858–1920* (London: Routledge, 1975).
17. V.Y. Mudimbe, *The Invention of Africa: Gnosis, Philosophy, and the Order of Knowledge* (Indianapolis: Indiana University Press, 1988), p. 44.
18. Brookes, 'Suit, Tie', p. 474.
19. Virgil Hawkins, 'The Other Side of the CNN Factor: The Media and Conflict', *Journalism Studies* 3/2 (2002), pp. 228–9.
20. Kothari, 'The Framing of the Darfur', p. 209; Brookes, 'Suit, Tie', p. 465; See also: Beverly Hawk (ed.), *Africa's Media Image* (Westport, CT: Praeger Publishers, 1992).
21. Brookes, 'Suit, Tie', p. 479; See also: Johnson-Cartee, *News Narratives*, p. 235.
22. Arnold S. de Beer, 'News From and In The "Dark Continent": Afro-pessimism, News Flows, Global Journalism and Media Regimes', *Journalism Studies* 11/4 (2010), p. 602.
23. Brookes, 'Suit, Tie', p. 488.
24. Ibid., p. 467.

25. Melvern, *A People Betrayed: The Role of the West in Rwanda's Genocide* (London: Zed Books, 2000), p. 229.

26. Mohamed Adhikari, 'Hotel Rwanda – The challenges of historicising and commercialising genocide', *Development Dialogue* 50 (2008), p. 173.

27. Danuta Reah, *The Language of Newspapers* (London: Routledge, 2005), p. 9.

28. Only the *Guardian*, which produced one front page article in June and none whatsoever in May, did not see June as its worst 'month' against this measure.

29. Reah, *The Language of Newspapers*, p. 28.

30. 'Rwanda toll grows', *Independent on Sunday*, 5 June 1994, p. 1.

31. Power, '*A Problem From Hell*', p. xv; Gourevitch, *We Wish to Inform You*, p. 170.

32. *Broadcasting Genocide: Censorship, Propaganda and State-sponsored Violence in Rwanda 1990–1994*, Article 19. (London: International Centre Against Censorship, 1996), p. 114.

33. Mark Doyle, 'Reporting the Genocide', pp. 153–4.

34. Reah, *The Language of Newspapers*, p. 4.

35. Melvern, 'Missing the Story', p. 208; Melvern, *Conspiracy to Murder*, p. 266.

36. It is possible that the selected newspapers received far more letters than they actually printed. Indeed, MP Tony Worthington stated in correspondence to the *Independent* that he, 'like all MPs' was receiving 'dozens of cards and letters about Rwanda,' – Tony Worthington, 'Government silence on Rwanda genocide', *Independent*, 29 June 1994, p. A1.

37. Cited in: Linda Melvern, *Conspiracy to Murder*, p. 236.

38. Entman, *Projections of Power*, p. 43.

39. Richard Dowden, 'Sweet sour stench of death fills Rwanda', *Independent*, 7 May 1994, p. 13.

40. Jerry Gray, 'Contest for farmland fuels centuries-old African feud', *Guardian*, 12 April 1994, p. 12; William E. Schmidt, 'Deaths in Rwanda fighting said to be 20,000 or more', *New York Times*, 11 April 1994, p. A 12.

41. Letter from Clay Caldwell, 'Tribal conflict', *Chicago Tribune*, 5 May 1994, p. 30.

42. 'A tide of misery', *Washington Post*, 24 July 1994, p. 26.

43. Bernard Levin, 'Poisoning the mind', *The Times*, 12 July 1994, p. 18.

44. Gray, 'Contest for farmland', p. 12; Editorial, 'The means of mercy in Rwanda', *Independent*, 2 May 1994, p. 13; Jonathan Howard, 'Rwanda split by its bloody feudal legacy', *Daily Telegraph*, 10 April 1994, p. 23.

45. Bernard Levin, 'Poisoning the mind', *The Times*, 12 July 1994, p. 18.

46. Jeffrey Lite, 'Before the bloodletting, and after', *Los Angeles Times*, 6 May 1994, p. B7.

47. Tribune Wires, 'Rwanda descends into bloody chaos', *Chicago Tribune*, 8 April 1994, p. 4; Editorial, 'Help Africans help Rwanda', *Chicago Tribune*, 3 May 1994, p. 18.

48. Editorial, 'Double tragedy in Rwanda', *New York Times*, 10 April 1994, sec. 4, p. 18; Reuter, 'Army on orgy of killing in Kigali', *Guardian*, 8 April 1994, p. 8; see also: Edward Luce, 'Killings soar in Rwanda anarchy', *Guardian*, 22 April 1994, p. 20.

49. Tribune Wires, 'Rwanda descends into bloody chaos', *Chicago Tribune*, 8 April 1994, p. 4.

50. Richard Dowden, 'Africa's return to our planet', *Independent*, 16 June 1994, p. 18.

51. Martin Woolacott, 'Africa excludes itself from the map of our moral concern', *Guardian*, 13 April 1994, p. 20.

52. Editorial, 'South Africa's near abroad', *The Times*, 20 June 1994, p. 19; Barbara Amiel, 'There is a Rwandan in all of us', *Sunday Times*, 3 July 1994, section 4, p. 4.

53. Letter from Michael H. Taylor, 'Complexities of Rwanda terror', *The Times*, 14 April 1994, p. 17.

54. Donatella Lorch, 'In the upheaval in Rwanda, few answers yet', *New York Times*, 5 May 1994, p. 3.

55. Richard Dowden, 'A wound at the heart of Africa', *Independent*, 11 May 1994, p. 19.

56. 'Blurred roots of conflict', *Guardian*, 10 May 1994, eG section, p. 13.

57. Kenan Malik, 'Rwanda's unnatural tragedy', *Independent*, 20 July 1994, p. 14.

58. Matthew Parris, 'Britain's lack of interest in Rwanda, in contrast to its stance in Bosnia, is the most insidious form of racism', *The Times*, 11 April 1994, p. 16.

59. Stephen Kinzer, 'European leaders reluctant to send troops to Rwanda', *New York Times*, 25 May 1994, p. 1.

60. Robert D. Kaplan, 'Into the bloody new world', *Washington Post*, 17 April 1994, p. C2.

61. Editorial, 'France's risky Rwanda plan', *New York Times*, 24 June 1994, p. A26; Editorial, 'Washington's Rwanda problems', *Chicago Tribune*, 17 June 1994, p. 20.

62. Henry S. Bienan, 'The morality of selective intervention', *Los Angeles Times*, 22 June 1994, p. B7.

63. Editorial, 'Horror in Rwanda, shame in the U.N.', *New York Times*, 3 May 1994, p. 22.

64. Adonis E. Hoffman, 'A policy of fine words, no actions', *Los Angeles Times*, 12 May 1994, p. B7.

65. Editorial, 'Help Africans help Rwanda', *Chicago Tribune*, 3 May 1994, p. 18.

66. Richard Dowden, 'Don't blame the UN for an American mess', *Independent*, 18 May 1994, p. 16.

67. Editorial, 'Help Africans help Rwanda', *Chicago Tribune*, 3 May 1994, p. 18; Editorial, 'Deadly reality: Rwanda is dying', *Los Angeles Times*, 4 May 1994, p. B6.
68. George B.N. Ayittey, 'Africa's salvation lies within itself', *Los Angeles Times*, 14 April 1994, p. B7.
69. Charles Krauthammer, 'Mandela should lead humanitarian efforts in Rwanda', *Chicago Tribune*, 27 May 1994, p. 21.
70. Stephen Chapman, 'Foreign tragedies test the limits of US obligations', *Chicago Tribune*, 21 April 1994, p. 29.
71. Editorial, 'Who lost Rwanda?', *Washington Post*, 27 July 1994, p. 26.
72. Peter Pringle, 'Can good come from this hell?', *Independent*, 5 May 1994, p. 20; Editorial, 'Look before plunging into Rwanda', *New York Times*, 18 May 1994, p. 22.
73. Editorial, 'Rwanda's descent into hell', *Chicago Tribune*, 24 April 1994, Perspective, p. 2.
74. Julia Preston, 'Rwanda death toll said to top 100,000', *Washington Post*, 22 April 1994, p. A1.
75. Quoted in Jean Davidson, 'Newspaper editor ask: After you report the genocide, then what?', *Chicago Tribune*, 17 April 1994, Chicagoland Final Edition, section 1, p. 22.
76. Moeller, *Compassion Fatigue*, p. 298.
77. Prunier, *The Rwanda Crisis*, p. 273–4; Dallaire, *Shake Hands*, p. 305.
78. Thompson, 'Introduction', p. 4.
79. In *The Times*, for example, the word did not appear until very late in April: Michael Binyon, 'Oxfam warning of Rwanda genocide', *The Times*, 29 April 1994, p. 29; Interestingly, the word actually appeared in the title of a *New York Times* article on 9 April, though this failed to greatly influence subsequent reporting: Jerry Gray, '2 nations joined by common history of genocide', *New York Times*, 9 April 1994, p. A6.
80. Jennifer Parmelee, 'Rebels advance in Rwanda, vow to take over capital', *Washington Post*, 12 April 1994, p. 13.
81. Donatella Lorch, 'Rwanda forces shell stadium full of refugees', *New York Times*, 20 April 1994, p. A8.
82. For example, see: Reuter, 'Terrified UN soldiers pull out of Rwanda', *Independent*, 21 April 1994, p. 12; 'UN troops flee from bloodbath in Kigali', *The Times*, 21 April 1994, p. 10; Reuters, 'Rebel official calls a truce for Rwanda', *New York Times*, 24 April 1994, p. A9; Reuter, 'Rebels call cease-fire', *Washington Post*, 24 April 1994, p. A22.
83. Reuter, 'Rwandan guerrillas declare ceasefire', *Independent*, 24 April 1994, p. 13; Reuter, 'Rwanda appeal', *The Times*, 28 April 1994, p. 15.
84. AFP, 'Kigali Threat', *The Times*, 27 April 1994, p. 10.

85. Times Wire Services, 'Rwanda massacre', *Los Angeles Times*, 21 April 1994, p. B6; Associated Press, 'Hundreds of UN troops exit Rwanda – One group puts death toll at 100,000', *Chicago Tribune*, 21 April 1994, North Sports Final Edition, p. 4.
86. Scott Peterson, '100,000 dead in Rwanda fighting', *Daily Telegraph*, 22 April 1994, p. 14.
87. Sarah Lambert, ' "8,000" butchered in Rwanda capital', *Independent on Sunday*, 10 April 1994, p. 1.
88. Power, *'A Problem From Hell'*, p. 307.
89. Kuperman, *The Limits of Humanitarian*, p. vii.
90. Kinglsey Moghalu, *Rwanda's Genocide: The Politics of Global Justice* (Hampshire: Palgrave MacMillan, 2005), p. 17; Barnett, *Eyewitness*, p. 150.
91. Associated Press, 'Rwanda rebels shell capital and army units', *New York Times*, 11 May 1994, p. A9; other examples include: Thaddee Nsengiyaremye, 'Hutus urged to take up arms as fighting rages', *Independent*, 6 May 1994, p. 12; Associated Press, 'U.N. Rwandan toll is more than 200,000', *Chicago Tribune*, 19 May 1994, North Sports Final Edition, p. 6; Paul Lewis, '3 African lands offer troops for Rwanda', *New York Times*, 25 May 1994, p. A12.
92. Associated Press, 'Rwandan death toll may exceed 200,000', *Washington Post*, 19 May 1994, p. A32.
93. For example: Reid Miller, 'Rwandan rebels gaining ground', *Daily Telegraph*, 7 May 1994, p. 15.; Hugh Davies & Jonathan Petre, 'UN rejects Rwanda troops plea', *Sunday Telegraph*, 1 May 1994, p. 2.
94. Editorial from the Orlando Sentinel, 'UN correct on Rwanda', *Chicago Tribune*, 23 May 1994, North Sports Final Edition, Section 1, p. 13.
95. Moeller, *Compassion Fatigue*, p. 252.
96. Ibid., p. 57.
97. This is described in: Aidan Hartley, *The Zanzibar Chest: A Memoir of Love and War* (London: HarperCollins, 2003), p. 381.
98. For example: Associated Press, 'Rwanda tragedy compared to Cambodia', *Chicago Tribune*, 4 May 1994, North Sports Final Edition, p. 12; Times Wire Services, 'Enemies negotiate U.N. control of Rwanda airport', *Los Angeles Times*, 19 May 1994, p. A13.
99. Reuter, '"Up to 500,000 killed" in Rwanda', *Guardian*, 14 May 1994, p. 14; Patrick Bishop, 'UN is urged not to delay intervention in Rwanda conflict', *Daily Telegraph*, 13 May 1994, p. 14.
100. Patrick Bishop, '500,000 reported dead in Rwanda bloodbath', *Daily Telegraph*, 19 May 1994, p. 12.
101. Steven Livingstone, 'Limited Vision', p. 190.

102. Cited in: Moeller, *Compassion Fatigue*, p. 34.
103. Tina Susman, '20,000 may have died in massacre at convent', *Daily Telegraph*, 1 June 1994, p. 14.
104. For example: Colin Smith, 'Stand still as I slaughter you', *Sunday Times*, 12 June 1994, p. 19.
105. Reuter, 'Tutsi rebels closing in', *Independent on Sunday*, 5 June 1994, p. 14: Cited in: Moeller, Compassion Fatigue, p. 22; These 'death ratios' are also discussed in Virgil Hawkins, 'The Other Side of the CNN Factor: The Media and Conflict', *Journalism Studies* Vol.3 (1), (2002), p. 230; See also: Herman & Chomsky, *Manufacturing Consent*, p. 39.
106. Moeller, *Compassion Fatigue*, p. 36.
107. Mark Huband, 'World sits on its hands as Rwanda bleeds to death', *Observer*, 19 June 1994, p. 19.
108. Roger Winter, 'Journey Into Genocide: A Rwanda Diary', *Washington Post*, 5 June 1994, p. 1; Richard Dowden, 'A wound at the heart of Africa', *Independent*, 11 May 1994, p. 19.
109. Charles Krauthammer, 'Mandela should lead humanitarian efforts in Rwanda', *Chicago Tribune*, 23 May 1994, North Sports Final Edition, p. 21; see also – Adrian Hamilton, 'Risky gestures that kill hope', *Observer*, 24 April 1994, p.27.
110. Charles Krauthammer, 'Stop the genocide in Rwanda', *Washington Post*, 27 May 1994, p. A25.
111. See: David Fetherstonhaugh, Paul Slovic, Stephen M. Johnson & James Friedrich, 'Insensitive to the value of human life: A study of psychophysical numbing', *Journal of Risk and Uncertainty* 14 (1997), p. 298; S. Slovic & P. Slovic, 'Numbers and nerves: Toward an affective apprehension of environmental risk', *Whole Terrain* 13, pp. 14–18.
112. Andrew Nastios, 'Illusions of influence: The CNN effect in complex emergencies', in Rotberg & Weiss (eds), *From Massacres to Genocide*, pp. 149–68.
113. Gourevitch, *We Wish to Inform*, p. 165.
114. Cited in: Moeller, Compassion Fatigue, p. 281.
115. Herman Cohen, 'Getting Rwanda wrong', *Washington Post*, 3 June 1994, p. A23.
116. Keith B. Richburg, 'Westerners begin fleeing Rwanda', *Washington Post*, 10 April 1994, p. 1; for examples of focus on western evacuation, as opposed to the genocide, see: Annabel Heseltine, 'Westerners airlifted out of Rwandan bloodbath', *Sunday Times*, 10 April 1994, p. 1; Jennifer Parmelee, 'Americans are out of Rwanda', *Washington Post*, 11 April 1994, p. 1; Melissa Healy & Tyler Marshall, 'Amid Chaos in Rwanda, U.S. Plans for Evacuation', *Los Angeles Times*, 9 April 1994, p. 1.
117. Keane, *Season of Blood*, p. 7.

118. Woollacott, 'Africa excludes itself', p. 20.
119. Editorial, 'Africa is not a lost continent', *Independent*, 11 April 1994, p. 15.
120. Parris, 'Britain's lack of interest', p. 16.
121. Alan Kuperman, 'How the media missed the Rwandan genocide', in Thompson (ed.), *The Media and the Rwanda Genocide*, p. 257.
122. As well as the *Guardian*, these were the *Independent*, *Los Angeles Times* & *The Times*.
123. Letter from Chris Boles, Bernard Elliot & Stephen Power, 'Back to fear?', *Guardian*, 14 April 1994, p. 23.
124. Steven Livingstone, 'Limited Vision', p. 189.
125. Editorial, 'The worst killing since Cambodia', *Independent*, 24 May 1995, p. 15.
126. Donatella Lorch, 'Bodies from Rwanda cast a pall on lakeside villages in Rwanda', *New York Times*, 28 May 1994, p. A1; see also: Reuter, 'Agony by the shores of Lake Victoria', *Guardian*, 27 May 1994, p. 13; David Lamb, 'Rwandan dead glut the waters of Lake Victoria', *Los Angeles Times*, 29 May 1994, p. 1; Donatella Lorch, 'Thousands of Rwanda dead wash down to Lake Victoria', *New York Times*, 21 May 1994, p. 1.
127. Richard Dowden, 'French press on with Rwanda mission', *Independent*, 21 June 1994, p. 11.
128. Editorial, 'Let France act in Rwanda', *Chicago Tribune*, 22 June 1994, p. 22.
129. Editorial, 'France helps in Rwanda', *New York Times*, 14 July 1994, p. 22.
130. Scott Kraft, 'France's big gamble pays off in Rwanda', *Los Angeles Times*, 16 July 1994, p. A1.
131. Associated Press, 'French troops warmly welcomed in Rwanda', *Chicago Tribune*, 26 June 1994, p. 4; Andrew Gumbel, 'French aim in Rwanda "is to save lives"', *Guardian*, 20 June 1994, p. 9; Robert Block, 'Rwandan put their faith in God and their trust in paratroopers', *Independent*, 27 June 1994, p. 1.
132. Paul Webster, 'France ducks as the shells whistle in', *Guardian*, 7 July 1994, p. 26; see also: Foreign Staff, 'French Foreign Legion rolls into Rwanda', *Guardian*, 24 June 1994, p. 1; Scott Peterson, 'French troops move in but killing continues', *Daily Telegraph*, 28 June 1994, p. 16; Associated Press, 'France arms joint African force', *Daily Telegraph*, 15 July 1994, p. 13.
133. Victoria Brittain, 'France's fatal impact', *Guardian*, 24 June 1994, p. 22.
134. Editorial, 'Going wrong in Rwanda', *Guardian*, 6 July 1994, p. 23.
135. Richard Dowden, 'A very French affair in Rwanda', *Independent*, 6 July 1994, p. 16.
136. Mark Huband, 'World sits on its hands as Rwanda bleeds to death', *Guardian*, 19 June 1994, p. 19.

137. Letter from Tony Carter, 'France's unacceptable role in Rwanda', *Guardian*, 12 July 1994, p. 19.
138. Editorial, 'A rash French venture in Rwanda', *Independent*, 21 June 1994, p. 15.
139. Ibid.
140. Letter from Donald Hart, 'Before we applaud France's mission to Rwanda', *New York Times*, 1 July 1994, p. 24.
141. Tribune Wires, '"The exodus of a nation"', *Chicago Tribune*, 18 July 1994, North Sports Final Edition, p. 1.
142. Dowden, *The Media's Failure*, p. 250.
143. Edward Luce & John Carvel, 'UN faces Rwanda crisis', *Guardian*, 20 July 1994, p. 1.
144. Tribune Wires, 'Emergency aid for Rwanda', *Chicago Tribune*, 29 July 1994, p. 1.
145. Anna Quidlen, 'Rwanda's appeal to the heart fades as compassion fails', *Chicago Tribune*, 25 July 1994, p. 13.
146. Editorial, 'Rwandan rescue', *The Times*, 23 July 1994, p. 15.
147. Herman & Chomsky, *Manufacturing Consent*, p. 228.
148. Prunier, *The Rwanda Crisis*, p. 268.
149. Editorial, 'Get help to Rwanda in a hurry', *Chicago Tribune*, 22 July 1994, p. 22.
150. Editorial, 'But is the world equal to this catastrophe?', *Los Angeles Times*, 22 July 1994, p. B6; Editorial, 'Help for haemorrhaging Rwanda', *Chicago Tribune*, 16 July 1994, North Sports Final Edition, p. 20; see also: Editorial, 'To help Africa', *The Times*, 25 July 1994, p. 17; Editorial, '"Who lost Rwanda?"', *Washington Post*, 27 July 1994, p. 26.
151. Editorial, 'Rwanda shows aid is not enough', *Observer*, 24 July 1994, p. 26; Editorial, 'Get help to Rwanda', *Chicago Tribune*, p. 22.
152. Editorial, 'The hell of reproach that is Goma', *Guardian*, 23 July 1994, p. 24.
153. Robert B. Oakley, 'A slow response on Rwanda', *Washington Post*, 27 July 1994, p. 27.
154. Romeo Dallaire, 'The media dichotomy', in Thompson, *The Media and the Rwanda Genocide*, p. 16.
155. Kenneth W. Harrow, '"Ancient Tribal Warfare": Foundational Fantasies of Ethnicity and History', *Research in African Literatures* 36/2 (2005), p. 40.
156. John Darnton, 'Does the world still recognise a holocaust?', *New York Times*, 25 April 1993, sec. 4, p. 1.
157. Dallaire, *Shake Hands With*, p. 513.
158. Richard Cohen, 'In no man's land', *Washington Post*, 31 May 1994, p. A17.

Chapter 5   From Disbelief to Disinterest

1. Philip Gourevitch, *We Wish to Inform You That Tomorrow We Will Be Killed With Our Families* (London: Picador, 2000), p. 165.

2. Mark Mazower, *The Balkans: From the End of Byzantium to the Present Day* (London: Phoenix Press, 2001), p. 4.

3. Roland Oliver, quoted in: Jonathan Benthall, *Disaster, Relief and the Media* (London: Flamingo, 2003), p. 307.

4. Samantha Power, *'A Problem From Hell': America and the Age of Genocide* (London: Flamingo, 2003), p. 307.

5. Wolfgang Sofsky, *Violence: Terrorism, Genocide, War* (London: Granta Books, 2003), p. 79.

6. Cited in: Heike Harting, 'Global humanitarianism, race, and the spectacle of the African corpse in current western representations of the Rwandan genocide', *Comparative Studies of South Asia, Africa and the Middle East* 28/1 (2008), p. 62.

7. Ian Kershaw, *Hitler, The Germans, and the Final Solution* (London: Yale University Press, 2008), p. 148.

8. Susan Sontag, *Regarding the Pain of Others* (London: Penguin Books, 2003), p. 96.

9. Elliott Cohen, 'Letters', *Commentary* 4 (October 1947), p. 348.

10. Geoffrey Hartman, *The Longest Shadow: In the Aftermath of the Holocaust* (London: Palgrave, 2002), pp. 100.

11. Sontag, *Regarding the Pain*, pp. 18–19.

12. Michael Barnett, *Eyewitness to a Genocide: The United Nations and Rwanda* (New York: Cornell University Press, 2002), p. 131; Gourevitch, *We Wish to Inform You*, p. 19.

13. Susan D. Moeller, *Compassion Fatigue: How the Media Sell Disease, Famine, War and Death* (London: Routledge, 1999), p. 304.

14. Sofsky, *Violence*, p. 16.

15. Ibid, p. 28.

16. Hartman, *The Longest Shadow*, p. 145.

17. Cited in: Tony Judt, '"The problem of evil in postwar Europe"', *New York Review*, 14 February 2008, p. 33.

18. Letter from Yahya R. Kamalipour, 'The world's shames', *Chicago Tribune*, 31 January 1994, p. 14.

19. Judith E. Doneson, *The Holocaust in American Film* – 2nd edition (New York: Syracuse University Press, 2002), pp. 187–8.

20. Moeller, *Compassion Fatigue*, p. 223.

21. Sofsky, *Violence*, p. 77.

22. Ibid., p. 86.
23. Patrick Cockburn, 'Sight that shook the world', *Independent*, 9 August 1992, p. 23.
24. Cited in: Katherine Bischoping & Andrea Kalmin, 'Public opinion about comparisons to the Holocaust', *Public Opinion Quarterly* 63 (1999), p. 486.
25. Peter Novick, *The Holocaust in American Life* (New York: Mariner Books, 2000), p. 197.
26. Cited in: Tim Cole, *Selling the Holocaust: How History is Bought, Packaged and Sold* (New York: Routledge, 2000), p. 13.
27. Novick, *The Holocaust in American Life*, p. 255.
28. Cited in: Matthew Krain, 'International intervention and the severity of genocides and politicides', *International Studies Quarterly* 49/3 (2005), p. 363.

Bibliography

Books

Abzug, R. *Inside the Vicious Heart: Americans and the Libesration of Nazi Concentration Camps* (New York: Oxford University Press, 1987).

Adelman, H. and Suhrke, A. (eds) *The Path of Genocide: The Rwanda Crisis from Uganda to Zaire* (New Brunswick, NJ: Transaction, 1999).

Aharoni, Z. & Dietl, W. *Operation Eichmann: Pursuit and Capture* (London: Weidenfeld & Nicholson, 1997).

Ambrose, S.E. *Band of Brothers* (London: Simon & Schuster, 2001).

Andreas, P. *Blue Helmets and Black Markets: The Business of Survival in the Siege of Sarajevo* (London: Cornell University Press, 2008).

Anyidoho, H.K. *Guns Over Kigali* (Accra: Woeli Publishing Services, 1997).

Arnold, G. *Africa: A Modern History* (London: Atlantic Books, 2005).

Asante, M.K. *The History of Africa: The Quest for Eternal Harmony* (London: Routledge, 2007).

Avisar, I. *Screening the Holocaust: Cinema's Images of the Unimaginable* (Indianapolis: Indiana University Press, 1988).

Axtell, J. *Beyond 1492: Encounters in Colonial North America* (New York: Oxford University Press, 1992).

Balakian, P. *The Burning Tigris: A History of the Armenian Genocide* (London: Pimlico, 2005).

Bankier, D. *The Germans and the Final Solution: Public Opinion Under Nazism* (Oxford: Blackwell, 1992).

Bardgett, S. & Cesarani, D. (eds) *Belsen 1945: New Historical Perspectives* (London: Vallentine Mitchell, 2006).

Barnett, M. *Eyewitness to a Genocide: The United Nations and Rwanda* (New York: Cornell University Press, 2002).

Bartov, O. *Murder in Our Midst: The Holocaust, Industrial Killing, and Representation* (Oxford: Oxford University Press, 1996)

Baum, S.K. *The Psychology of Genocide: Perpetrators, Bystanders, and Rescuers* (New York: Cambridge University Press, 2008).

Benthall, J. *Disasters, Relief and the Media* (London: I.B.Tauris, 1993).

Berkeley, B. *The Graves Are Not Yet Full: Race, Tribe and Power in the Heart of Africa* (New York: Basic Books, 2001).

241

Bibliography

Bieber, F., Galijas, A. & Archer, R. (eds) *Debating the End of Yugoslavia* (London: Routledge, 2014).

Biondich, M. *The Balkans: Revolution, War, and Political Violence Since 1878* (Oxford: Oxford University Press, 2011).

Breitman, R. *Official Secrets: What the Nazis Planned; What the British and Americans Knew* (London: Penguin Books, 2000).

Brooks, B.S., Kennedy, G., Moen, D. & Ranly, D. *News Reporting and Writing* – 6th edition (Boston: Bedford, 1999).

Browning, C. *Ordinary Men: Reserve Battalion 101 and the Final Solution in Poland* (New York: Harper Perennial, 1998).

Burleigh, M. *The Third Reich: A New History* (London: Pan MacMillan, 2001).

Butcher, T. *Blood River: A Journey to Africa's Broken Heart* (London: Vintage Books, 2008).

Bryce, J. & Toynbee, A.J. (eds) *The Treatment of Armenians in the Ottoman Empire, 1915–1916: Documents Presented to Viscount Grey of Falloden* (London: Gomidas Institute, 2005).

Cargas, H. *Problems Unique to the Holocaust* (Kentucky: The University Press of Kentucky, 1999).

Cesarani, D. *Eichmann: His Life and Crimes* (London: Vintage, 2005).

Chan, S. *Grasping Africa: A Tale of Tragedy and Achievement* (London: I.B.Tauris, 2007).

Chouliaraki, L. *The Spectatorship of Suffering* (London: Sage Publications, 2006).

Churchill, W. *A Little Matter of Genocide: Holocaust and Denial in the America's 1492 to Present* (San Francisco: City Lights Books, 1997).

Cigar, N. *Genocide in Bosnia: The Policy of 'Ethnic Cleansing'* (Texas: Texas A&M University Press, 1995).

Cohen, J. *One Hundred Days of Silence: America and the Rwanda Genocide* (Lanham: Rowman and Littlefield Publishers Inc, 2007).

Cole, T. *Selling the Holocaust: From Auschwitz to Schindler: How History is Bought, Packaged and Sold* (New York; Routledge, 2000).

Conboy, M. *Journalism Studies: The Basics* (London: Routledge, 2013).

Cushman, T. & Mestrovic, S. (eds) *This Time We Knew: Western Responses to Genocide in Bosnia* (New York: New York University Press, 1996).

Dallaire, R. *Shake Hands with the Devil: The Failure of Humanity in Rwanda* (London: Arrow Books Ltd, 2003).

Dean, C.J. *The Fragility of Empathy After the Holocaust* (London: Cornell University Press, 2004).

Des Forges, A. *Leave None to Tell the Story: Genocide in Rwanda* (New York: Human Rights Watch, 1999).

Diamond, Jared. *The Rise and Fall of the Third Chimpanzee* (London: Vintage Books, 2002).

Bibliography

——— *Collapse: How Societies Choose to Fail or Succeed* (New York: Viking Books, 2005).

Doneson, J. *The Holocaust in American Film* – 2nd edition (New York: Syracuse University Press, 2002).

Donia, R. *Radovan Karadzic: Architect of the Bosnian Genocide* (Cambridge: Cambridge University Press, 2014).

Doxtader, E. & Villa-Vecencio, C. (eds) *Through Fire and Water: The Roots of Division and the Potential for Reconciliation in Africa* (South Africa: David Philip Publishers, 2003).

Drew, E. *On the Edge: The Clinton Presidency* (New York: Simon and Schuster, 1994).

Durham, M.E. *Twenty Years of Balkan Tangle* (London: George Allen & Unwin, 1920).

Eckhardt, A. (ed.) *Burning Memory: Times of Testing and Reckoning* (Oxford: Pergamon Press, 1993).

Eltringham, N. *Accounting for Horror: Post-Genocide Debates in Rwanda* (London: Pluto Press, 2004).

Entman, R.M. *Projections of Power: Framing News, Public Opinion, and U.S. Foreign Policy* (Chicago: University of Chicago Press, 2004).

Evensen, B.J. *The Responsible Reporter: News Gathering and Writing with the Highest Standards of Professional and Personal Conduct* – 2nd edition (Northport: Vision Press, 1997).

Favez, J. *The Red Cross and the Holocaust* – edited and translated by John and Beryl Fletcher (Cambridge: Cambridge University Press, 1999).

Fein, H. *Genocide: A Sociological Perspective* (London: Sage, 1993).

Ferguson, N. *The Pity of War* (London: Allen Lane, 1998).

——— *Colossus: The Rise and Fall of the American Empire* (London: Penguin, 2005).

——— *The War of the World: History's Age of Hatred* (London: Penguin Books, 2006).

Filstiner, J. *Paul Celan: Poet, Survivor, Jew* (New Haven: Yale University Press, 2001).

Finkelstein, N.G. *The Holocaust Industry: Reflections on the Exploitation of Jewish Suffering* – 2nd paperback edition (London: Verso, 2003).

Flanzbaum, H. *The Americanization of the Holocaust* (London: The John Hopkins University Press, 1999).

Fowler, R. *Language in the News: Discourse and Ideology in the Press* (London: Routledge, 1991).

Fox, J. *Teaching the Holocaust: The report of a survey in the United Kingdom – 1987* (Leicester: National Yad Vashem Charitable Trust, 1989).

Frere, M. *The Media and Conflicts in Central Africa* (London: Lynne Riener Publishers, Inc., 2007)

Friedlander, S. (ed.) *Probing the Limits of Representation: Nazism and the 'Final Solution'* (Cambridge MA: Harvard University Press, 1992).

Bibliography

—— *The Years of Extermination: Nazi Germany and the Jews, 1939–1945* (London: Weidenfeld & Nicolson, 2007).

Gardner, D. *Risk: The Science and Politics of Fear* (London: Virgin Books, 2009).

Garrard, E. & Scarre, G. (eds) *Moral Philosophy and the Holocaust* (Aldershot: Ashgate Publishing Limited, 2003).

Geras, N. *The Contract of Mutual Indifference: Political Philosophy After the Holocaust* (London: Verso, 1999).

Geshkof, T.I. *Balkan Union: A Road to Peace in Southeastern Europe* (New York: Columbia University Press, 1940).

Gilbert, M. *The Holocaust: The Jewish Tragedy* (London: Fontana Press, 1987).

—— *First World War* (London: Weidenfeld and Nicolson, 1994).

—— *Auschwitz and The Allies* (London: Pimlico, 2001).

Gladwell, M. *The Tipping Point: How Little Things Can Make a Big Difference* (London: Abacus, 2008).

Glenny, M. *The Fall of Yugoslavia* – 3rd edition (London: Penguin, 1996).

—— *The Balkans: 1804–1999 – Nationalism, War and the Great Powers* (London: Granta Books, 2000).

Glover, J. *Humanity: A Moral History of the Twentieth Century* (London: Yale University Press, 2001).

Goldhagen, D. *Hitler's Willing Executioners* (New York: Knopf, 1996).

Gourevitch, P. *We Wish to Inform You That Tomorrow We Will Be Killed with Our Families*, paperback edition (London: Picador, 2000).

Graber, D. *Mass Media and American Politics* (Washington, DC: Congressional Quarterly Press, 1980).

Graber, G.S. *History of the SS* (London: Robert Hale, 1978).

Gutman, R. *A Witness to Genocide* (Dorset: Element Books, 1993).

Habermas, J. *The New Conservartism: Cultural Criticism and Historians Debate* (Cambridge: Polity Press, 1989).

Hackett, D. (tran.) *The Buchenwald Report* (Colorado: Westview Press, 1995).

Haggith, T. & Newman, J. (eds) *Holocaust and the Moving Image: Representations in Film and Television Since 1933* (London: Wallflower Press, 2005).

Hammond, P. & Herman, E. *Degraded Capability: The Media and the Kosovo Crisis* (London: Pluto Press, 2000).

Hansen, L. *Security as Practice: Discourse Analysis and the Bosnian War* (London: Routledge, 2006).

Hartley, A. *The Zanzibar Chest: A Memoir of Love and War* (London: Harper Collins, 2003).

Harms, K., Reuter, L.R. & Durr, V. *Coping with the Past: Germany and Austria after 1945* (Winconsin: The University of Winconsin Press, 1990).

Hartman, G. *The Longest Shadow: In the Aftermath of the Holocaust* (London: Palgrave, 2002).

Bibliography

Hausner, G. *Justice in Jerusalem* (London: Nelson, 1967).

Hawk, B. (ed.) *Africa's Media Image* (Westport, CT: Praeger Publishers, 1992).

Hayes, P. (ed.) *Lessons and Legacies: The Meaning of the Holocaust in a Changing World* (Illinois: Northwestern Press, 1991).

Herman, E.S. & Chomsky, N. *Manufacturing Consent: The Political Economy of the Mass Media* (London: Vintage, 1994).

Hinton, A. & O'Neill, K.L. *Genocide: Truth, Memory, and Representation* (London: Duke University Press, 2009).

Hitchcock, W. *Liberation: The Bitter Road to Freedom, Europe 1944-1945* (London: Faber and Faber Limited, 2009).

Hodgkin, T. *Nationalism in Colonial Africa* (New York: New York University Press, 1957).

Holbrooke, R. *To End a War* (New York: The Modern Library, 1999).

Honig, J.W. & Both, N. *Srebrenica: Record of a War Crime* (London: Penguin Books, 1996).

Horne, J.H. & Kramer, A. *German Atrocities 1914: A History of Denial* (London: Yale University Press, 2002).

Huntington, S.P. *The Clash of Civilizations and the Remaking of the World Order* (London: Simon and Schuster, 2002).

Ignatieff, M. *The Warrior's Honor: Ethnic War and the Modern Conscience* (New York: Metropolitan Holt, 1997).

Insdorf, A. *Indelible Shadows: Film and the Holocaust*, 3rd edition (Cambridge: Cambridge University Press, 2003).

James, D. *Schindler's List: Images of the Steven Spielberg Film* (New York: Newmarket, 2004).

James, L. *The Rise and Fall of the British Empire* (London: Abacus, 1998).

Jamieson, K.H. and Waldman, P. *The Press Effect: Politicians, Journalists, and the Stories that Shape the Political World* (New York: Oxford University Press, 2003).

Jennings, C. *Across the Red River: Rwanda, Burundi and the Heart of Darkness* (London: Victor Gollancz, 2000).

Johnson, E.A. & Reuband, K. *What We Knew: Terror, Mass Murder, and Everyday Life in Nazi Germany* (Cambridge: Basic Books, 2005).

Johnson-Cartee, K.S. *News Narratives and News Framing: Constructing Political Reality* (Oxford: Rowman & Littlefield, 2005).

Jones, A. *Genocide: A Comprehensive Introduction* (London: Routledge, 2006).

Kapuscinski, R. *The Other* (London: Verso, 2008).

Keane, F. *Season of Blood: A Rwandan Journey*, 2nd edition (London: Penguin Books, 1996).

Kemp, P. (ed.) *The Relief of Belsen: April 1945 Eye Witness Accounts* (London: Imperial War Museum, 1991).

Bibliography

Kent, G. *Framing War and Genocide: British Policy and News Media Reaction to the War in Bosnia* (New York: Hampton Press, 2005).

Kershaw, I. *Hitler, The Germans, and the Final Solution* (London: Yale University Press, 2008).

—— *Fateful Choices: Ten Decisions That Changed the World, 1940–1941* (London: Penguin, 2008).

Knapp, G.H. *The Tragedy of Bitlis* (New York: F.H. Revell, 1919).

Kuper, L. *Genocide: Its Political Use in the Twentieth Century* (London: Yale University Press, 1981).

Kuperman, A.J. *The Limits of Humanitarian Intervention: Genocide in Rwanda* (Washington, DC: Brookings, 2001).

Kushner, T. *The Holocaust and the Liberal Imagination: A Social and Cultural History* (Oxford: Blackwell, 1994).

Lang, B. *Post-Holocaust: Interpretation, Misinterpretation and the Claims of History* (Bloomington: Indiana University Press, 2005).

Lanzmann, C. *Shoah: An Oral History of the Holocaust* (New York: Pantheon Books, 1985).

Laqueur, W. *The Terrible Secret: Suppression of the Truth About Hitler's 'Final Solution'* (Boston: Littlehampton Books, 1980).

Lawrence, J. *Warrior Race: A History of the British at War* (London: Abacus, 2002).

Lee, S.J. *Hitler and Nazi Germany* (London: Routledge, 2001).

Leff, L. *Buried by The Times: The Holocaust and America's Most Important Newspaper* (New York: Cambridge University Press, 2005).

Lemkin, R. *Axis Rule in Occupied Europe: Laws of occupation, analysis of Government, Proposals for Redress* (Washington, DC: Carnegie Endowment for International Peace, 1944).

Levene, M., Johnson, R. & Roberts, P. *History at the End of the World? History, Climate Change and the Possibility of Change* (Penrith: Humanities E-Books, 2010).

Levy, D. & Sznaider, N. *The Holocaust and Memory in the Global Age* (Philadelphia: Temple University Press, 2006).

Lindemann, A.S. *Anti-Semitism Before the Holocaust* (Essex: Pearson Education Limited, 2000).

Lipstadt, D. *Beyond Belief: The American Press & The Coming of the Holocaust 1933–1935* (New York: The Free Press, 1986).

—— *Denying the Holocaust: The Growing Assault on Truth and Memory* (London: Penguin, 1993).

Lochner, L.P. *What About Germany?* (New York: Dodd, Mead & Co, 1942).

Lookstein, H. *Were We Our Brothers' Keepers? The Public Response of American Jews to the Holocaust 1938–1944* (New York: Vintage Books, 1988).

Bibliography

Loshitzky, Y. *Spielberg's Holocaust: Critical Perspectives on Schindler's List* (Indianapolis: Indiana University Press, 1997).

Lule, J. *Daily News, Eternal Stories: The Mythological Role of Journalism* (New York: Guilford Press, 2001).

Mamdani, M. *When Victims Become Killers: Colonialism, Nativism and the Genocide in Rwanda* (Princeton: Princeton University Press, 2001).

Malcolm, N. *Bosnia: A Short History* (London: Pan Books, 1996).

—— *Bosnia: A Short History* (London: Pan MacMillan, 2002).

Marcuse, H. *Legacies of Dachau: The Uses and Abuses of a Concentration Camp, 1933–2001* (Cambridge: Cambridge University Press, 2001).

Marrus, M. *The Holocaust in History* (Toronto: Key Porter Books, 2000).

Mazower, M. *Dark Continent: Europe's Twentieth Century* (London: Penguin Books, 1999).

—— *The Balkans: From the End of Byzantium to the Present Day* (London: Phoenix Press, 2001).

McCormick, P. *The Other Balkan Wars. A 1913 Carnegie Endowment Inquiry in Retrospect with a New Introduction and Reflections on the Present Conflict by George F. Kennan* (Washington, DC: Carnegie Endowment for International Peace, 1993).

McLuhan, M. *Understanding Media: The Extensions of Man* (Cambridge: MIT Press, 1994).

McNair, B. *News and Journalism in the UK*, 2nd edition (London: Routledge, 1996).

—— *The Sociology of Journalism* (London: Arnold, 1998).

—— *Journalism and Democracy: An Evaluation of the Political Public Sphere* (London: Routledge, 2000).

Mead, G. *Mind, Self, and Society: From the Standpoint of a Social Behaviorist* (Chicago: University of Chicago Press, 1934).

Melvern, L. *A People Betrayed: The Role of the West in Rwanda's Genocide* (London: Zed Books, 2000).

—— *Conspiracy to Murder: The Rwandan Genocide* (London: Verso, 2006).

Mills, N. & Brunner, K. *The New Killing Fields: Massacre and the Politics of Intervention*, 2nd edition (New York: Basic Books, 2003).

Mintz, A. *Popular Culture and the Shaping of Holocaust Memory in America* (Seattle: University of Washington Press, 2001).

Moghalu, K. *Rwanda's Genocide: The Politics of Global Justice* (Hampshire: Palgrave MacMillan, 2005).

Moeller, S. *Compassion Fatigue: How the Media Sell Disease, Famine, War and Death* (London: Routledge, 1999).

Moore, J. (ed.) *Hard Choices: Moral Dilemmas in Humanitarian Intervention* (Oxford: Rowman & Littlefield Publishers, Inc, 1998).

Bibliography

Morse, A.D. *While Six Million Died: A Chronicle of American Apathy* (New York: Random House, 1967).

Mudimbe, V.Y. *The Invention of Africa: Gnosis, Philosophy, and the Order of Knowledge* (Indianapolis: Indiana University Press, 1988).

Naughtie, J. *The Accidental American: Tony Blair and the Presidency* (London: Pan Books, 2005).

Nimmo, D. & Combs, J. *Mediated Political Realities* (New York: Longman, 1983).

Nettelfield, L. & Wagner, S. *Srebrenica in the Aftermath of Genocide* (New York: Cambridge University Press, 2014).

Neufeld, M. & Berenbaum, M. *The Bombing of Auschwitz: Should the Allies Have Attempted It?* (Kansas: University Press of Kansas, 2003).

Newbury, C. *The Cohesion of Oppression: Clientship and Ethnicity in Rwanda, 1860– 1950* (New York: Columbia University Press, 1988).

Novick, P. *The Holocaust in American Life* (New York: Mariner Books, 2000).

Off, C. *The Lion, the Fox, and the Eagle: A Story of Generals and Justice in Rwanda and Yugoslavia* (Toronto: Random House Canada, 2001).

Parenti, M. *Inventing Reality: The Politics of News Media* (New York: St Martin's Press, 1993).

Pearce, C. *Contemporary Germany and the Nazi Legacy: Remembrance, Politics and the Dialectic of Normality* (New York: Palgrave MacMillan, 2008).

Penkower, M. *The Jews Were Expendable: Free World Diplomacy and the Holocaust* (Detroit: Wayne State University Press, 1988).

Peterson, S. *Me Against My Brother: At War in Somalia, Sudan, and Rwanda* (New York: Routledge, 2000).

Power, S. *'A Problem From Hell': America and the Age of Genocide* (London: Flamingo, 2003).

Prunier, G. *The Rwanda Crisis: History of a Genocide*, 5th impression (London: Hurst & Company, 2005).

Reader, J. *Africa: A Biography of the Continent* (London: Penguin Books, 1998).

Reah, D. *The Language of Newspapers* (London: Routledge, 2005).

Rees, L. *Auschwitz: The Nazis and the Final Solution* (London: BBC Books, 2005).

—— *The Nazis: A Warning from History* (London: BBC Books, 2005).

Reid, R.J. *A History of Modern Africa: 1800 to the Present* (Chichester: Wiley-Blackwell, 2009).

Reilly, J. *Belsen: The Liberation of a Concentration Camp* (London: Routledge, 1998).

Reilly, J., Cesarani, D., Kushner, T. & Richmond, C. (eds) *Belsen in History and Memory* (London: Frank Cass, 1997).

Richardson, J.E. *Analysing Newspapers: An Approach from Critical Discourse Analysis* (New York: Palgrave MacMillan, 2007).

Rieff, D. *Slaughterhouse: Bosnia and the Failure of the West* (New York: Touchstone, 1996).

Bibliography

Rohde, D. *End Game: The Betrayal and Fall of Srebrenica: Europe's Worst Massacre Since World War II* (Colorado: Westview Press, 1998).

Roosevelt, T. *Fear God and Take Your Own Part* (New York: George H. Duran, 1916).

Rosenbaum, A.S. *Is the Holocaust Unique? Perspectives on Comparing Genocide* (Boulder: Westview Press, 1996).

Rotberg, R.I. & Weiss, T.G. (eds) *From Massacres to Genocide: The Media, Public Policy and Humanitarian Crisis* (Washington, DC: The Brookings Institution, 1996).

Roth, J.K. *Genocide and Human Rights: A Philosophical Guide* (New York: Palgrave MacMillan, 2005).

Rubenstein, R. *The Cunning of History: The Holocaust and the American Future* (New York: Harper & Row Publishers, 1985).

Rubinstein, W.D. *The Myth of Rescue: Why the Democracies Could Not Have Saved More Jews From the Nazis*, reprint (New York: Routledge, 2000).

—— *Genocide: A History* (Harlow: Pearson Education Limited, 2004).

Salzman, J. *Making the News: A Guide for Nonprofits and Activists* (Boulder: Westview, 1998).

Schlesinger Jr, A. *The Age of Roosevelt: The Politics of Upheaval, 1935–1936* (New York: Houghton Mifflin, 1966).

Sells, M. *The Bridge Betrayed: Religion and Genocide in Bosnia* (Los Angeles: University of California Press, 1998).

Semelin, J. *Purify and Destroy: The Political Uses of Massacre and Genocide* (London: Hurst & Company, 2007).

Shawcross, W. *Deliver Us from Evil: Warlords and Peacekeepers in a World of Endless Conflict* (London: Simon & Schuster, 2000).

Shephard, B. *A War of Nerves: Soldiers and Psychiatrists, 1914–1994* (London: Pimlico, 2002).

—— *After Daybreak: The Liberation of Belsen, 1945* (London: Pimlico, 2006).

Shimoni, G. (ed), *The Holocaust in University Teaching* (Oxford: Pergamon Press, 1991).

Silber, L. & Little, A. *The Death of Yugoslavia* (London: Penguin, 1996).

Simms, B. *Unfinest Hour: Britain and the Destruction of Bosnia* (London: Penguin, 2002).

Sinclair, A. *An Anatomy of Terror: A History of Terrorism* (London: MacMillan, 2003).

Smith, T. *Holocaust Denial: What the Survey Data Reveal* (New York: American Jewish Commitee, 1994).

Sofsky, W. *Violence: Terrorism, Genocide, War*, transl. Anthea Bell (London: Granta Books, 2003).

Sontag, S. *Regarding the Pain of Others* (London: Penguin Books, 2003).

Stember, C.H. et al. *Jews in the Mind of America* (New York: Basic Books, 1966).

Bibliography

Straus, S. *The Order of Genocide* (Ithaca, NY: Cornell University Press, 2006).

Street, B.V. *The Savage in Literature: Representations of 'Primitive' Society in English Fiction, 1858–1920* (London: Routledge, 1975).

Sujo, G. *Legacies of Silence: The Visual Arts and Holocaust Memory* (London: Philip Wilson Publishers, 2001).

Tester, K. *Compassion, Morality and the Media* (Philadelphia: Open University Press, 2001).

Thompson, A. (ed.) *The Media and the Rwanda Genocide* (London: Pluto Press, 2007).

Todorova, M. *Imagining the Balkans* (Oxford: Oxford University Press, 2009).

Tomasevich, J. *War and Revolution in Yugoslavia, 1941–1945: Occupation and Collaboration* (San Francisco: Stanford University Press, 2001).

Tosh, J. *The Pursuit of History* (Harlow: Longman, 1999).

Tuchman, G. *Making News: A Study in the Construction of Reality* (New York: Free Press, 1978).

Tyner, J.A. *War, Violence, and Population: Making the Body Count* (London: The Guilford Press, 2009).

Vice, S. (ed.) *Representing the Holocaust* (London: Vallentine Mitchell, 2003).

Waller, J. *Becoming Evil: How Ordinary People Commit Genocide and Mass Killing*, 2nd edition (Oxford: Oxford University Press, 2007).

Wekker, G. *White Innocence: Paradoxes of Colonialism and Race* (London: Duke University Press, 2016).

Williamson, D.G. *The Third Reich*, 3rd edition (London: Pearson Education Limited, 2002).

Woodward, S. *Balkan Tragedy* (Washington, DC: Brookings, 1995).

Wright, R. *A Short History of Progress* (Edinburgh: Canongate, 2006).

Wundt, Wilhelm Max *Outlines of Psychology* (Leipzig: Engleman, 1907).

Wyman, D. *The Abandonment of the Jews: America and the Holocaust, 1941–1945* (New York: Pantheon Books, 1984).

—— (ed.) *The World Reacts to the Holocaust* (Baltimore: The John Hopkins, 1996).

Zeldin, T. *An Intimate History of Humanity* (London: Vintage Books, 1998).

Zelizer, B. *Remembering to Forget: Holocaust Memory Through the Camera's Eye* (Chicago: The University of Chicago Press, 1998).

Zimbardo, P. *The Lucifer Effect: How Good People Turn Evil* (London: Rider, 2007).

Book Chapters and Articles

Adhikari, M. "*Hotel Rwanda* – The Challenges of Historicising and Commercialising genocide", *Development Dialogue* 50 (December 2008), pp. 173–95.

Bibliography

Allen, C.J. & Hamilton, J.M. "Normalcy in Foreign News", *Journalism Studies* 11/5 (September 2010), pp. 634–49.

Alozie, E.C. "What Did They Say? African Media Coverage of the First 100 Days of the Rwanda Crisis", in Allan Thompson (ed.), *The Media and the Rwanda Genocide* (London: Pluto Press, 2007), pp. 211–30.

Amishai-Maisels, Z. "The Visual Arts as an Aid for Teaching About the Holocaust", in Gideon Shimoni (ed.), *The Holocaust in University Teaching* (Oxford: Pergamon Press, 1991), pp. 1–8.

Amon, M. "Oppression, Mass Violence and State Persecution: Some Neglected Considerations", *Journal of Genocide Research* 5/3 (2003), pp. 361–82.

Aretxaga, B. "Maddening of States", *Annual Review of Anthropology* 32 (2003), pp. 393–410.

Auerbach, Y. & Bloch-Elkon, Y. "Media Framing and Foreign Policy: The Elite Press vis-a-vis US Policy in Bosnia, 1992–95", *Journal of Peace Research* 42/1 (January 2005), pp. 83–99.

Baer, A. "Consuming History and Memory Through Mass Media Products", *European Journal of Cultural Studies* 4/4 (2001), pp. 491–501.

Baer, U. "To Give Memory a Place: Holocaust Photography and the Landscape Tradition", *Representations* 69 (Winter 2000), pp. 38–62.

Banks, W.C. & Straussman, J.D. "A New Imperial Presidency? Insights from U.S. Involvement in Bosnia", *Political Science Quarterly* 114/2 (Summer 1999), pp. 195–217.

Bardgett, S. "Film and the Making of the Imperial War Museum's Holocaust Exhibition", in Toby Haggith & Joanna Newman (eds), *Holocaust and the Moving Image: Representations in Film and Television Since 1933* (London: Wallflower Press, 2005), pp. 19–23.

—— "What Wireless Listeners Learned: Some Lesser-Known BBC Broadcasts about Belsen", in Suzanne Bardgett & David Cesarani (eds), *Belsen 1945: New Historical Perspectives* (London: Vallentine Mitchell, 2006), pp. 123–36.

Bardgett, S. & Dodds, A. "Exploring the Common Threads of Genocide: The Crimes Against Humanity Exhibition at the Imperial War Museum", in Toby Haggith & Joanna Newman (eds), *Holocaust and the Moving Image: Representations in Film and Television Since 1933* (London: Wallflower Press, 2005), pp. 280–7.

Barnett, M. "The Politics of Indifference at the United Nations and Genocide in Rwanda and Bosnia", in Thomas Cushman & Stjepan G. Mestrovic (eds), *This Time We Knew: Western Responses to Genocide in Bosnia* (New York: New York University Press, 1996), pp. 128–62.

—— "The UN Security Council, Indifference, and Genocide in Rwanda", *Cultural Anthropology* 12/4 (1997), pp. 551–78.

Bibliography

Baron, L. "The Holocaust and American Public Memory, 1945-1960", *Holocaust and Genocide Studies* 17/1 (Spring 2003), pp. 62-88.

—— "Not in Kansas Anymore: Holocaust Films for Children", *The Lion and the Unicorn* 27 (2003), pp. 394-409.

—— "X-Men as J-Men: The Jewish Subtext of a Comic Book Movie", *Shofar: An Interdisciplinary Journal of Jewish Studies* 22/1 (Fall 2003), pp. 44-52.

Bartov, O. "Hollywood Tries Evil", in Yosefa Loshitzky, *Spielberg's Holocaust: Critical Perspectives on Schindler's List* (Indianapolis: Indiana University Press, 1997), pp. 41-60.

—— "Chambers of Horror: Holocaust Museums in Israel and the United States", *Israel Studies* 2/2 (Fall 1997), pp. 66-87.

—— "Defining Enemies, Making Victims: Germans, Jews, and the Holocaust", *American Historical Review* 103/3 (1998), pp. 771-816.

Bartrop, P. "The Relationship Between War and Genocide in the Twentieth Century: A Consideration", *Journal of Genocide Research* 4/4 (2002), pp. 519-32.

Baudrillard, J. "No Pity for Sarajevo", in Thomas Cushman & Stjepan G. Mestrovic (eds), *This Time We Knew: Western Responses to Genocide in Bosnia* (New York: New York University Press, 1996), pp. 80-4.

Bauer, Y. "Is the Holocaust Explicable?", *Holocaust and Genocide Studies* 5/2 (1990), pp. 145-55.

Baum, M.A. "Sex, Lies, and War: How Soft News Brings Foreign Policy to the Inattentive Public", *American Political Science Review* 96/1 (March 2002), pp. 91-109.

—— "Circling the Wagon: Soft News and Isolationism in American Public Opinion", *International Studies Quarterly* 48/2 (June 2004), pp. 313-38.

Becker, L.B., Hollifield, C.A., Jacobsson, A., Jacobsson, E. & Vlad, T. "Is More Always Better? Examining the Adverse Effects of Competition on Media Performance", *Journalism Studies* 10/3 (2009), pp. 368-85.

de Beer, A.S. "News from and in The 'Dark Continent': Afro-pessimism, News Flows, Global Journalism and Media Regimes", *Journalism Studies* 11/4 (2010), pp. 596-609.

Berkeley, B. "Road to a Genocide", in Nicolaus Mills & Kira Brunner, *The New Killing Fields: Massacre and the Politics of Intervention*, 2nd edition (New York: Basic Books, 2003), pp. 103-16.

Bernard-Donals, M. "Forgetful Memory and Images of the Holocaust", *College English* 66/4 (March 2004), pp. 380-402.

Bethge, R. "The 8th of May: 1945 and the Years After", in: Alice L. Eckhardt (ed.), *Burning Memory: Times of Testing and Reckoning* (Oxford: Pergamon Press, 1993), pp. 221-40.

Bibliography

Bhavani, R. "Ethnic Norms and Interethnic Violence: Accounting for Mass Participation in the Rwandan Genocide", *Journal of Peace Research* 43/6 (2006), pp. 651-69.

Bieber, F. "Bosnia-Herzegovina and Lebanon: Historical Lessons of Two Multireligious States", *Third World Quarterly* 21/2 (April 2000), pp. 269-81.

Bingham, A. "Ignoring the First Draft of History", *Media History* 18/3-4 (September 2012), pp. 311-26.

Bischoping, K. "Method and Meaning in Holocaust Knowledge Surveys", *Holocaust and Genocide Studies* 12/3 (Winter 1998), pp. 454-74.

Bischoping, K. & Kalmin, K. "Public Opinion About Comparisons to the Holocaust", *Public Opinion Quarterly* 63 (1999), pp. 485-507.

Bloomstein, R. "Human Rights: Does Anyone Care?", in Toby Haggith & Joanna Newman (eds), *Holocaust and the Moving Image: Representations in Film and Television Since 1933* (London: Wallflower Press, 2005), pp. 259-70.

Bloxham, D. "British War Crimes Trial Policy in Germany, 1945-1947: Implementation and Collapse", *The Journal of British Studies* 42/1 (January 2003), pp. 91-118.

—— "Britain's Holocaust Memorial Days: Reshaping the Past in the Service of the Present", in: Sue Vice (ed.), *Representing the Holocaust* (London: Vallentine Mitchell, 2003), pp. 41-62.

Blum, L. et al. "Tellers and Listeners: The Impact of Holocaust Narratives", in Peter Hayes (ed.), *Lessons and Legacies: The Meaning of the Holocaust in a Changing World* (Illinois: Northwestern Press, 1991), pp. 316-28.

Boose, L.E. "National Countermemories: Crossing the River Drina: Bosnian Rape Camps, Turkish Impalement, and Serb Cultural Memory", *Signs* 28/1 (Autumn 2002), pp. 71-96.

Boskovic, A. "Distinguishing 'Self' and 'Other': Anthropology and National Identity in Former Yugoslavia", *Anthropology Today* 21/2 (April 2005), pp. 8-13.

Bowlby, C. "Nazis on the Silver Screen", *BBC History Magazine*, 9/9 (September 2008), pp. 40-1.

Braiterman, Z. "Against Holocaust-Sublime: Naive Reference and the Generation of Memory", *History and Memory* 12/2 (2000), pp. 7-28.

Braun, R. "The Holocaust and Problems of Historical Representation", *History and Theory* 33/2 (May 1994), pp. 172-97.

Breitman, R. "Auschwitz Partially Decoded", in Michael J. Neufeld & Michael Berenbaum, *The Bombing of Auschwitz: Should the Allies Have Attempted It?* (Kansas: University Press of Kansas, 2003), pp. 27-34.

Brookes, H.J. "'Suit, Tie and a Touch of Juju' - The Ideological Construction of Africa: A Critical Discourse Analysis of News on Africa in the British Press", *Discourse Society* 6/4 (1995), pp. 461-94.

Bibliography

Brown, M. "The Holocaust as an Appropriate Topic for Interdisciplinary Study", in: Gideon Shimoni (ed.), *The Holocaust in University Teaching* (Oxford: Pergamon Press, 1991), pp. 9–14.

Brubaker, R. & Laitin, D.D. "Ethnic and Nationalist Violence", *Annual Review of Sociology* 24 (1998), pp. 423–52.

Bruce, S. "Religion and Violence: What Can Sociology Offer?", *Numen* 52/1 (2005), pp. 5–28.

Brugel, J.W. "The Crime of Genocide", *The Central European Observer* (17 October, 1947), p. 293.

Brunk, D.C. "Curing the Somalia Syndrome: Analogy, Foreign Policy Decision Making, and the Rwandan Genocide", *Foreign Policy Analysis* 4 (2008), pp. 301–20.

Campbell, D. "Atrocity, memory, photography: Imagining the amps of Bosnia – the case of ITN versus *Living Marxism*, Part 2", *Journal of Human Rights* 1/2 (2002), pp. 143–72.

Capet, A. "The Liberation of the Bergen-Belsen Camp as seen by Some British Official War Artists in 1945", in Suzanne Bardgett & David Cesarani (eds), *Belsen 1945: New Historical Perspectives* (London: Vallentine Mitchell, 2006), pp. 170–85.

Caplan, G. "Rwanda: Walking the Road to Genocide", in Allan Thompson (ed.), *The Media and the Rwanda Genocide* (London: Pluto Press, 2007), pp. 20–37.

Carroll, J. "Shoah in the News: Patterns and Meanings of News Coverage of the Holocaust", Discussion Paper D-27, Harvard University, (October 1997).

Carter, H. "Punishing Serbia", *Foreign Policy* 96 (Autumn 1994), pp. 49–56.

Cate, F. "Communications, Policy-Making, and Humanitarian Crises", in Robert I. Rotberg & Thomas G. Weiss (eds), *From Massacres to Genocide: The Media, Public Policy and Humanitarian Crisis* (Washington, DC: The Brookings Institution, 1996), pp. 15–44.

Cesarani, D. "Great Britain", in David S. Wyman (ed.), *The World Reacts to the Holocaust* (Baltimore: The John Hopkins, 1996), pp. 599–641.

—— "Seizing the Day: Why Britain Will Benefit from Holocaust Memorial Day", *Patterns of Prejudice* 34/4 (2000), pp. 61–6.

—— "Introduction", in Suzanne Bardgett & David Cesarani (eds), *Belsen 1945: New Historical Perspectives* (London: Vallentine Mitchell, 2006), pp. 1–10.

—— "A Brief History of Bergen-Belsen", in Suzanne Bardgett & David Cesarani (eds), *Belsen 1945: New Historical Perspectives* (London: Vallentine Mitchell, 2006), pp. 13–21.

Cesarani, D. et al., "Approaching Belsen: An Introduction", in Jo Reilly, David Cesarani, Tony Kushner & Colin Richmond (eds), *Belsen in History and Memory* (London: Frank Cass, 1997), pp. 3–33.

Bibliography

Chalk, F. "Genocide in the 20th Century: Definitions of Genocide and Their Implications for Prediction and Prevention", *Holocaust and Genocide Studies* 4/2 (1989), pp. 149–60.

—— "Intervening to Prevent Genocidal Violence: The Role of the Media", in Allan Thompson (ed.), *The Media and the Rwanda Genocide* (London: Pluto Press, 2007), pp. 375–80.

Chang, H.I., Lewis, S.C. & Zheng, N. "A Matter of Life and Death? Examining How Newspapers Covered the Newspaper 'Crisis'", *Journalism Studies* 13/3 (November 2011), pp. 305–24.

Chang, T. and Lee, J. "Factors Affecting Gatekeepers' Selection of Foreign News: A National Survey of Newspaper Editor", *Journalism Quarterly* 69/3 (Fall 1992), pp. 554–61.

Chase, J.L. "The Development of the Morgenthau Plan Through the Quebec Conference", *The Journal of Politics* 16/2 (May 1954), pp. 325–59.

Cheyette, B. "The Uncertain Certainty of Schindler's List", in Yosefa Loshitzky, *Spielberg's Holocaust: Critical Perspectives on Schindler's List* (Indianapolis: Indiana University Press, 1997), pp. 226–38.

Choan, A. "Who Failed in Rwanda, Journalists or the Media?", in Allan Thompson (ed.), *The Media and the Rwanda Genocide* (London: Pluto Press, 2007), pp. 160–6.

Clark, M.M. "Holocaust Video Testimony, Oral History, and Narrative Medicine: The Struggle against Indifference", *Literature and Medicine* 24/2 (Fall 2005), pp. 266–82.

Clark, R. "Looking Back at Mr Spectator, Given Srebrenica: A Tail-Piece", *Media History* 14/3 (December 2008), pp. 373–88.

Coleman, S., Morrison, D.E. & Anthony, S. "A Constructivst Study of Trust in the News", *Journalism Studies* 13/1 (2012), pp. 37–53.

Conversi, D. "Moral Relativism and Equidistance in British Attitudes to the War in the Formr Yugoslavia", in Thomas Cushman & Stjepan G. Mestrovic (eds), *This Time We Knew: Western Responses to Genocide in Bosnia* (New York: New York University Press, 1996), pp. 244–81.

Cope, J. "On Reading History as a Mental Health Issue", in Mark Levene, Rob Johnson & Penny Roberts, *History at the End of the World? History, Climate Change and the Possibility of Change* (Penrith: Humanities E-Books, 2010), pp. 188–204.

Coulson, M. "Looking Behind the Violent Breakup of Yugoslavia", *Feminist Review* 45 (Autumn 1993), pp. 86–101.

Cox, C. "Film as Documentation, Social Comment, Satire and Spoof", *The English Journal* 76/4 (April 1987), pp. 85–7.

Crane, S. "Choosing Not to Look: Representation, Repatriation, and Holocaust Atrocity Photography", *History and Theory* 47 (October 2008), pp. 309–30.

Bibliography

Crowe, E. "Seeing and Hearing for Ourselves: The Spectacle of Reality in the Holocaust Documentary", in Toby Haggith & Joanna Newman (eds), *Holocaust and the Moving Image: Representations in Film and Television Since 1933* (London: Wallflower Press, 2005), pp. 182–8.

Cushman, T. & Mestrovic, S. "Introduction", in Thomas Cushman & Stjepan G. Mestrovic (eds), *This Time We Knew: Western Responses to Genocide in Bosnia* (New York: New York University Press, 1996), pp. 1–38.

Dadrian, V. "Patterns of Twentieth Century Genocides: The Armenian, Jewish, and Rwandan Cases", *Journal of Genocide Research* 6/4 (2004), pp. 487–522.

Dallaire, R. "The Media Dichotomy", in Allan Thompson (ed.), *The Media and the Rwanda Genocide* (London: Pluto Press, 2007), pp. 12–19.

Danner, M. "America and the Bosnia Genocide", *New York Review of Books*, 4 December 1997, pp. 55–65.

Darlow, M. "Baggage and Responsibility: *The World at War* and the Holocaust", in Toby Haggith & Joanna Newman (eds), *Holocaust and the Moving Image: Representations in Film and Television Since 1933* (London: Wallflower Press, 2005), pp. 140–5.

Davis, R.G. "The Bombing of Auschwitz: Comments on a Historical Speculation", in Michael & Michael Berenbaum (eds), *The Bombing of Auschwitz: Should the Allies Have Attempted It?* (Kansas: University of Kansas Press, 2003), pp. 214–26.

Davis, S. "Genocide, Despair, and Religious Hope: An Essay on Human Nature", in John K. Roth, *Genocide and Human Rights: A Philosophical Guide* (New York: Palgrave MacMillan, 2005), pp. 35–45.

Day, A.G. & Golan, G. "Source and Content Diversity in Op-Ed Pages: Assessing Editorial Strategies in *The New York Times* and *The Washington Post*", *Journalism Studies* 6/1 (2005), pp. 61–71.

Dean, C.J. "History Writing, Numbness, and the Restoration of Dignity", *History of the Human Sciences* 17 (2&3), pp. 57–96.

Delage, C. "*Nuit et Brouillard*: A Turning Point in the History and Memory of the Holocaust", in Toby Haggith & Joanna Newman (eds), *Holocaust and the Moving Image: Representations in Film and Television Since 1933* (London: Wallflower Press, 2005), pp. 127–39.

Delano, A. "No Sign of a Better Job: 100 Years of British Journalism", *Journalism Studies* 1/2 (2000), pp. 261–72.

Denich, B. "Dismembering Yugoslavia: Nationalist Ideologies and the Symbolic Revival of Genocide", *American Ethnologist* 21/2 (May 1994), pp. 367–90.

Denitch, B. "Learning from the Death of Yugoslavia: Nationalism and Democracy", *Social Text* 34 (1993), pp. 3–16.

Bibliography

Depelchin, J. "The History of Mass Violence Since Colonial Times – Trying to understand the roots of a mindset", *Development Dialogue* 50 (December 2008), pp. 13–31.

DeRouen Jr, K.R. "Putting the Numbers to Work: Implications for Violence Prevention", *Journal of Peace Research* 42/1 (January 2005), pp. 27–45.

Doder, D. "Yugoslavia: New War, Old Hatreds", *Foreign Policy* 91 (Summer 1993), pp. 3–23.

Doherty, T. "Art Spiegelman's Maus: Graphic Art and the Holocaust", *American Literature* 68/1 (March 1996), pp. 69–84.

Doneson, J. "The American History of Anne Frank's Diary", *Holocaust and Genocide Studies* 2/1 (1987), pp. 149–60.

—— "The Use of Film in Teaching About the Holocaust", in: Gideon Shimoni (ed.), *The Holocaust in University Teaching* (Oxford: Pergamon Press, 1991), pp. 15–23.

—— "*Holocaust* Revisited: A Catalyst for Memory or Trivialisation?", *Annals of the American Academy of Political and Social Science* 548 – The Holocaust: Remembering for the Future (November 1996), pp. 70–7.

Dorland, M. "PG – Parental Guidance or Portrayal of Genocide: The Comparative Depiction of Mass Murder in Contemporary Cinema", in Allan Thompson (ed.), *The Media and the Rwanda Genocide* (London: Pluto Press, 2007), pp. 417–32.

Douglas, L. "Film as Witness: Screening *Nazi Concentration Camps* Before the Nuremberg Tribunal", *The Yale Law Journal* 105/2 (November 1995), pp. 449–81.

Dowden, R. "Comment: The Rwandan Genocide: How the Press Missed the Story. A Memoir", in *African Affairs* 103 (2004), pp. 283–90.

—— "The Media's Failure: A Reflection on the Rwanda Genocide", in Allan Thompson (ed.), *The Media and the Rwanda Genocide* (London: Pluto Press, 2007), pp. 248–55.

Doyle, M. "Reporting the Genocide", in Allan Thompson (ed.), *The Media and the Rwanda Genocide* (London: Pluto Press, 2007), pp. 145–59.

Eckhardt, A. "Memory: Blessing, Burden, or Curse? The *Shoah* as a Burning Memory", in: Alice L. Eckhardt (ed.), *Burning Memory: Times of Testing and Reckoning* (Oxford: Pergamon Press, 1993), pp. 1–17.

Eichenberg, R. "Victory Has Many Friends: US Public Opinion and the Use of Military Force, 1981–2005", *International Security* 30/1 (Summer 2005), pp. 140–77.

Entman, R.M. "Framing: Toward Clarification of a Fractured Paradigm", *Journal of Communication* 43 (1993), pp. 51–8.

Eribo, F. "Russian Newspaper Coverage of Somalia and the Former Yugoslavia", *Issue: A Journal of Opinion* 22/1 (Winter-Spring, 1992), pp. 30–4.

Bibliography

Fair, J.E. & Parks, L. "Africa on Camera: Television News Coverage and Aerial Imaging of Rwandan Refugees", *Africa Today* 48/2 (Summer 2001), pp. 35–57.

Fallace, T. "The Origins of Holocaust Education in American Public Schools", *Holocaust and Genocide Studies* 20/1 (Spring 2006), pp. 80–102.

Fawcett, L. "Why Peace Journalism Isn't News", *Journalism Studies* 3/2 (2002), pp. 213–23.

Faye, E. "Missing The 'Real' Trace of Trauma: How the Second Generation Remember The Holocaust", *American Imago* 58/2 (2001), pp. 525–44.

Ferro, M. "Film as an Agent, Product and Source of History", *Journal of Contemporary History* 18/3 (July 1983), pp. 357–64.

Fetherstonhaugh, D., Slovic, P., Johnson, S. & Friedrich, J. "Insensitivity to the Value of Human Life: A Study of Psychophysical Numbing", *Journal of Risk and Uncertainty* 14 (1997), pp. 283–300.

Fettweis, C. "War as Catalyst: Moving World War II to the Centre of Holocaust Scholarship", *Journal of Genocide Research* 5/2 (June 2003), pp. 225–36.

Fink, S. "The Anti-Genocide Movement on American College Campuses: A Growing Response to the Balkan War", in Thomas Cushman & Stjepan G. Mestrovic (eds), *This Time We Knew: Western Responses to Genocide in Bosnia* (New York: New York University Press, 1996), pp. 313–49.

Fixdal, M. & Smith, D. "Humanitarian Intervention and Just War", *Mershon International Studies Review* 42/2 (November 1998), pp. 283–312.

Fox, J. "The Rise of Religious Nationalism and Conflict: Ethnic Conflict and Revolutionary Wars, 1945–2001", *Journal of Peace Research* 41/6 (November 2004), pp. 715–31.

Franks, S. "How Famine Captured the Headlines", *Media History* 12/3 (2006), pp. 37–53.

Freeman, M. "The Theory and Prevention of Genocide", *Holocaust and Genocide Studies* 6/2 (1991), pp. 185–99.

―――― "Is Limited Altruism Morally Wrong?", in Eve Garrard & Geoffrey Scarre (eds), *Moral Philosophy and the Holocaust* (Aldershot: Ashgate Publishing Limited, 2003), pp. 137–53.

Frey, R. "Is Objectivity Morally Defensible in Discussing the Holocaust?", in: Harry James Cargas, *Problems Unique to the Holocaust* (Kentucky: The University Press of Kentucky, 1999), pp. 98–108.

Friedrich, J., Barnes, P., Chapin, K., Dawson, I., Garst, V. & Kerr, D. "Psychophysical Numbing: When Lives Are Valued Less as the Lives at Risk Increase", *Journal of Consumer Psychology* 8/3 (1999), pp. 277–99.

Fujii, L.A. "Transforming the Moral Landscape: The Diffusion of a Genocidal Norm in Rwanda", *Journal of Genocide Research* 6/1 (March 2004), pp. 99–114.

Bibliography

Fulton, E. & Roberts, P. "The Wrath of God: Explanations of Crisis and Natural Disaster in Premodern Europe", in Mark Levene, Rob Johnson & Penny Roberts, *History at the End of the World? History, Climate Change and the Possibility of Change* (Penrith: Humanities E-Books, 2010), pp. 67–79.

Gamson, W.A. "News as Framing", *American Behavioral Scientist* 33 (1989), pp. 157–61.

Gamson, W.A., Croteau, D., Hoynes, W. & Sasson, T. "Media Images and the Social Construction of Reality", *Annual Review of Sociology* 18 (1992), pp. 373–93.

Geras, N. "In a Class of its Own", in Eve Garrard & Geoffrey Scarre (eds), *Moral Philosophy and the Holocaust* (Aldershot: Ashgate Publishing Limited, 2003), pp. 25–56.

Giles, T. "Media Failure over Rwanda's Genocide", in Allan Thompson (ed.), *The Media and the Rwanda Genocide* (London: Pluto Press, 2007), pp. 235–7.

Giradet, E.R. "Are the New Electronic Media Making a Difference?", in Robert I. Rotberg & Thomas G. Weiss (eds), *From Massacres to Genocide: The Media, Public Policy and Humanitarian Crisis* (Washington, DC: The Brookings Institution, 1996), pp. 45–67.

Gladstone, K. "Separate Intentions: The Allied Screening of Concentration Camp Documentaries in Defeated Germany in 1945–46: *Death Mills* and *Memory of the Camps*", in Toby Haggith & Joanna Newman (eds), *Holocaust and the Moving Image: Representations in Film and Television Since 1933* (London: Wallflower Press, 2005), pp. 50–64.

Glanville, L. "Is 'Genocide' Still a Powerful Word?", *Journal of Genocide Research* 11/4 (2009), pp. 467–86.

Glaurdic, J. "Yugoslavia's Dissolution: Between the Scylla of Facts and the Charybdis of Interpretation", in Florian Bieber, Armina Galijas & Rory Archer (eds), *Debating the End of Yugoslavia* (London: Routledge, 2014), pp. 23–8.

Golan, G. "Inter-Media Agenda Setting and Global News Coverage: Assessing the Influence of the *New York Times* on Three Network Television Evening News Programs", *Journalism Studies* 7/2 (2006), pp. 323–33.

Gold, T. "An Overview of Hollywood Cinema's Treatment of the Holocaust", in Toby Haggith & Joanna Newman (eds), *Holocaust and the Moving Image: Representations in Film and Television Since 1933* (London: Wallflower Press, 2005), pp. 193–7.

Greenspan, H. "Imagining Survivors: Testimony and the Rise of Holocaust Consciousness", in: Hilene Flanzbaum, *The Americanization of the Holocaust* (London: The John Hopkins University Press, 1999), pp. 45–67.

Haggith, T. "Filming the Liberation of Bergen-Belsen", in Toby Haggith & Joanna Newman (eds), *Holocaust and the Moving Image: Representations in Film and Television Since 1933* (London: Wallflower Press, 2005), pp. 33–49.

259

Bibliography

—— "British Relief Teams in Belsen Concentration Camp: Emergency Relief and the Perception of Survivors", in Suzanne Bardgett & David Cesarani (eds), *Belsen 1945: New Historical Perspectives* (London: Vallentine Mitchell, 2006), pp. 89–122.

Hakansson, P. & Sjoholm, F. "Who Do You Trust? Ethnicity and Trust in Bosnia and Herzegovina", *Europe-Asia Studies* 59/6 (September 2007), pp. 961–76.

Hallahan, K. "Seven Models of Framing: Implications for Public Relations", *Journal of Public Relations Research* 11 (1999), pp. 205–42.

Haller, B. & Ralph, S. "Not Worth Keeping Alive? News Framing of Assisted Suicide in the United States and Great Britain", *Journalism Studies* 2/3 (2001), pp. 407–21.

Halpern, J. & Weinstein, H. "Rehumanizing the Other: Empathy and Reconciliation", *Human Rights Quarterly* 26/3 (August 2004), pp. 561–83.

Hammond, P. "Reporting Humanitarian Warfare: Propaganda, Moralism and NATO's Kosovo War", *Journalism Studies* 1/3 (2000), pp. 365–86.

Hannon, J.T. & Marullo, S. "Education for Survival: Using Films to Teach War as a Social Problem", *Teaching Sociology* 16/3 (July 1988), pp. 245–55.

Hansen, M.B. "*Schindler's List* Is Not *Shoah*: The Second Commandment, Popular Modernism, and Public Memory", *Critical Inquiry* 22/2 (Winter 1996), pp. 292–312.

Harcup, Tony & Deirdre O'Neill, "What Is News? Galtung and Ruge revisited", *Journalism Studies*, 2/2 (2001), pp. 261–80.

Harff, B. "No Lessons Learned from the Holocaust? Assessing Risks of Genocide and Political Mass Murder since 1955", *American Political Science Review* 97/1 (February 2003), pp. 57–73.

Harrison, D.G. "Journey Into Darkness", in Toby Haggith & Joanna Newman (eds), *Holocaust and the Moving Image: Representations in Film and Television Since 1933* (London: Wallflower Press, 2005), pp. 265–70.

Harrow, K.W. "'Ancient Tribal Warfare': Foundational Fantasies of Ethnicity and History", *Research in African Literatures* 36/2 (Summer 2005), pp. 34–45.

Harting, H. "Global Humanitarianism, Race, and the Spectacle of the African Corpse in Current Western Representations of the Rwandan Genocide", *Comparative Studies of South Asia, Africa and the Middle East* 28/1 (2008), pp. 61–77.

Harvey, F.P. "Primordialism, Evolutionary Theory and Ethnic Violence in the Balkans: Opportunities and Constraints for Theory and Policy", *Canadian Journal of Political Science* 33/1 (March 2000), pp. 37–65.

Hasian Jr. M. "Anne Frank, Bergen-Belsen, and the Polysemic Nature of Holocaust Memories", *Rhetoric & Public Affairs* 4/3 (2001), pp. 349–74.

Bibliography

Hawkins, V. "The Other Side of the CNN Factor: The Media and Conflict", *Journalism Studies* 3/2 (2002), pp. 225–40.

Hayden, R. "Imagined Communities and Real Victims: Self-Determination and Ethnic Cleansing in Yugoslavia", *American Ethnologist* 23/4 (November 1996), pp. 783–801.

—— "Moral Vision and Impaired Insight: The Imagining of Other People's Communities in Bosnia", *Current Anthropology* 48/1 (February 2007), pp. 105–31.

—— "'Genocide Denial' Laws as Secular Heresy: A Critical Analysis with Reference to Bosnia", *Slavic Review* 67/2 (Summer 2008), pp. 384–407.

Hayes, P. "Introduction", in Peter Hayes (ed), *Lessons and Legacies: The Meaning of the Holocaust in a Changing World* (Illinois: Northwestern Press, 1991), pp. 1–10.

Herf, J. "The 'Jewish War': Goebbels and the Antisemitic Campaigns of the Nazi Propaganda Ministry", in *Holocaust and Genocide Studies* 19/1 (Spring 2005), pp. 51–80.

Hilberg, R. "Opening Remarks: The Discovery of the Holocaust", in Peter Hayes (ed.), *Lessons and Legacies: The Meaning of the Holocaust in a Changing World* (Illinois: Northwestern Press, 1991), pp. 11–19.

Himmelstein, H. & Faithorn, E.P. "Eyewitness to Disaster: How Journalists Cope with the Psychological Stress Inherent in Reporting Traumatic Events", *Journalism Studies* 3/4 (2002), pp. 537–55.

Hintjens, H. "When Identity Becomes a Knife", *Ethnicities* 1/1 (2001), pp. 25–55.

Hirsch, M. "Surviving Images: Holocaust Photographs and the Work of Postmemory", *The Yale Journal of Criticism* 14/1 (2001), pp. 5–37.

Hoijer, B. "The Discourse of Global Compassion: The Audience and Media Reporting of Human Suffering", *Media Culture Society* 26/4 (2004), pp. 513–31.

Holdsworth, A. "'Television Resurrections': Television and Memory", *Cinema Journal* 47/3 (Spring 2008), pp. 137–44.

Holroyd, P. "Lest We Forget: The Importance of Holocaust Education", *NASSP Bulletin* 79 (1995), pp. 16–25.

Hormuth, S. & Stephan, W.G. "Effects of Viewing 'Holocaust' on Germans and Americans: A Just-World Analysis", *Journal of Applied Social Psychology* 11/3 (1981), pp. 240–51.

Horowitz, S.R. "But Is It Good for the Jews? Spielberg's Schindler and the Aesthetics of Atrocity", in Yosefa Loshitzky, *Spielberg's Holocaust: Critical Perspectives on Schindler's List* (Indianapolis: Indiana University Press, 1997), pp. 119–39.

Hughes, N. "Exhibit 467: Genocide Through a Camera Lens", in Allan Thompson (ed.), *The Media and the Rwanda Genocide* (London: Pluto Press, 2007), pp. 231–4.

Bibliography

Hume, M. "Nazifying the Serbs, from Bosnia to Kosovo", in Philip Hammond & Edward S. Herman, *Degraded Capability: The Media and the Kosovo Crisis* (London: Pluto Press, 2000), pp. 70–8.

Hunter, A. "Intruding on Private Grief", in Harry James Cargas, *Problems Unique to the Holocaust* (Kentucky: The University Press of Kentucky, 1999), pp. 122–34.

Huttenbach, H. "The *Kristallnacht* in Holocaust Context: Between Burning Books (1933) and Burning Bodies (1943)", in Alice L. Eckhardt (ed.), *Burning Memory: Times of Testing and Reckoning* (Oxford: Pergamon Press, 1993), pp. 43–55.

Ignatieff, M. "The Stories We Tell: Television and Humanitarian Aid", in Jonathan Moore (ed), *Hard Choices: Moral Dilemmas in Humanitarian Intervention* (Oxford: Rowman & Littlefield Publishers, Inc, 1998), pp. 287–302.

—— "Intervention and State Failure", in Mills, Nicolaus & Brunner, Kira, *The New Killing Fields: Massacre and the Politics of Intervention*, 2nd edition (New York: Basic Books, 2003), pp. 229–44.

James, E. "Media, Genocide and International Response: Another Look at Rwanda", *Small Wars & Insurgencies* 19/1 (March 2008), pp. 89–115.

Jonassohn, K. "Prevention without Prediction", *Holocaust and Genocide Studies* 8/1 (1993), pp. 1–13.

Jones, D.H. "The Right to Life, Genocide, and the Problem of Bystander States", in John K. Roth, *Genocide and Human Rights: A Philosophical Guide* (New York: Palgrave MacMillan, 2005), pp. 265–76.

Judt, T. "The 'Problem of Evil' in Postwar Europe", *New York Review*, 14 February 2008, pp. 33–5.

Kahneman, D. & Tversky, A. "Prospect Theory: An Analysis of Decision Under Risk", *Econometrica* 47 (1979), pp. 263–91.

Kansteiner, W. "Testing the Limits of Trauma: The Long-Term Psychological Effects of the Holocaust on Individuals and Collectives", *History of the Human Sciences* 17/2–3 (2004), pp. 97–123.

Karnik, N.S. "Rwanda & the Media: Imagery, War & Refuge", in *Review of African Political Economy* 25/78 (Whose News? Control of the Media in Africa), (December 1998), pp. 611–23.

Katongole, E.M. "Christianity, Tribalism, and the Rwandan Genocide: A Catholic Reassessment of Christian 'Social Responsibility'", *Logos* 8/3 (Summer 2005), pp. 67–93.

Kaufman, S.J. "Escaping the Symbolic Politics Trap: Reconciliation Initiatives and Conflict Resolution in Ethnic Wars", *Journal of Peace Research* 43/2 (March 2006), pp. 201–18.

Keats, P.A. "Vicarious Witnessing in European Concentration Camps: Imagining the Trauma of Another", *Traumatology* 11/3 (September 2005), pp. 171–87.

Bibliography

Keenan, T. "Publicity and Indifference (Sarajevo on Television)", *PMLA* 117/1 (January 2002), pp. 104–16.

―――― "Mobilizing Shame", *The South Atlantic Quarterly* 103/2–3 (Spring/Summer 2004), pp. 435–49.

Kemp, P. "The British Army and the Liberation of Bergen-Belsen, April 1945", in Jo Reilly, David Cesarani, Tony Kushner & Colin Richmond (eds), *Belsen in History and Memory* (London: Frank Cass, 1997), pp. 134–48.

Kinzer, S. "Big Gamble in Rwanda", *New York Review* (29 March 2007), pp. 23–6.

Kissi, E. "Rwanda, Ethiopia and Cambodia: Links, Faultlines and Complexities in a Comparative Study of Genocide", *Journal of Genocide Research* 6/1 (2004), pp. 115–33.

Koepnick, L. "Reframing the Past: Heritage Cinema and Holocaust in the 1990s", *New German Critique* 87 (Autumn 2002), pp. 47–82.

Kogon, E. & Gutman, R.A. "Hitler's Concentration Camps – An Examination of Conscience", *The Review of Politics* 9/1 (January 1947), pp. 34–46.

Kothari, A. "The Framing of the Darfur Conflict in the *New York Times*: 2003–2006", *Journalism Studies* 11/2 (2010), pp. 209–24.

Kovner, A. "From Generation to Generation", *Holocaust and Genocide Studies* 8/1 (Spring 1994), pp. 107–13.

Krain, M. "International Intervention and the Severity of Genocides and Politicides", *International Studies Quarterly* 49/3 (September 2005), pp. 363–87.

Kritz, N.J. "Coming to Terms with Atrocities: A Review of Accountability Mechanisms for Mass Violations of Human Rights", *Law and Contemporary Problems* 59/4 (Autumn 1996), pp. 127–52.

Krome, F. "The True Glory and the Failure of Anglo–American Film Propaganda in the Second World War", *Journal of Contemporary History* 33/1 (January 1998), pp. 21–34.

Kuperman, A.J. "How the Media Missed the Rwandan Genocide", in Allan Thompson (ed.), *The Media and the Rwanda Genocide* (London: Pluto Press, 2007), pp. 256–60.

Kushner, T. "Ambivalence or Antisemitism? Christian Attitudes and Responses in Britain to the Crisis of European Jewry During the Second World War", *Holocaust and Genocide Studies* 5/2 (1990), pp. 175–89.

―――― "Rules of the Game: Britain, America and the Holocaust in 1944", *Holocaust and Genocide Studies* 5/4 (1990), pp. 381–402.

―――― "The Memory of Belsen", in Jo Reilly, David Cesarani, Tony Kushner & Colin Richmond (eds), *Belsen in History and Memory* (London: Frank Cass, 1997), pp. 181–205.

―――― "From 'This Belsen Business' to 'Shoah Business':History, Memory and Heritage, 1945-2005", in Suzanne Bardgett & David Cesarani (eds), *Belsen 1945: New Historical Perspectives* (London: Vallentine Mitchell, 2006), pp. 189–216.

263

Bibliography

Kuusisto, R. "Framing the Wars in the Gulf and in Bosnia: The Rhetorical Definitions of the Western Power Leaders in Action", *Journal of Peace Research* 35/5 (September 1998), pp. 603–20.

Lal, V. "The Concentration Camp and Development: The Pasts and Future of Genocide", *Patterns of Prejudice* 39/2 (2005), pp. 222–43.

Landsberg, A. "America, the Holocaust, and the Mass Culture of Memory: Toward a Radical Politics of Empathy", *New German Critique* 71 (Spring-Summer 1997), pp. 63–86.

Lang, B. "Is It Possible to Misrepresent the Holocaust?", *History and Theory* 34/1 (February 1995), pp. 84–9.

—— "Philosophy's Contribution to Holocaust Studies", in Eve Garrard & Geoffrey Scarre (eds), *Moral Philosophy and the Holocaust* (Aldershot: Ashgate Publishing Limited, 2003), pp. 1–8.

—— "The Evil in Genocide", in John K. Roth, *Genocide and Human Rights: A Philosophical Guide* (New York: Palgrave MacMillan, 2005), pp. 5–17.

Lasker-Wallfisch, A. "A Survivor's Memories of Liberation", in Suzanne Bardgett & David Cesarani (eds), *Belsen 1945: New Historical Perspectives* (London: Vallentine Mitchell, 2006), pp. 22–6.

Lavsky, H. "A Community of Survivors: Bergen-Belsen as a Jewish Centre after 1945", in Jo Reilly, David Cesarani, Tony Kushner & Colin Richmond (eds), *Belsen in History and Memory* (London: Frank Cass, 1997), pp. 162–77.

Leff, L. "When the Facts Didn't Speak for Themselves: The Holocaust in the *New York Times*, 1939-1945", *Press / Politics* 5/2 (2000), pp. 52–72.

Lemarchand, R. "Disconnecting the Threads: Rwanda and Holocaust Reconsidered", *Journal of Genocide Research* 4/4 (2002), pp. 499–518.

Lennon, H. "A Witness to Atrocity: Film as Evidence in International War Crimes Tribunals", in Toby Haggith & Joanna Newman (eds), *Holocaust and the Moving Image: Representations in Film and Television Since 1933* (London: Wallflower Press, 2005), pp. 65–73.

Levene, M. "Why Is the Twentieth Century the Century of Genocide?", *Journal of World History* 11/2 (2000), pp. 305–36.

—— "Introduction: A Chronicle of a Death Foretold?", in Mark Levene, Rob Johnson & Penny Roberts, *History at the End of the World? History, Climate Change and the Possibility of Change* (Penrith: Humanities E-Books, 2010), pp. 13–33.

Levinson, J. "The Maimed Body and the Tortured Soul: Holocaust Survivors in American Film", *The Yale Journal of Criticism* 17/1 (2004), pp. 141–60.

Lewy, G. "Can There Be Genocide Without the Intent to Commit Genocide?", *Journal of Genocide Research* 9/4 (December 2007), pp. 661–74.

Bibliography

Li, D. "Echoes of Violence", in Mills, Nicolaus & Brunner, Kira, *The New Killing Fields: Massacre and the Politics of Intervention*, 2nd edition (New York: Basic Books, 2003), pp. 117–28.

Light, M.B. "Research for the Social Good: Information, Persuasion, Illumination", *The English Journal* 84/2 (February 1995), pp. 95–8.

Lippman, M. "A Road Map to the 1948 Convention on the Prevention and Punishment of the Crime Genocide", *Journal of Genocide Research* 4/2 (2002), pp. 177–95.

Lipstadt, D. "Pious Sympathies and Sincere Regrets: The American News Media and the Holocaust from Kristallnacht to Bermuda, 1938–1943", *Modern Judaism* 2/1 (February 1982), pp. 53–72.

—— "America and the Memory of the Holocaust, 1950–1956", *Modern Judaism* 16/3 (October 1996), pp. 195–214.

—— "'The Failure to Rescue and Contemporary American Jewish Historiography of the Holocaust: Judging from a Distance", in Michael J. Neufeld & Michael Berenbaum, *The Bombing of Auschwitz: Should The Allies Have Attempted It?* (Kansas: University Press of Kansas, 2003), pp. 227–36.

Lisus, N. & Ericson, R. "Misplacing Memory: The Effect of Television Format on Holocaust Remembrance", *The British Journal of Sociology* 46/1 (March 1995), pp. 1–19.

Littell, F.H. "Holocaust and Genocide: The Essential Dialectic", *Holocaust and Genocide Studies* 2/1 (1987), pp. 95–104.

Littell, F.L. "Essay: Early Warning", *Holocaust and Genocide Studies* 3/4 (1988), pp. 483–90.

Livingston, S. "Limited Vision: How Both the American Media and Government Failed Rwanda", in Allan Thompson (ed.), *The Media and the Rwanda Genocide* (London: Pluto Press, 2007), pp. 188–97.

Loshitzky, Y. "Introduction", in Yosefa Loshitzky, *Spielberg's Holocaust: Critical Perspectives on Schindler's List* (Indianapolis: Indiana University Press, 1997), pp. 1–17.

Losson, N. "Notes on the Images of the Camps", trans. Annette Michelson, *October* 90 (Autumn, 1999), pp. 25–35.

Lumsden, M. "Breaking the Cycle of Violence", *Journal of Peace Research* 34/4 (November 1997), pp. 377–83.

Maas, P. "Paying for the Powell Doctrine", in Mills, Nicolaus & Brunner, Kira, *The New Killing Fields: Massacre and the Politics of Intervention*, 2nd edition (New York: Basic Books, 2003), pp. 71–87.

Mace, J.E. "The Politics of Famine: American Government and Press Response to the Ukrainian Famine, 1932–1933", *Holocaust and Genocide Studies* 3/1 (1988), pp. 75–94.

Bibliography

Magilow, D.H. "Counting to Six Million: Holocaust Memorialization", *Jewish Social Studies: History, Culture, Society* 14/1 (Fall 2007), pp. 23–39.

Manchel, F. "A Reel Witness: Steven Spielberg's Representation of the Holocaust in *Schindler's List*", *The Journal of Modern History* 67/1 (March 1995), pp. 83–100.

Marrus, M.R. "The Use and Misuse of the Holocaust", in Peter Hayes (ed.), *Lessons and Legacies: The Meaning of the Holocaust in a Changing World* (Illinois: Northwestern Press, 1991), pp. 106–19.

Martin, S.E. "US Media Pools and Military Interventions in the 1980s and 1990s", *Journal of Peace Research* 43/5 (September 2006), pp. 601–16.

Maxwell, N. "The Urgent Need for an Academic Revolution", in Mark Levene, Rob Johnson & Penny Roberts, *History at the End of the World? History, Climate Change and the Possibility of Change* (Penrith: Humanities E-Books, 2010), pp. 80–93.

Maynes, C.W. "Relearning Intervention", *Foreign Policy* 98 (Spring 1995), pp. 96–113.

Mazower, M. "Violence and the State in the Twentieth Century", *The American Historical Review* 107/4 (October 2002), pp. 1158–78.

Medoff, R. "'Retribution Is Not Enough': The 1943 Campaign by Jewish Students to Raise American Public Awareness of the Nazi Holocaust", *Holocaust and Genocide Studies* 1/2 (Fall 1997), pp. 171–89.

Melvern, L. "Rwanda and Darfur: The Media and the Security Council", *International Relations* 20/1 (2006), pp. 93–104.

—— "Missing the Story: The Media and the Rwanda Genocide", in Allan Thompson (ed.), *The Media and the Rwanda Genocide* (London: Pluto Press, 2007), pp. 198–210.

Melvern, L. & Williams, P. "Britannia Waived the Rules: The Major Government and the 1994 Rwandan Genocide", *African Affairs* 103 (2004), pp. 1–22.

Mermin, J. "Television News and American Intervention in Somalia: The Myth of a Media-Driven Foreign Policy", *Political Science Quarterly* 112/3 (Autumn 1997), pp. 385–403.

Miles, W.F. "Hamites and Hebrews: problems in 'Judaizing' the Rwandan Genocide", *Journal of Genocide Research* 2/1 (2000), p. 107–15.

Miller, D.B. "The Morality Play: Getting to the Heart of Media Influence on Foreign Policy", *Journalism Studies* 11/5 (2010), pp. 718–33.

Mills, N. "Preface", in Mills, Nicholaus & Brunner, Kira (eds), *The New Killing Fields: Massacre and the Politics of Intervention* (New York: Basic Books, 2003), pp. ix–xi.

—— "The Language of Slaughter", in Mills, Nicholaus & Brunner, Kira (eds), *The New Killing Fields: Massacre and the Politics of Intervention* (New York: Basic Books, 2003), pp. 3–17.

Bibliography

Moodie, M. "The Balkan Tragedy", *Annals of the American Academy of Political and Social Science* 541 (September 1995), pp. 101–15.

Moore, J.F. "Integrating Theological Analysis into a Course on the Holocaust", in: Gideon Shimoni (ed.), *The Holocaust in University Teaching* (Oxford: Pergamon Press, 1991), pp. 24–33.

Morgan, M. "Shame, the Holocaust, and Dark Times", in John K. Roth, *Genocide and Human Rights: A Philosophical Guide* (New York: Palgrave MacMillan, 2005), pp. 304–25.

Mueller, J. "The Banality of Ethnic War", *International Security* 25/1 (Summer 2000), pp. 42–70.

Murigande, C. "Lessons Learned from the 1994 Rwanda Genocide", *Mediterranean Quarterly* 19/2 (2008), pp. 5–10.

Murray, W. "Monday-Morning Quarterbacking and the Bombing of Auschwitz", in Michael J. Neufeld & Michael Berenbaum, *The Bombing of Auschwitz: Should the Allies Have Attempted It?* (Kansas: University Press of Kansas, 2003), pp. 204–13.

Myers,G., Klak, T. & Koehl, T. "The Inscription of Difference: News Coverage of the Conflicts in Rwanda and Bosnia", *Political Geography* 15/1 (1996), pp. 21–46.

Nastios, A. "Illusions of Influence: The CNN Effect in Complex Emergencies", in Robert I. Rotberg & Thomas G. Weiss (eds), *From Massacres to Genocide: The Media, Public Policy and Humanitarian Crisis* (Washington, DC: The Brookings Institution, 1996), pp. 149–68.

Nelson, T.E., Clawson, R. & Oxley, Z.M. "Media Framing of a Civil Liberties Conflict and its Effect on Tolerance", *American Political Science Review* 91 (1997), pp. 567–83.

Neufeld, M. "Introduction to the Controvery", in Michael J. Neufeld & Michael Berenbaum, *The Bombing of Auschwitz: Should the Allies Have Attempted It?* (Kansas: University Press of Kansas, 2003), pp. 1–10.

Neuman, W.R. "Television and American Culture: The Mass Medium and the Pluralist Audience", *Public Opinion Quarterly* 46 (1982), pp. 471–87.

Ngesi, S. & Villa-Vicencio, C. "Rwanda: Balancing the Weight of History", in Erik Doxtader & Charles Villa-Vecencio (eds), *Through Fire and Water: The Roots of Division and the Potential for Reconciliation in Africa* (South Africa: David Philip Publishers, 2003), pp. 1–34.

Novak, S.A. & Rodseth, L. "Remembering Mountain Meadows: Collective Violence and the Manipulation of Social Boundaries", *Journal of Anthropological Research* 62/1 (Spring 2006), pp. 1–25.

Oberschall, A. "The manipulation of ethnicity: from ethnic cooperation to violence and war in Yugoslavia", *Ethnic and Racial Studies* 23/6 (November 2000), pp. 982–1001.

Bibliography

Ochsner, J.K. "Understanding the Holocaust Through the U.S. Holocaust Memorial Museum", *Journal of Architectural Education* 48/4 (May 1995), pp. 240–9.

O'Gorman, H.J. "The Discovery of Pluralistic Ignorance", *Journal of the History of the Behavioral Sciences* 22 (1986), pp. 333–47.

Okuizimi, K. "Peacebuilding Mission: Lessons from the UN Mission in Bosnia and Herzegovina", *Human Rights Quarterly* 24/3 (August 2002), pp. 721–35.

Olujic, M.B. "Embodiment of Terror: Gendered Violence in Peacetime and Wartime in Croatia and Bosnia-Herzegovina", *Medical Anthropology Quarterly* 12/1 (March 1998), pp. 31–50.

O'Neill, K.L. & Hinton, A.L. "Genocide, Truth, Memory, and Representation", in Alexander Laban Hinton & Kevin Lewis O'Neill (eds), *Genocide: Truth, Memory, and Representation* (London: Duke University Press, 2009), pp. 1–26.

O'Tuathail, G. & Agnew, J. "Geopolitics and discourse: practical geopolitical reasoning in American foreign policy", *Political Geography* 11/2 (1992), pp. 190–204.

Packer, G. "Justice on a Hill", in Mills, Nicolaus & Brunner, Kira, *The New Killing Fields: Massacre and the Politics of Intervention*, 2nd edition (New York: Basic Books, 2003), pp. 129–53.

Patterson, D. "The Annihilation of Exits: The Problem of Liberation in the Holocaust Memoir", *Holocaust and Genocide Studies* 9/2 (Fall 1995), pp. 208–30.

Pavkovic, A. "The Serb National Idea: A Revival – 1986–92", *The Slavonic and East European Review* 72/3 (July 1994), pp. 440–55.

Pavlowitch, S. "Who is 'Balkanizing' Whom? The Misunderstandings Between the Debris of Yugoslavia and an Unprepared West", *Daedalus* 123/2 (Spring 1994), pp. 203–23.

Payne, D. & Dagne, T. "Rwanda: Seven Years after the Genocide", *Mediterranean Quarterly* (Winter 2002), pp. 38–43.

Pietrse, J.N. "Sociology of Humanitarian Intervnetion: Bosnia, Rwanda and Somalia Compared", *International Political Science Review* 18/1 (Jan 1997), pp. 71–93.

Piiparinen, T. "Reconsidering the silence over the ultimate crime: a functional shift in crisis management from the Rwandan genocide to Darfur", *Journal of Genocide Research* 9/1 (2007), pp. 71–91.

Pleasants, N. "The concept of learning from the study of the Holocaust", *History of the Human Sciences* 17/2-3 (2004), pp. 187–210.

Pollefeyt, D. "Victims of Evil or Evil of Victims", in Harry James Cargas, *Problems Unique to the Holocaust* (Kentucky: The University Press of Kentucky, 1999), pp. 67–82.

Power, S. "To Suffer by Comparison?", *Daedalus* 128/2 (Spring 1999), pp. 31–66.

—— "Raising the Cost of Genocide", in Mills, Nicolaus & Brunner, Kira (eds), *The New Killing Fields: Massacre and the Politics of Intervention*, 2nd edition (New York: Basic Books, 2003), pp. 245–64.

Bibliography

Postone, M. "After the Holocaust: History and Identity in West Germany", in: Kathy Harms, Lutz R. Reuter & Volker Durr, *Coping with the Past: Germany and Austria after 1945* (Winconsin: The University of Winconsin Press, 1990), pp. 233–51.

Price, V. & Tewksbury, D. "News Values and Public Opinion: A Theoretical Account of Priming and Framing", in George A. Barnett & Franklin J. Boster (eds), *Progress in Communication Sciences: Advances in Persuasion* – Vol. 13 (Greenwich, Connecticut: Ablex, 1997), pp. 173–212.

Pronay, N. "The 'Moving Picture' and Historical Research", *Journal of Contemporary History* 18/3 (July 1983), pp. 365–95.

Reading, A. "Young People's Viewing of Holocaust Films in Different Cultural Contexts", in Toby Haggith & Joanna Newman (eds), *Holocaust and the Moving Image: Representations in Film and Television Since 1933* (London: Wallflower Press, 2005), pp. 211–16.

Rees, L. "The Nazis: A Warning From History", in Toby Haggith & Joanna Newman (eds), *Holocaust and the Moving Image: Representations in Film and Television Since 1933* (London: Wallflower Press, 2005), pp. 146–53.

Reilly, J. "Cleaner, Carer and Occasional Dance Partner? Writing Women Back into the Liberation of Bergen-Belsen", in Jo Reilly, David Cesarani, Tony Kushner & Colin Richmond (eds), *Belsen in History and Memory* (London: Frank Cass, 1997), pp. 149–61.

Riggs, F.W. "The Modernity of Ethnic Identity and Conflict", *International Political Science Review* 19/3 (July 1998), pp. 269–88.

Robben, A. "Epilogue: The Imagination of Genocide", in Alexander Laban Hinton & Kevin Lewis O'Neill, *Genocide: Truth, Memory, and Representation* (London: Duke University Press, 2009), pp. 317–31.

Roizen, R. "Herschel Grynszpan: The Fate of a Forgotten Assassin", *Holocaust and Genocide Studies* 1/2 (1986), pp. 217–28.

Ron, S. "Varying Methods of State Violence", *International Organisation* 51/2 (Spring 1997), pp. 275–300.

——— "Boundaries and Violence: Repertoires of State Action along the Bosnia / Yugoslavia Divide", *Theory and Society* 29/5 (October 2002), pp. 609–49.

Rosenfeld, A. "Popularization and Memory: The Case of Anne Frank", in Peter Hayes (ed.), *Lessons and Legacies: The Meaning of the Holocaust in a Changing World* (Illinois: Northwestern Press, 1991), pp. 243–78.

——— "Holocaust Fictions and the Transformation of Historical Memory", *Holocaust and Genocide Studies* 3/3 (1988), pp. 323–36.

Rosenfeld, G. "The Politics of Uniqueness: Reflections on the Recent Polemical Turn in Holocaust and Genocide Scholarship", *Holocaust and Genocide Studies* 13/1 (Spring 1999), pp. 28–61.

——— "A Flawed Propehcy? *Zakhor*, the Memory Boom, and the Holocaust", *The Jewish Quarterly Review* 97/4 (Fall 2007), pp. 508–20.

Bibliography

Rosenzveig, C. "Foreword", in David S. Wyman (ed.), *The World Reacts to the Holocaust* (Baltimore: The John Hopkins, 1996), pp. xiii–xviii.

Roskis, E. "A Genocide Without Images: White Film Noirs", in Allan Thompson (ed.), *The Media and the Rwanda Genocide* (London: Pluto Press, 2007), pp. 238–41.

Ross, S. "What Photographs Can't Do", *The Journal of Aesthetics and Art Criticism* 41/1 (Autumn 1982), pp. 5–17.

Rotberg, R.I. & Weiss, T. "Introduction", in Robert I. Rotberg & Thomas G. Weiss (eds), *From Massacres to Genocide: The Media, Public Policy and Humanitarian Crisis* (Washington, DC: The Brookings Institution, 1996), pp. 1–11

—— "Coping with the New World Order: The Media, Humanitarians, and Policy-Makers", in Robert I. Rotberg & Thomas G. Weiss (eds), *From Massacres to Genocide: The Media, Public Policy and Humanitarian Crisis* (Washington, DC: The Brookings Institution, 1996), pp. 149–68.

Roth, J.K. "Reflections on Post-Holocaust Ethics", in: Harry James Cargas, *Problems Unique to the Holocaust* (Kentucky: The University Press of Kentucky, 1999), pp. 169–81.

—— "Prologue: Philosophy and Genocide", in John K. Roth, *Genocide and Human Rights: A Philosophical Guide* (New York: Palgrave MacMillan, 2005), pp. xvi–xxi.

—— "The Problem of Evil: How Does Genocide Affect Philosophy", in John K. Roth, *Genocide and Human Rights: A Philosophical Guide* (New York: Palgrave MacMillan, 2005), pp. 1–4.

Rubinstein, R. "Waldheim, The Pope and the Holocaust", in Alice L. Eckhardt (ed.), *Burning Memory: Times of Testing and Reckoning* (Oxford: Pergamon Press, 1993), pp. 263–79.

Sadowski, Y. "Ethnic Conflict", *Foreign Policy* 111 (Summer 1998), pp. 12–23.

Schatzker, C. "The Teaching of the Holocaust: Dilemmas and Considerations", *The Annals of the American Academy of Political and Social Science* 450 (July 1980), pp. 218–26.

Schear, J.A. "Bosnia's Post-Dayton Traumas", *Foreign Policy* 104 (Autumn 1996), pp. 86–101.

Schulze, R. "Forgetting and Remembering: Memories and Memorialisation of Bergen-Belsen", in Suzanne Bardgett & David Cesarani (eds), *Belsen 1945: New Historical Perspectives* (London: Vallentine Mitchell, 2006), pp. 217–35.

Seaton, J. "The BBC and the Holocaust", *European Journal of Communication* 2 (1987), pp. 53–80.

Sells, M. "Crosses of Blood: Sacred Space, Religion, and Violence in Bosnia-Herzegovina", *Sociology of Religion* 64/3 (Autumn 2003), pp. 309–31.

Shandler, J. "Schindler's Discourse: America Discusses the Holocaust and Its Mediation, from NBC's Miniseries to Spielberg's Film", in Yosefa Loshitzky,

Bibliography

Spielberg's Holocaust: Critical Perspectives on Schindler's List (Indianapolis: Indiana University Press, 1997), pp. 153–68.

—— "Aliens in the Wasteland: American Encounters with the Holocaust on 1960s Science Fiction Television", in Hilene Flanzbaum, *The Americanization of the Holocaust* (London: The John Hopkins University Press, 1999), pp. 33–44.

Shawcross, W. "Lessons of Cambodia", in Mills, Nicolaus & Brunner, Kira (eds), *The New Killing Fields: Massacre and the Politics of Intervention*, 2nd edition (New York: Basic Books, 2003), pp. 37–49.

Shehata, A. & Hopmann, D.N. "Framing Climate Change: A Study of US and Swedish Press Coverage of Global Warming", *Journalism Studies* 13/2 (2012), pp. 175–92.

Shiras, P. "Big Problem, Small Print: A Guide to the Complexity of Humanitarian Emergencies and the Media", in Robert I. Rotberg & Thomas G. Weiss (eds), *From Massacres to Genocide: The Media, Public Policy and Humanitarian Crisis* (Washington, D.C., The Brookings Institution, 1996), pp. 93–114.

Simms, B. "Bosnia: The Lessons of History?", in Thomas Cushman & Stjepan G. Mestrovic (eds), *This Time We Knew: Western Responses to Genocide in Bosnia* (New York: New York University Press, 1996), pp. 65–78.

Skoco, M. & Woodger, W. "War Crimes", in Philip Hammond & Edward S. Herman, *Degraded Capability: The Media and the Kosovo Crisis* (London: Pluto Press, 2000), pp. 31–8.

Slack, J.A. & Doyon, R.R. "Population Dynamics and Susceptibility for Ethnic Conflict: The Case of Bosnia and Herzegovina", *Journal of Peace Research* 38/2 (March 2001), pp. 139–61.

Slovic, P. "If I look at the mass I will never act": Psychic numbing and genocide", *Judgement and Decision Making* 2/2 (April 2007), pp. 79–97.

Smith, B. "Public Memory and Active Recall in Two Holocaust Films: *Partisans of Vilna* (1986) and *Come and See* (1985)", in: Sue Vice (ed.), *Representing the Holocaust* (London: Vallentine Mitchell, 2003), pp. 89–107.

Sobel, R. "Trends: United States Intervention in Bosnia", *The Public Opinion Quarterly* 62/2 (Summer 1998), pp. 250–78.

Spyer, P. "Fire Without Smoke and Other Phantom's of Ambon's Violence: Media Effects, Agency, and the Work of Imagination", *Indonesia* 74 (October 2002), pp. 21–36.

Stanton, G. "Could the Rwandan genocide have been prevented?", *Journal of Genocide Research* 6/2 (2004), pp. 211–28.

Staub, E. "Genocide and Mass Killings: Origins, Prevention, Healing and Reconciliation", *Political Psychology* 21/2 (June 2000), pp. 367–82.

Steinert, J. "British Relief Teams in Belsen Concentration Camp: Emergency Relief and the Perception of Survivors", in Suzanne Bardgett & David Cesarani (eds), *Belsen 1945: New Historical Perspectives* (London: Vallentine Mitchell, 2006), pp. 62–78.

271

Bibliography

Steinweis, A.E. "The Holocaust and American Culture: An Assessment of Recent Scholarship", *Holocaust and Genocide Studies* 15/2 (2001), pp. 296–310.

—— "The Auschwitz Analogy: Holocaust Memory and American Debates over Intervention in Bosnia and Kosovo in the 1990s", *Holocaust and Genocide Studies* 19/2 (2005), pp. 276–89.

Sterling, E. "Indifferent Accomplices", in: Harry James Cargas, *Problems Unique to the Holocaust* (Kentucky: The University Press of Kentucky, 1999), pp. 109–21.

Stojsavljevic, J. "Women, Conflict, and Culture in Former Yugoslavia", *Gender and Development* 3/1 (February 1995), pp. 36–41.

Stone, D. "Day of Remembrance or Day of Forgetting? Or, Why Britain Does Not Need a Holocaust Memorial Day", *Patterns of Prejudice* 34/4 (2000), pp. 53–9.

—— "Raphael Lemkin on the Holocaust", *Journal of Genocide Research* 7/4 (2005), pp. 539–50.

Storey, A. "Structural Adjustment, State Power & Genocide: The World Bank & Rwanda", *Review of African Political Economy* 28/89 (September 2001), pp. 365–85.

Straus, S. "How Many Perpetrators Were There in the Rwandan genocide? An estimate", *Journal of Genocide Research* 6/1 (March 2004), pp. 85–98.

Stromback, J., Karlsson, M. & Hopmann, D.N. "Determinants of News Content: Comparing Journalists' Perception of the Normative and Actual Impact of Different Properties When Declaring What's News", *Journalism Studies* 13/5 (2012), pp. 718–28.

Suny, R.G. "Towards a Social History of the October Revolution", *The American Historical Review* 88/1 (February, 1983), pp. 31–52.

Taylor, P.M. "Strategic Communications or Democratic Propaganda", *Journalism Studies* 3/3, (2002), pp. 437–41.

Thompson, A. "Introduction", in Allan Thompson (ed.), *The Media and the Rwanda Genocide* (London: Pluto Press, 2007), pp. 1–11.

—— "The Responsibility to Report: A New Journalistic Paradigm", in Allan Thompson (ed) *The Media and the Rwanda Genocide* (London: Pluto Press, 2007), pp. 433–45.

Tuck, S. "Fighting the Government with its Own Propaganda: The Struggle for Racial Equality in the USA During the Second World War", in Toby Haggith & Joanna Newman (eds), *Holocaust and the Moving Image: Representations in Film and Television Since 1933* (London: Wallflower Press, 2005), pp. 116–23.

Van Schaak, B. "The Crime of Political Genocide: Repairing the Genocide Convention's Blind Spot", *The Yale Law Journal* 106/7 (May 1997), pp. 2259–91.

Veremis, T. "The Balkans in Search of Multilaterlism", *Eurobalkan* 17 (Winter 1994/5), pp. 4–9.

Verwimp, P. "Death and Survival During the 1994 Genocide in Rwanda", *Population Studies* 58/2 (2004), pp. 233–45.

Bibliography

—— "Machetes and Firearms: The Organisation of Massacres in Rwanda", *Journal of Genocide Research* 43/1 (2006), pp. 5–22.

Vice, S. "Binjamin Wilkomirski's *Fragments* and Holocaust Envy: 'Why Wasn't I There, Too?'", in Sue Vice (ed.), *Representing the Holocaust* (London: Vallentine Mitchell, 2003), pp. 249–68.

Vulliamy, E. "Bosnia: The Crime of Appeasement", *International Affairs* 74/1 (January 1998), pp. 73–91.

Wahl-Jorgenen, K. "Playground of the Pundits or Voice of the People? Comparing British and Danish Opinion Pages", *Journalism Studies* 5/1 (2004), pp. 59–70.

Wall, I. "The Holocaust, Film and Education", in Toby Haggith & Joanna Newman (eds), *Holocaust and the Moving Image: Representations in Film and Television Since 1933* (London: Wallflower Press, 2005), pp. 203–10.

Wall, M. "An Analysis of News Magazine Coverage of the Rwanda Crisis in the United States", in Allan Thompson (ed.), *The Media and the Rwanda Genocide* (London: Pluto Press, 2007), pp. 261–73.

Wallensteen, P. & Sollenberg, M. "Armed Conflict, 1989–2000", *Journal of Peace Research* 38/5 (September 2001), pp. 629–44.

Walzer, M. "Arguing for Humanitarian Intervention", in Mills, Nicolaus & Brunner, Kira (eds), *The New Killing Fields: Massacre and the Politics of Intervention*, 2nd edition (New York: Basic Books, 2003), pp. 19–35.

Warbrick, C. "The United Kingdom and the United Nations", *The International Comparative Law Quarterly* 42/4 (October 1993), pp. 938–45.

Wegner, B. "The Ideology of Self Destruction: Hitler and the Choreography of Defeat", *German Historical Institute, London Bulletin* 26/2 (November 2004), pp. 18–33.

Weinberg, G.L. "The Allies and the Holocaust", in Michael J. Neufeld & Michael Berenbaum (eds), *The Bombing of Auschwitz: Should the Allies Have Attempted It?* (Kansas: University Press of Kansas, 2003), pp. 15–26.

Western, J. "Sources of Humanitarian Intervention: Beliefs, Information, and Advocacy in the U.S. Decisions on Somalia and Bosnia", *International Security* 26/4 (Spring 2002), pp. 112–42.

Wheeler, D. "Goddard's List: Why Spielberg and Auschwitz are Number One", *Media History* 15/2 (2009), pp. 185–203.

Wheeler, N.J. "Making Sense of Humanitarian Outrage", *Irish Studies in International Affairs* 7 (1996), pp. 31–40.

White, K.R. "Scourge of Racism: Genocide in Rwanda", *Journal of Black Studies* 39/3 (2009), pp. 471–81.

Williams, K. "Flattened Visions from Timeless Machines: History in the Mass Media", *Media History* 13/2–3 (2007), pp. 127–48.

Winston, M. "The Prevention of Institutionalized Intergroup Violence", *Health and Human Rights* 2/3 (1997), pp. 15–26.

273

Bibliography

Winter, D.G. "Power, Sex, and Violence: A Psychological Reconstruction of the 20th Century and an Intellectual Agenda for Political Psychology", *Political Psychology* 21/2 (June 2000), pp. 383–404.

Wood, W. "Geographic Aspects of Genocide: A Comparison of Bosnia and Rwanda", *Transactions of the Institute of British Geographers* 26/1 (2001), pp. 57–75.

Woodward, S.L. "Genocide or Partition: Two Faces of the Same Coin?", *Slavic Review* 55/4 (Winter 1996), pp. 755–61.

Wouters, J. & Naert, F. "How Effective Is the European Security Architecture? Lessons from Bosnia and Kosovo", *The International and Comparative Law Quarterly* 50/3 (July 2001), pp. 540–76.

Wyman, D. "Introduction", in David S. Wyman (ed.), *The World Reacts to the Holocaust* (Baltimore: The John Hopkins, 1996), pp. xix–xxiii.

—— "The United States", in David S. Wyman (editor), *The World Reacts to the Holocaust* (Baltimore: The John Hopkins, 1996), pp. 693–748.

Yadin, O. "But is it Documentary?", in Toby Haggith & Joanna Newman (eds), *Holocaust and the Moving Image: Representations in Film and Television Since 1933* (London: Wallflower Press, 2005), pp. 168–72.

Young, J.E. "The Texture of Memory: Holocaust Memorials and Meaning", *Holocaust and Genocide Studies* 4/1 (1989), pp. 63–76.

Zaller, J. & Chiu, D. "Government's Little Helper: U.S. Press Coverage of Foreign Policy Crises, 1945–1991, *Political Communication* 13 (1996), pp. 385–405.

Zelizer, B. "Schindler's List and the Shaping of History", in Yosefa Loshitzky, *Spielberg's Holocaust: Critical Perspectives on Schindler's List* (Indianapolis: Indiana University Press, 1997), pp. 18–35.

Zukier, H. "The Twisted Road to Genocide: On the Psychological Development of Evil During the Holocaust", *Social Research* 61/2 (Summer 1994), pp. 423–54.

Audio-Visual & Electronic Sources

BBC Radio 4, "The Archive Hour: Images of Belsen", recorded 14 May 2000 – IWM sound files.

Dimbleby, R. (Dispatch from Belsen), 15 April 1945 – IWM sound files (17714).

Hawley, A. IWM Transcript from Sound Files (19575).

IWM Film No: A70 302-1

IWM Film No: A70 304/03 P 3 A 35.

IWM Film A 70 304/04-06 P 3 A35.

IWM Film MGH 3349 P 2 A 35.

Pronay, N. IWM sound files (19573).

Main Newspaper Sources for Chapters 2 & 3

Chicago Tribune
Daily Telegraph (and *Sunday Telegraph*)
Guardian (and *Observer*)
Independent (and *Independent on Sunday*)
Los Angeles Times
New York Times
The Times (and *Sunday Times*)
Washington Post

All editions of the titles above were analysed for the following date ranges:

1 August – 28 August 1992;
29 January – 26 February 1994;
7 April – 29 July 1994;
7 July – 3 August 1995;
21 August – 18 September 1995.

Index

Index

Index

Index

Index

Fettweis, Christopher
  on war and genocide 132
Fiennes, Ralph
  as Amon Goeth 53, 56
Filipovic, Zlata 94
  and Anne Frank 94
framing
  of policy options 116
France
  colonial past in Africa 172
  debate on intervention 170, 171,
    172, 173
  intervention in Rwanda 157, 166,
    169, 170, 171, 172, 173
Frank, Anne
  cultural legacy 41, 42, 46, 57
  Diary of Anne Frank 40, 41, 42
  as introduction to Holocaust 40, 41
front page
  in American press 68
  importance of 67

Geneva Convention 27
genocide
  Armenian 1, 3
  in Bosnia 59, 61, 103, 110, 117, 118,
    119, 128
  creation of term 39
  definition of 2, 39, 194
  Herero 3
  in history 32
  lack of focus in media 102, 119, 133,
    159, 160, 161, 162, 166, 173,
    175, 177, 178, 179, 182, 185
  media landmarks in exposure to 11,
    16, 20, 21, 22, 32, 34, 36, 46,
    49, 181
  psychological aspects 25, 26, 190
  in Rwanda 131, 132, 146, 163,
    164, 178

Western conceptualisation of
    4, 45, 61
Genocide Convention (1948) 39
German Army
  in Yugoslavia (analogy) 114, 115
Germany (1945)
  calls for action against 24, 25,
    26, 27, 28
  collective guilt 26
  Western condemnation of 23,
    24, 25, 26
  World War I atrocities 34
Gilbert, Martin
  on postwar knowledge of
    Holocaust 37
Goebbels, Josef
  on Nazi aims 14
Goering, Hermann 39
Goeth, Amon
  depiction in *Schindler's List* 55
Goodman, Walter
  on influence of television images 96
Green, Gerald 46
Greenfield, Meg
  on ignoring atrocities 101
Gueye, Moctor
  on violence in Rwanda 151
Gutman, Roy
  camp revelations (1992) 71, 78

Habyarimana, Juvenal
  assassination of 131
Hackett, Albert and Frances 41
Hansen, Miriam
  on *Schindler's List* 55
Hardaga, Zeyneba 94
Harris, Robin
  on genocide in Bosnia 118
Harrow, Kenneth
  on banality of genocide 177

Index

Hartley, Aidan
  editor's comments on Rwanda 146
Hartman, Geoffrey
  on depiction of violence in
    media 124
Hausner, Gideon
  on Eichmann 43
Hawkins, Virgil
  on Western media depictions of
    Africa 135
Hilberg, Raul
  on *Holocaust* 46
Hitchcock, Alfred 18
Hitler, Adolf
  on Armenia 32
  in coverage of Bosnia 113
  death of 15
Hodgkin, Thomas
  on Western ideas regarding
    Africa 134
Holbrooke, Richard
  on Western alliance 112, 113
Holocaust, the
  in Anglo–American culture 4, 10,
    19, 34, 36, 37, 43, 45, 49, 50, 51,
    52, 54, 55, 56, 57, 78, 129, 190
  and concept of genocide 9, 10, 36,
    37, 57, 58, 81, 83, 191, 192, 193
  criticism of media depictions 48
  commoditisation of 48
  as defining moral event 28, 37, 81, 83
  denial 50
  growing awareness of 7, 9, 10, 39, 45,
    46, 47, 48, 49, 52, 53, 56, 58, 81,
    117, 129, 190
  image of perpetrators in 44, 47,
    53, 55, 56
  literature on 38, 40, 45
  survivors, testimony of 38, 39,
    43, 45, 46
  teaching of in schools 49, 51

  as unparalleled 34
  use in political rhetoric 57
  as widely recognised event 80, 192
Holocaust (TV series)
  awards 48
  debate regarding 48
  and other subsequent
    productions 49
  pre-broadcast publicity 47
  production of 46
  in raising Holocaust
    awareness 47, 48
  viewing figures 47, 48
'Horror in Our Time' 18
Hotel Rwanda 1
Howard, Jonathan
  on violence in Rwanda 149
Huband, Mark
  on French intervention in
    Rwanda 172
  on Rwanda and Holocaust 164
human rights 2
  Western support of 4, 7, 120, 143,
    187, 191
Hutton, Will
  on appeasement in Bosnia 113

Imperial War Museum
  Holocaust exhibit 51
Insdorf, Annette
  on Holocaust 47
intervention
  by France in Rwanda 157, 169, 186
  influence on focus of reporting 92,
    95, 96, 100, 114, 178
intervention (anti)
  in Bosnia 62, 65, 84, 85, 95, 96, 97,
    100, 102, 110, 113, 114, 115,
    116, 126, 128, 195
  in Rwanda 142, 149, 154, 155, 158,
    170, 172, 176, 177, 195

Index

Index

Index

Index

Index

Index

www.ingramcontent.com/pod-product-compliance
Lightning Source LLC
Chambersburg PA
CBHW060152280326
41932CB00012B/1730